Security Planning & Disaster Recovery

Eric Maiwald
William Sieglein

McGraw-Hill/Osborne

New York   Chicago   San Francisco
Lisbon   London   Madrid   Mexico City
Milan   New Delhi   San Juan
Seoul   Singapore   Sydney   Toronto

McGraw-Hill/Osborne
2600 Tenth Street
Berkeley, California 94710
U.S.A.

To arrange bulk purchase discounts for sales promotions, premiums, or fund-raisers, please contact **McGraw-Hill/**Osborne at the above address. For information on translations or book distributors outside the U.S.A., please see the International Contact Information page immediately following the index of this book.

Security Planning & Disaster Recovery

1234567890 FGR FGR 0198765432

ISBN 0-07-222463-0

Publisher	**Proofreader**
Brandon A. Nordin	Pam Vevea
Vice President & Associate Publisher	**Indexer**
Scott Rogers	Claire Splan
Acquisitions Editor	**Computer Designers**
Jane Brownlow	Kelly Stanton-Scott, Mickey Galicia
Project Editor	**Illustrators**
Janet Walden	Lyssa Wald, Michael Mueller
Acquisitions Coordinator	**Series Design**
Emma Acker	Peter Hancik, Lyssa Wald
Technical Editor	**Cover Series Design**
Ben Rothke	Jeff Weeks
Copy Editor	
Claire Splan	

This book was composed with Corel VENTURA™ Publisher.

This book is dedicated to my wife Kay and my two sons, Steffan and Joel, who put up with a lot of long days and lost time (again) during the writing of this book. *–EM*

This book is dedicated to my lovely wife Jane—'Tis naught Othello or King Lear, but that WS did not receive royalties. And to my children Kyle, Haley, and Maggy—YES, I can play now! *–WS*

About the Authors

Eric Maiwald is the Chief Technology Officer for Fortrex Technologies, where he oversees all security research and training activities for the company. He also manages the Fortrex Network Security Operations Center where all managed services are performed. Mr. Maiwald also performs assessments, develops policies, and implements security solutions for large financial institutions, services firms, and manufacturers. He has extensive experience in the security field as a consultant, security officer, and developer. Mr. Maiwald holds a Bachelors of Science degree in Electrical Engineering from Rensselaer Polytechnic Institute, a Masters of Engineering in Electrical Engineering from Stevens Institute of Technology, and is a Certified Information Systems Security Professional (CISSP).

Mr. Maiwald is a named inventor on patent numbers 5,577,209, "Apparatus and Method for Providing Multi-level Security for Communications Among Computers and Terminals on a Network"; 5.872.847, "Using Trusted Associations to Establish Trust in a Computer Network"; 5,940,591, "Apparatus and Method for Providing Network Security"; and 6,212.636, "Method for Establishing Trust in a Computer Network via Association."

Mr. Maiwald is a regular presenter at a number of well-known security conferences. He has also written *Network Security: A Beginner's Guide,* published by McGraw-Hill/Osborne, and is a contributing author for *Hacking Linux Exposed* and *Hacker's Challenge,* also published by McGraw-Hill/Osborne.

William Sieglein is the Manager of Security Services for Fortrex Technologies, where he oversees all security consulting and professional services for the company. Mr. Sieglein also manages information security projects for Fortrex clients, leads risk assessments, develops policies, and implements security solutions. He has over 20 years experience in the IT industry, specializing in information security. Mr. Sieglein holds a Bachelors of Science degree in Computer Science from the University of Maryland and a Masters of Science in Technical Management from Johns Hopkins University.

Mr. Sieglein has published numerous articles for various publications including *Business Credit Magazine, Security Advisor,* and *CMP's iPlanet,* where he was also the security expert for several months. Mr. Sieglein been a guest speaker for various organizations including the Information Systems Audit and Controls Association (ISACA), Joint Special Operations Command (JSOC), and the American Society for Industrial Security (ASIS).

About the Technical Reviewer

Ben Rothke (brothke@hotmail.com) is a Principal Consultant with trustEra (www.trustEra.com). His areas of expertise are in PKI, design and implementation of systems security, HIPAA, encryption, security architecture and analysis, firewall configuration and review, cryptography, and security policy development. Mr. Rothke previously worked for Baltimore Technologies, Ernst & Young, and Citibank and has provided information security solutions to many Fortune 500 companies.

He is a frequent speaker at industry conferences and has written for many computer periodicals. Currently, he writes a column for *Unix Review* as well as a monthly security book review for *Security Management* magazine.

Mr. Rothke is a Certified Information Systems Security Professional (CISSP), a Certified Confidentiality Officer (CCO), and a member of ISSA, ICSA, IEEE, ASIS & CSI, operating out of a New York-based office.

AT A GLANCE

Part IV   How to Respond to Incidents

Part V   Appendixes

CONTENTS

Part IV   How to Respond to Incidents

ACKNOWLEDGMENTS

This book could not have been written without the help of a number of people. Most notable in their help were those people we work with at Fortrex Technologies, Inc., especially Lee Kelly for his work on the HIPAA regulations and Andrew Waltz for his research on GLBA. We would also like to acknowledge the great support of our technical editor, Ben Rothke, who turned the chapters around very quickly. Of course, none of this could have been possible without the help from the people at McGraw-Hill/Osborne, most notably Jane Brownlow, Emma Acker, and Janet Walden.

INTRODUCTION

In this e-centric day and age organizations have come to rely on IT infrastructures not just as an aid to business, but for some, as the core of their business. Safe, secure, and reliable computing and telecommunications are essential to these organizations. As these organizations begin to understand the importance of information security, they are developing security programs that are often under the direction of the CIO.

An information security program includes more than just people and technology. The programs involve policies, procedures, audits, monitoring, and an investment of time and money. This book is meant to provide organizations with a broad overview of the security program, what it should be, who it should include, what it entails, and how it should fit into the overall organization.

This book is for the security professional who must answer to management about the security of the organization. In today's economy, many organizations do not have the ability to hire a person and dedicate that person to security. Often the person who is given this job is an IT professional with no specific security training. This book will provide the road map for such individuals.

The book is divided into four main parts plus some good information in appendices:

Part I: Guiding Principles in Plan Development   Part I is intended to provide guidance on fundamental issues with security planning. In this part we cover the basic concepts of the role of information security, laws and regulations, and risk identification.

- **Chapter 1: The Role of the Information Security Program**   Chapter 1 discusses the overall importance of the information security program. It describes where it fits into the organization and who should establish its charter, mission, responsibilities, and authority. It further talks about the relationship of the information security manager (and the department) to the rest of the organization. It is impossible to build a program in a vacuum or with bad relationships throughout the organization.

- **Chapter 2: Laws and Regulations**   Many industries have federal or state regulations that must be followed. Some of these regulations may affect the security program. It is therefore important for the security department to understand the regulation requirements. In some cases the existence of the information security program is clearly dictated by laws and regulations.

- **Chapter 3: Assessments**   This chapter focuses on how organizations go about identifying the state of their information security efforts. It includes information on various types of assessments and when they should and should not be used.

Part II: Plan Implementation   Part II discusses the basics of risk management and mitigation. Once risk has been identified, the mitigation steps must be taken. While the exact plan will vary for each organization, this part of the book provides the basics.

- **Chapter 4: Establishing Policies and Procedures**   This chapter discusses the importance of policies and procedures and describes policies and procedures that need to be created for the organization. The primary focus of this chapter is the order that they should be created and the approach to use in getting the organization to buy into what is created.

- **Chapter 5: Implementing the Security Plan**   Policies are nice documents but if they are not implemented, they do no good. This chapter talks about general guidelines for implementing good policies.

- **Chapter 6: Deploying New Projects and Technologies**   No organization can afford to develop everything internally. Security is no different in this regard. Since it is likely that products will be purchased for the organization and new projects will be developed internally, this chapter covers how to manage the risk to the organization through the development process.

- **Chapter 7: Security Training and Awareness**   This chapter discusses the programs and classes that must be established to make the organization aware of security issues. Security awareness is one of the most cost-effective components of the information security program. In a recent speech, Richard Clark, the President's cyber-security advisor, noted that the awareness of employees was critical to an organization's security program. He also noted that he and the federal government would be stressing this topic to industry in the coming months.

- **Chapter 8: Monitoring Security**   The security program is in place. How do you know that it is working? The only way to know is to monitor it. This chapter discusses the more useful methods for monitoring.

Part III: Plan Administration   Security programs are no different than any other program within an organization. Once they are set up and working properly, they must be managed and administered properly. This part talks about these tasks.

- **Chapter 9: Budgeting for Security**   Just about every organization has a budget process. The security department must go through it with every other department. Therefore, it is important for the security department to do it well.

- **Chapter 10: The Security Staff**   Not every security program has a staff but many do. Choosing the correct individuals for the staff and the correct mix of skills can make or break the program. This chapter talks about the mix of the team and how to find good people.

- **Chapter 11: Reporting**   Finally, there is reporting. Without some type of reporting there is no way for the organization to gauge the effectiveness of the security department. There is rarely an ROI for security (but this is changing) and thus there must be other metrics to use to measure the performance of the department.

Part IV: How to Respond to Incidents   All of the planning, risk identification, risk mitigation, and administration tasks can help an organization to manage risk. However, no one can ever completely remove risk. This part of the book discusses how to deal with incidents and disasters when they occur.

- **Chapter 12: Incident Response**   Bad things happen. The security program works diligently to try to prevent them but they happen anyway. When they do, the security department must be ready to take the lead in the response.

- **Chapter 13: Developing Contingency Plans**   Disasters of all shapes and sizes occur to businesses. Because organizations have become so dependent on their IT infrastructures it is essential that they develop an IT Disaster Recovery Plan and keep it up to date. This plan will provide policies, procedures, roles, and responsibilities for preparing for, responding to, and recovering from a variety of disasters. This chapter explains the key steps in developing an IT DRP.

- **Chapter 14: Responding to Disasters**   How an organization responds to a disaster is just as important as how an organization plans for a disaster. Often, the response to a disaster deviates from the plan due to unforeseen circumstances. This chapter discusses the proper response during a serious disaster.

Part V: Appendixes   Part V provides three sections that complement the purpose of the book. These sections are intended to assist the reader in answering particular questions about security and implementing a strong program.

- **Appendix A: Handling Audits**   Audits are a fact of life. Every organization goes through them. They may be internal audits or external. The security team must be a part of these audits and the organization's response.

- **Appendix B: Outsourcing Security**   The outsourcing of security has become a lively topic recently. Many new security firms exist that sell some type of service. This may impact the security of the organization or it may be a cost-effective way to fulfill the responsibilities of the security department.

- **Appendix C: Managing New Security Projects**   This appendix is a continuation of Chapter 6 that talks specifically about building new security projects as opposed to security in new business projects.

PART I

Guiding Principles in Plan Development

CHAPTER 1

The Role of the Information Security Program

S ecurity professionals today talk about the need for strong security programs. We hear calls for the latest products, more staff, and more funding. But what is a strong security program? If an organization has a weak program, how can it be strengthened? How much money does it take to create and maintain a strong program?

None of these questions have simple answers. However, one thing is very clear: A security program must have three things in order to be strong and successful:

- A well-defined mission
- Good relationships within the organization
- Intelligent, knowledgeable security professionals

The details of building and maintaining a strong security program will be left to the other chapters of this book. Identifying, hiring, and keeping security professionals will also be discussed in some detail later in the book (see Chapter 10). This chapter will focus on the first two items above—the mission and the relationships. In short, these two items identify the role that the security program will play within the organization.

GETTING OFF ON THE RIGHT FOOT

Perhaps the most important part of the security manager's job is the beginning. The person who leads the organization's information security department has a job that will touch every other department in the organization. Every employee will be affected by the decisions and policies that are developed by information security. Therefore, it is extremely important for the information security manager to establish good working relationships with other departments. We will talk more about these relationships later in this chapter.

 SECURITY ALERT!   The security manager who starts off on the wrong foot is destined for failure. Many security departments and security managers failed to help organizations manage their risk by ignoring the impact of relationships.

A new security manager must begin these relationships. In most cases, the information security manager will be the new kid on the block. The other departments will have well-established missions, roles, procedures, and reporting structures. The worst possible thing would be for the new information security manager to attempt to assert his authority over this existing structure. The rest of the organization would ignore the new manager and force the entire security effort to become ineffective.

CHALLENGE

You are a new security manager for an organization. The first task that you have on your plate is the development of a new information security policy. You complete the policy without the help of the rest of the organization since this is your job. Now you must go out and implement the policy.

As soon as you begin to work with system administrators, you get serious resistance. Then the administrators just stop working with you altogether. You approach your boss about the problem, thinking that pulling rank will get the policy implemented. Do you really think that this is the best course of action in this case? Even if your boss can or will help you put pressure on the administrators, will the policy implementation succeed?

Likely, the answer is no it will not. The administrators have no interest in the policy since they view it as being shoved down their throats. The best chance you have of getting any policy implemented now is to go to the system administration staff and beg for their help in writing a new policy (don't even try to start with the original one).

What then is the best way to get off on the right foot? First, remember that the information security department is likely to be new kid to the organization and thus must learn how the organization works before putting out directives that must be met or else. The security manager should start by talking to each department manager. He or she must also learn not to *direct* how security should be handled but to *learn* and *work with* the other departments.

Second, the information security department is charged with a mission. How this mission is accomplished is the primary job of the information security manager. The mission must be accomplished in conjunction with, not in spite of, the other departments and employees of the organization. Establishing a good working relationship so that everyone understands the need for security will go a long way to accomplishing the security department's mission.

ESTABLISHING THE ROLE OF SECURITY

The information security department was established for a reason. Depending on the organization the reason might be any of the following:

- Government regulation required it.
- An audit report recommended it.

- Senior management or the board decided it was necessary.
- The IT department decided it was necessary to have the function.

In any case, a reason exists for the security department and thus a scope of operations exists as well. The scope of operations is defined by the location of the department within the organization. For example, if the information security department was established by senior management, it may have a scope that includes the entire organization. If the information security department was established by the IT director, then the scope is likely to be more limited (the IT department for instance).

The reporting structure for security is only one part of establishing the role of security. The information security department should also have a mission statement and long-term goals. These should be developed and approved by the organization.

TIP   Work with senior management to develop the mission statement. Make sure the mission statement agrees with what senior management had in mind for the security department.

Reporting Structure

The reporting structure for the information security department is one of the most important aspects of the department's creation. If the department reports too low in the organization, the scope and authority of the department will be too limited to be effective. In some cases the reporting location may also cause conflicts of interest.

Figure 1-1 shows a very general organization chart with various placements for the information security department. Two of the locations are shown in medium shading. These indicate good places for the department. The first would have security reporting directly to the president or CEO. This location gives the information security department the largest possible scope and the highest possible visibility in the organization. While this reporting point is good for information security, it is not always possible. Some organizations do not wish to elevate the head of information security to the senior management team for example.

The second good alternative would place the information security department under the organization's general counsel. This moves the department from directly reporting to the President or CEO and yet still allows the department to have a large scope (the general counsel usually can act throughout the organization). Given that many security issues are also becoming legal issues, placement here is certainly appropriate.

Some organizations place the information security department under the CFO, as indicated in light shading in Figure 1-1. While this placement is not bad, it does pose some potential conflicts of interest. Since the CFO usually looks across the organization, the scope of the information security department would not be limited. However, the CFO usually also manages the internal audit department. Information security and internal audit have similar yet different roles within an organization (see the "Relationship" section for a more complete explanation of this relationship) and therefore should be

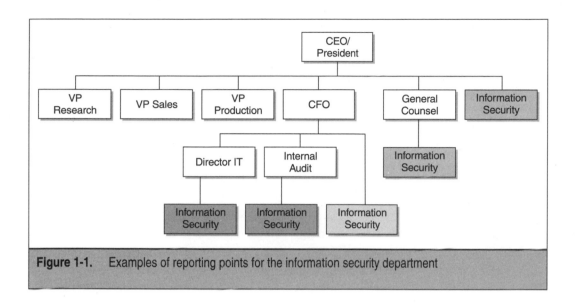

Figure 1-1.   Examples of reporting points for the information security department

kept as separate as possible. If the CFO manages this potential conflict properly, there is no reason why placing the information security department here would not work.

Information security departments are often placed below the IT department, as indicated in dark shading in Figure 1-1. This is because information security usually develops out of the IT department's need for security policy and incident response. Unfortunately, the placement of the organization's information security department here tends to limit the scope of the department unnecessarily. It often becomes difficult for the information security department to work effectively across the organization.

 SECURITY ALERT!   If the security department reports to the IT department, make sure that the mission statement for the department is focused primarily on IT issues. If the mission statement is too broad, conflicts with other departments may arise.

Placement of the information security department below the internal audit function (also indicated in dark shading in Figure 1-1) causes a serious conflict of interest. Information security is supposed to create and manage policy. The audit department is supposed to determine compliance. It is not appropriate for the audit department to both create policy and then determine compliance.

Mission Statement

In most cases, we don't see the point of a mission statement for a department within an organization. The simple reason for this is that most mission statements are self-evident. For example, the mission of the software development department is to develop good software according to the design requirements. This seems pretty obvious.

Unfortunately, the mission of the information security department is often misunderstood. The information security department cannot guarantee the security of the organization's information or systems. The information security department can assist in managing the information security risk to the organization but that is as far as we can go. Security in general (and information security in particular) are exercises in risk management. There are no guarantees. In fact, risk is an inevitable part of life. It is the job of the information security department to help manage the risk to the organization.

Given that, what are some appropriate mission statements for the information security department? The following statements are provided as examples of good mission statements for an information security department:

- To appropriately manage the information security risk to the organization by working with the various internal departments

- To appropriately manage the information security risk to the organization by operating various network and system security mechanisms

- To appropriately manage the information security risk to the organization by developing and managing organizational security policy

- To appropriately manage the information security risk to the IT department of the organization by managing the implementation of organization security policy

Please notice that each of these mission statements includes the scope of the work (the entire organization or the IT department) and the mechanism for the work. In some organizations the information security department only sets policy while in others the department will manage network devices such as firewalls and intrusion detection systems. The type of tasks that the department is expected to carry out will impact how the mission statement is worded.

So why is it so important that we get the mission statement of the information security department correct? Because from the mission statement all of the work of the department is derived (see Figure 1-2). Since the mission statement will also define how the work is to be done (at a very high level) and for whom the work is to be done (the scope of the department's authority), it is a very important statement.

Once the mission statement has been developed, it should be agreed to by the senior management of the organization.

Long-Term Goals

As can be seen in Figure 1-2, long-term goals for the information security department flow from the department's mission statement. Long-term goals are goals that may take several months to several years to accomplish. These are goals for the department that directly affect the ability of the department to meet the mission statement.

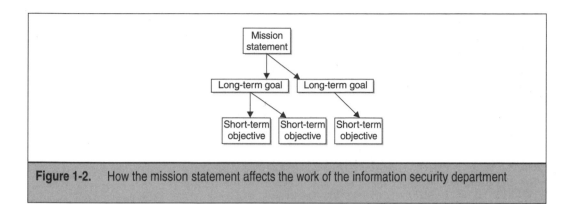

Figure 1-2.   How the mission statement affects the work of the information security department

A long-term goal for the department might be to be able to quantify the risk to the organization on a regular basis. Obviously, this goal will require significant work in various areas such as assessments, vulnerability tracking, threat identification, and policy compliance monitoring. Each of these systems may themselves take time and resources to implement.

Long-term goals should be part of strategies used by the department to manage the risk to the organization. Figure 1-3 shows another way to plan the direction for the department. Following a risk assessment (see Chapter 3), the major risks to the security of information within the organization should be identified. For each major risk, a strategy should be created to manage the risk. The management of these risks becomes the long-term goal for the department.

TIP   At least once a year, the long-term goals of the department should be reviewed to check on progress. The review of long-term goals may also identify completed goals and new goals that must be added to respond to changes in the organization.

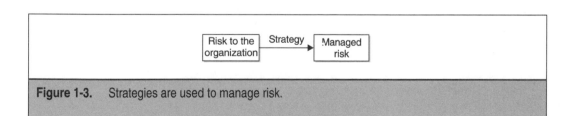

Figure 1-3.   Strategies are used to manage risk.

Short-Term Objectives

At least once a year short-term objectives should be identified to move the department toward meeting the long-term goals of security for the organization. These objectives can be turned into project plans for the coming year. Each project plan can be used for budgeting purposes (see Chapter 9).

Short-term objectives may be the installation of a new product or the creation of a process to monitor some aspect of security. No matter how the objectives are defined, the completion of any of the objectives should lead the department closer to the long-term goal.

RELATIONSHIPS

As mentioned before, relationships will make or break the effectiveness of the information security department. Regardless of the support from senior management or the authority given to the department, the relationships that are developed between security staff and management and the rest of the organization are critical to the overall success of the department.

There are two types of relationships that the security department must create:

- Technical
- Business

Technical relationships are those that build on the ability of the security staff to explain and understand technical issues. Business relationships are those that build on the ability of the security staff to understand the needs of the organization in order to accomplish the business of the organization.

Technical Relationships

As was already mentioned, technical relationships are those that build on the ability of security staff to explain and understand technical issues. In other words, technical relationships are built on mutual respect for the technical knowledge and capabilities of the security staff and the other employees or departments.

 SECURITY ALERT!   If the security staff shows that it has no understanding of networks, systems, software development, and so on, these groups will not believe that the security department will be able to help them or understand their problems.

It is also important to understand that the technical relationships between security and other departments are not always two-way relationships (see Figure 1-4). In many cases, the relationship may be one where security provides information, guidance, and assistance to the other department but does not really receive assistance in return.

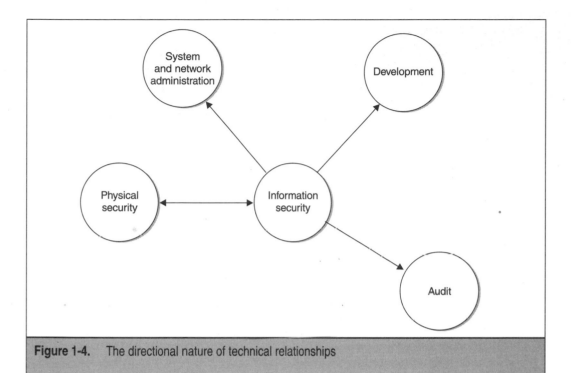

Figure 1-4.   The directional nature of technical relationships

Administrators

Both system and network administrators are very technical professionals who tend to have more work then they do hours in the day. Therefore, when the issue of security comes up, the administrator is unlikely to be favorably disposed to taking on more work. How then can the security department form a relationship with system and network administrators?

It is painfully obvious to anyone who has tried that attempting to threaten or force administrators to secure their systems does not work. The primary job of system and network administrators is to keep the systems up and running. They do this very well. Anything that is perceived as reducing their ability to keep the systems up is unlikely to be done. (This is not to say the administrators do not wish their systems to be secure. On the contrary, they do.) Therefore, the security department must provide information to the administrators that shows how security can assist them in keeping the systems up. In this way, the security department shows a value to the administrators. Once a value is shown, the job of security becomes easier.

Another issue that hurts the relationship between security and administrators is the perception that the security department does not understand the technical system or network issues. Often this is in fact the case and leads to security staff making recommendations or even demands that do not make sense in the technical environment of the organization.

In order to build a good working relationship with administrators, the security staff needs to have technical knowledge in the following areas:

- Network architecture
- Network protocols (specifically TCP/IP or whatever protocols are used on site)
- Basic Unix administration (basic commands and where to find files)
- Basic Windows NT/2000 administration

With this basic knowledge, the security staff will understand why a sniffer may not work in a switched environment or why the Unix passwd file has to be readable by all processes but the shadow file does not.

Development

Development staff are also very technical individuals who have project deadlines that must be met. In many cases, these deadlines are imposed by senior management for new product offerings. As with administrators, if security attempts to dictate to the developers, the relationship will fail.

Security must work within the framework of the developers' world. In most organizations, the development staff uses a development methodology. This methodology is the perfect way for security to work with the development staff. Throughout project development there are tasks that would benefit from security involvement. For example, the requirements phase of a project should consider security requirements. If the project does not take into account security during the requirements phase, the project may find that the new system has security holes when it is time for the project to go into production. By showing the development staff how security can alleviate some of the back-end headaches, the development staff can be shown a benefit to security's involvement.

As with the administration staff, development will not look kindly upon security staff who lack an understanding of the development methodology and the technical issues involved in the development process. This is not to say that the security staff must understand how to code C++, but the members of the staff that work with the developers should have some understanding of how systems are developed and coded. *Building Secure Software: How to Avoid Security Problems the Right Way* by John Viega and Gary McGraw (Addison Wesley Professional, 2001) is an excellent reference on how to write secure code.

In addition, knowledge in the following areas will assist the security staff when working with development:

- System architecture
- Performance testing
- Software development
- System integration issues (making products work together)
- The organization's development methodology

Physical Security

In most organizations, the department that handles the door locks, guards, cameras, and other physical security mechanisms is separate from the information security department. Yet physical security is a very important component of the overall information security of the organization. This makes it doubly important that the information security department have a good relationship with the people that handle physical security.

The relationship with physical security should be a peer-to-peer relationship. The two departments should be able to reinforce and assist each other in the overall goal of improved security and reduced risk to the organization. This means that the physical security department should be involved in risk assessments and in risk management. Often, it may be found that changing physical security procedures may be cheaper and easier than enhancing computer or network security.

Audit

Unfortunately, the audit department is often looked at as an adversary or an antagonist by information security. Clearly, this is the wrong way to look at this relationship. The audit department serves a very important role in organizations. They are the watchdogs and the checkers who make sure that policies and procedures are followed. Auditors make sure that trust relationships between the organization and its employees are upheld.

Information security and audit serve very similar roles. Both have the job of reducing the overall risk to the organization. And yet, the two departments are not direct competitors for funds and prestige. Therefore, there should be a good working relationship between the two departments.

When we worked in organizations that had internal audit departments, we made it our business to meet the internal auditors and to find out how they did their jobs. In doing this, we have found individuals who wish to learn about the technology that is used in information security so that they could do their jobs better.

TIP   The information security department can and should provide information to the audit department about the technology and procedures that are being used to manage risk. When the auditors request to perform an audit, the information security department should be completely open with them and provide all the necessary information.

Business Relationships

If the security staff understands nothing else, they must understand that their job is to assist the organization in performing its primary business function. With that said, the security department must form business relationships within the organization. These are relationships where security supports the primary business function (see Figure 1-5). No business functions will support the security department. Why? Because the security department is a support organization. Its job is to assist the business to function. It is not the function of the business departments to assist the security department.

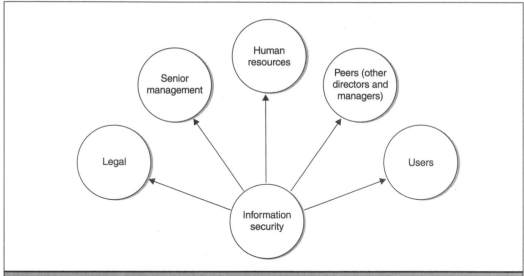

Figure 1-5. The security department supports the business of the organization.

 SECURITY ALERT! It is essential to reiterate that the information security staff must understand the business role of the organization they are working to protect. An ideal manager of the security department will be able to merge the business and the technical.

Senior Management

Security supports the senior management of the organization in its job of managing the organization. This means that security provides information to the top managers of the organization to assist them in making decisions. We will talk more about this when we discuss reporting in Chapter 11. At this point we need to talk about the relationship between the security department and the senior management of the organization.

It sometimes appears that security will use the support of senior management to accomplish its tasks. For example, a letter from the CEO about compliance with security policies is often key in gaining organization buy-in. But in reality, during this whole process security is supporting the organization. The reason for this is that the development of the security policy and the organization's compliance with it actually support the management of risk for the entire organization. The leaders of the organization are supposed to make money for the owners (or stockholders) and make the organization successful. They do this by making decisions about risk and reward.

Security supports this by providing information on risk and helping to manage the security risk to the organization. Therefore, the activities of the security department should all be targeted to manage security risk. The development and deployment of a security policy is a means of doing just that. Therefore the support of the organization's senior management is actually senior management agreeing that security is helping them manage risk to the organization.

Enough of a philosophic view of the relationship. Let's talk more down to earth. First off, the senior management of the organization must be able to trust the information that comes from the security department. This means that the security department must provide appropriate information. There should be no grand-standing and no inflation of the risks (that is, security should not go around yelling that the sky is falling). Note that an effective security department manager will know what to worry about and, to a degree more importantly, what not to worry about.

It also means that security should be staffed by professionals who have a good understanding of security and the technologies that security must affect (networks, systems, and so on). In the performance of its duty, security may be asked to comment on technical solutions. If security does not understand the technical aspects of the problem and proposed solution, how can a valid comment be made?

The second key aspect of the relationship between security and senior management is that security must understand the business of the organization. This understanding is important because recommended solutions to manage risk must take into account that business must continue. Recommendations that clearly prevent business or that adversely affect the business of the organization without providing a clear benefit will not be taken seriously. If this occurs, senior management will no longer trust the opinions of the security department and thus security will not be able to provide assistance in managing business risk.

The relationship with senior management is thus one of assistance and advice. Security must be trusted to know security and the business of the organization in order to supply both of these.

Peers

For the purpose of this discussion, we will consider all other managers, department heads, and directors who do not fit in the senior management category as peers to the security manager. For the same reason that it is important for security to support senior management, it is also important for security to support peers and peer departments. Some of these peer departments will be departments that do the business of the organization. Other peer departments will be supporting departments who assist the organization in doing business (just like security does).

Security will help these other departments manage their risk and perform the functions of the business in a manner that manages the security risk to the organization. This means that the heads of these departments must understand that some things they do may cause risk. Therefore, security will be constantly educating other departments on the ramifications to the organization if a risk were to actually occur.

Security must build a trust relationship with these other departments so that the other departments will follow security recommendations and come to the security department with questions. Nowhere will this relationship be more important than with the IT and development groups. We have already talked about the technical relationship with these departments. In addition to this technical relationship, there must also be a business relationship. Technically, both departments must see that security has knowledge about systems, networks, and development. From the business perspective, both departments need to see that security understands how the business functions and how IT and development assist in the business functions.

The User Community

The relationship between the security department and the user community of the organization may be the most important. The reason for this is very simple. The organization can spend hundreds of thousands or even millions of dollars on security systems and technologies but a single employee who is unaware of the security policies of the organization can allow an intruder to bypass it all. This means that every employee in the organization must understand the need for security (see Chapter 7 on security awareness training). Remember that behind most security breaches are authorized users who did not follow the rules.

This does not mean that the security department or the security manager will have a personal relationship with every single employee. However, employees should understand what the security department is and what its function is with regard to the organization. Employees are human and thus they will seek the path of least resistance when performing their jobs. This is not to say that employees are by nature lazy, only that human nature will seek to perform a task while expending the least amount of effort. Understanding this fact will enable the security department to develop programs and its relationship with the user community in such a way that the security risk to the organization can be managed.

Since the relationship with the user community is generally not a personal one (as most other relationships will likely be), the security department will interact and relate to users in a different way. Successful security departments will provide information to the user community in such a way that the users find the information interesting. For example, the security department may run a lunch-time seminar on how to protect your kids from the dangers of the Internet. While conducting the seminar, security can provide the employees with good practices that are also in line with organization policy. Likewise, the security department could provide hints and suggestions on keeping home computers free of viruses. The information provided to the users can be the same as that required of them when performing their jobs. In both cases, the users are provided with something that can be useful and perhaps take some risk out of their lives as well as their work. These actions show the users that security can be of help to them and not just a hindrance to their work.

In the best of all possible worlds, the organization will take violations of security policy as seriously as it does violations of sexual harassment policies. Most companies have a zero tolerance policy for sexual harassment. But if that same employee violates an information security policy, there is much greater tolerance.

 SECURITY ALERT!   The security awareness of employees is perhaps the most important single factor in the overall risk to the organization. A security manager who ignores the employees will almost always fail.

Legal

The general counsel's office is the department that is perhaps the closest to the security department in function. Both are in place to assist in the performance of the organization's primary function and both are used to reduce the likelihood that something bad will happen to the organization. As more and more government regulations, such as the Health Information Portability and Accountability Act (HIPAA), are created that call for information security and information privacy, the general counsel and the security department will work more and more closely to develop appropriate policies and implement appropriate mechanisms to reduce the organization's exposure to fines and lawsuits.

Given this, the relationship between the legal office and security should be very obvious and easy to build. The security department will need the advice and guidance of the general counsel's office when defining policy. The legal office will need to work with the security department to determine if government regulations are being complied with and what potential legal exposures the organization may have.

During a security incident (see Chapter 12), the general counsel and the security department must work very closely, with mutual trust and respect in order to limit the damage to the organization.

Human Resources

HR is another support department that is very important to the success of the information security department. The reason for this is simple: HR is the source of many policies that affect the overall information security risk of the organization. For example, HR may be the source of a policy that allows telecommuting. This policy has security ramifications since the employees who are working from home may have sensitive information with them or on their computers. At the same time, these computers may need connectivity back into the organization's internal network. Both of these issues are key information security risks that must be managed by the information security department.

Another important reason for a relationship with HR is that HR handles the hiring and termination of employees. This is another key risk area that the information security department must deal with. A good working relationship with HR will make the work of training new employees on the need for security much easier. At the same time, this relationship will assist in the identification of people who are no longer employees and whose access should be rescinded.

If those two reasons are not enough, HR is also usually the location of the organization's training department. Any type of security awareness program will not succeed without the assistance of HR.

None of this is meant to imply that the relationship with HR is one-way. The relationship should be one of mutual trust and assistance. The security department will rely on HR to educate employees and identify the status of employees. HR will rely on the security department for the implementation of policies such as computer use, telecommuting, and so on and for the material that must be provided to the employees of the organization.

CHECKLIST: KEY ROLES OF THE PROGRAM

The following is a checklist of key steps in the establishment of an information security program:

- ☐ Identify the reporting structure for the information security department— try to locate the department at an appropriate place within the organization.
- ☐ Learn how the organization works and what it does.
- ☐ Develop a sound mission statement.
- ☐ Get approval and support from management for the mission.
- ☐ Identify long -term goals and a risk management strategy.
- ☐ Develop short-term objectives.
- ☐ Develop good technical relationships with administrators, development, physical security, and audit.
- ☐ Develop good business relationships with peers, the user community, and human resources.
- ☐ Develop a good reporting mechanism for senior management.
- ☐ Work with the legal department to understand the legal issues surrounding information security within the organization.

CHAPTER 2

Laws and Regulations

Many companies are regulated by federal, state, and local statutes. As more companies utilize information technology as a core part of their business operations, there are more regulations specifically aimed at ensuring that information is appropriately protected. Without doubt the most regulated are the financial services and medical industries. These industries have long had requirements for protecting the privacy of customer and patient data. With the increased usage and dependence on information systems and networks, the government has begun to pass legislation specifically aimed at controlling access to and protecting the confidentiality of such information.

You must ensure that your information security program helps the company stay compliant with all relevant regulations. Most recently, the Gramm-Leach-Bliley Act (GLBA) and the Health Insurance Portability and Accountability Act (HIPAA) have put very specific requirements on the way financial services firms and healthcare organizations protect information. HIPAA even has criminal penalties for failure to comply. Specifically, violations of the provisions in HIPAA can result in $100 for each violation, subject to a $25,000 limit for all violations of the same "requirement or prohibition" during the same calendar year. Given the numerous "requirements or prohibitions" under HIPAA, a $25,000 limit per requirement or prohibition can add up quickly. The law is even harsher on those who intentionally violate HIPAA. The lowest penalty is a fine of up to $50,000 and imprisonment for up to a year, which increases to $100,000 and up to five years in prison if the offense is committed under false pretenses, and which tops out at $250,000 and up to ten years in prison if the violation is committed "with intent to sell, transfer, or use individually identifiable health information for commercial advantage, personal gain, or malicious harm." This is pretty serious business.

GLBA and HIPAA will have a significant impact on financial services and healthcare organizations. They require formal information security programs to be established and recognized by senior management. The GLBA states that the board of directors must approve the information security plan. Similarly, HIPAA mandates a formal information security and privacy infrastructure. HIPAA is a huge endeavor that will cost healthcare organizations a huge amount of money.

For the first time information security risk is being laid in the hands of the most senior management. These new regulations are forcing organizations to create formal information security programs and spend money to ensure they are adequately protecting information systems. For some these laws might seem like a burden. For others it might be a blessing because now there is less guessing about what the program should include and it will likely bring more funding for the information security budget.

In addition to the fact that there are laws that drive the way we run our information security programs, there are also laws that protect us as corporations against hackers and malicious internal employees who would steal information from our computer systems. These laws pertain to such things as cyber-crime, domain name theft (cyber-squatting), intellectual property protection, defamation, and trademark infringement. The crimes against companies—usually theft and fraud—are not new. The difference is that the Internet has brought about new ways of conducting those same old crimes.

In this chapter we will cover some of the laws and regulations that dictate the way we must control access to the systems and information in our enterprises, and what we can use to protect ourselves. There are more laws and regulations than there are pages permitted for this chapter. There is also an entire series of regulations that pertains specifically to the way that federal information systems are to be protected. For this chapter we focus only on laws that pertain to general commerce and not specifically to federal government information security programs.

NOTE   The information in this chapter is not legal advice. The authors are not lawyers. For information on how these or other regulations pertain to your specific situation, you should consult with your company's legal counsel.

WORKING WITH THE LEGAL AND COMPLIANCE DEPARTMENTS

Before we discuss any specific regulations we should understand the importance of a good working relationship between the information security department and the legal/compliance department. They will be extremely helpful in keeping current with the federal, state, local, and industry-specific regulations that affect your program. You should establish a process that allows you to meet regularly with the legal and compliance organizations to exchange information on changes to the regulatory environment. To ensure that you are being most efficient and not duplicating effort, you should establish roles within your information security regulatory team. We'd suggest that you let the legal folks track what they are best at tracking—the laws.

The compliance department will be critical to ensuring that you are staying in line with federal, state, and local statutes. These laws will most likely be the ones that specify the types of controls you must have in place to protect the confidentiality and privacy of the sensitive information you process. This may include customer, member, client, partner, vendor, and/or employee data. The compliance department might have internal auditors that will periodically want to check to see if the controls you have emplaced are functioning and that they meet the minimum standards specified by law.

TIP   The legal department will be your best resource if you think that a breach of security might warrant prosecution. It is very important to remember that if, as an information security professional, you think that legal action will result from that breach, you must preserve evidence in accordance with government standards. It is very easy to make evidence inadmissible or less likely to go unchallenged if you improperly handle it. Computer evidence, although not very new, is still not widely understood by the legal system and jury members. Later in this chapter we will discuss evidence in more detail. Additionally, you may want to consider an internal protocol to have only the legal department be the one to contact and interface with the legal authorities.

LEGAL BACKGROUND

Laws that pertain specifically to computer security started to appear in the 1980s as computer systems were becoming more vital to business and government operations. As those computers came under increasingly frequent attacks by "hackers" the government decided that legislation was necessary to protect systems from unauthorized access. In 1981 no clear laws were in place to deal with a 24-year-old known as "Captain Zap" and three others who used the White House switchboard to make long distance connections to other computers around the world. These hackers were eventually tried under some existing laws that had nothing to do with computer misuse. "Captain Zap" was fined $1000 and sentenced to two and a half years probation.

It became obvious that existing laws, even those dealing with wiretapping and eavesdropping, were not sufficient to charge this new breed of criminals. Legislators began putting their heads together to develop laws that would help them place stiff penalties against unauthorized computer intrusions. One of the first of those laws was the Computer Fraud and Abuse Act of 1986.

Some of these laws will be helpful in protecting your business from would-be hackers and crackers. Others might be used against you if you are not careful in how you implement the controls of your information security program.

Computer Fraud and Abuse Act of 1986

Part 1 of Title 18 of the US Code Chapter 47 Section 1030, The Computer Fraud and Abuse Act of 1986, was the culmination of several years of research and discussion among lawmakers. The law took quite some time to develop because legislators had a much more difficult time than expected collecting enough testimony from victims in the private sector. Companies were very reluctant to reveal that they had been the victim of computer hacking for fear of losing public confidence and business.

The Act enhanced and strengthened an intermediate Fraud and Abuse Act established in 1984. It also complemented the Electronic Communications Privacy Act of 1986, which outlawed the unauthorized interception of digital communications and had just recently been passed. President Ronald Reagan signed it into law on October 16, 1986.

The law established two primary felonies; one addressed the unauthorized access of a "federal interest computer" with the intention to commit fraudulent theft. The other felony addressed "malicious damage," involving alteration of information in, or preventing the use of, a federal interest computer. To be covered by the law, a malicious damage violation would have to result in a loss to the victim of $1000 or more, except in cases involving the alteration of medical records.

The law was carefully crafted to address only federal and interstate computer crimes because of concern that it could infringe on individual states' rights to develop their own computer crime laws. A "federal interest computer," according to the law, is one:

...exclusively for the use of a financial institution or the United States Government, or, in the case of a computer not exclusively for such use, used by or for a financial institution or the United States Government, and the conduct constituting the offense affects such use, or which is one of two or more computers used in committing the offense, not all of which are located in the same State.

Financial institutions covered by the law specifically include

- Federally insured banks, thrifts, and credit unions
- Registered securities brokers
- Members of the Federal Home Loan Bank System, the Farm Credit Administration, and the Federal Reserve System

The penalty for a violation resulting in conviction under this law could result in a prison term of five years for a first offense and ten years for a second offense.

The Act also made it a federal misdemeanor to traffic in computer passwords with the intent to commit fraud that affects interstate commerce. This provision was meant to cover the creation, maintenance, and use of "pirate bulletin boards" where confidential computer passwords are revealed. The legislation applied to anyone who:

...knowingly and with the intent to defraud, traffics, transfers, or otherwise disposes of, to another, or obtains control of, with intent to transfer or dispose of in any password through which a computer may be accessed without authorization, if such trafficking affects interstate or foreign commerce or such computer is used by or for the Government of the United States.

The two most prominent cases to test the new legislation involved Robert Morris, a 22-year-old Cornell graduate student, and Herbert Zinn, a high school dropout. Zinn, whose hacker codename was "Shadowhawk," was the first person convicted under the new law. He was only 16 years old when he broke into AT&T and Department of Defense computer systems. He was convicted on January 23, 1989, of destroying $174,000 worth of files, copying programs valued at millions of dollars, and publishing passwords and instructions on how to violate computer security systems. Zinn's sentence was nine months in prison and he was fined $10,000. If he had not been a minor at the time of his crimes, Zinn could have received 13 years in prison and a fine of $800,000.

The second case tried by the Computer Fraud and Abuse Act of 1986 involved Robert Morris and his infamous "Internet Worm." In November 1988, Morris launched the "worm" program that he claims was designed to navigate the Internet on its own to search for system vulnerabilities. The worm grew out of control very quickly and consumed computer resources until more than 6000 systems had crashed or were seriously crippled. Morris was convicted and sentenced to three years of probation, 400 hours of community service, and a $10,000 fine under the Computer Fraud and Abuse Act.

Electronic Communications Privacy Act of 1986

The Electronic Communications Privacy Act (ECPA) became law less than one week after the Computer Fraud and Abuse Act of 1986 was signed by President Reagan. ECPA replaced Title III of the Omnibus Crime Control and Safe Streets Act of 1968, which had previously established the procedures that governed electronic surveillance. A 1967 case determined that the FBI's use of electronic surveillance devices to record and listen to telephone conversations without a warrant was a violation of the Fourth Amendment to the Constitution. This amendment provides for protection from unreasonable searches and seizures. The 1967 ruling allowed the courts to establish more specific criteria for allowable government surveillance.

The ruling stated that government agencies were required to demonstrate probable cause; identify the specific suspect, crime, telephone to be used, and time of conversation; and secure a warrant before they could legally execute a wiretap. By 1986 there had been very few significant abuses of earlier privacy legislation, but lawmakers felt pressure from industry and civil liberties groups to take notice of and address the dramatic expansion in the use of new technologies like electronic mail. An October 1985 report from the congressional Office of Technology Assessment stated that "many innovations in electronic surveillance technology" employed by law enforcement agencies "have outstripped constitutional and statutory protections, leaving areas in which there is currently no legal protection against … new surveillance devices."

ECPA was developed in anticipation of new privacy issues, relating to both government surveillance and "recreational eavesdropping" by private parties, that were likely to emerge along with the widespread use of new communication technologies such as those provided by the rapidly expanding Internet.

ECPA extended the privacy protection found in Title III to the transmission and storage of digitized textual information such as that included in electronic mail. The Act redefined the term *intercept* "to make it clear that it is illegal to intercept the non-voice portion of a wire communication such as the data or digitized portion of a voice communication." The "non-voice portion" includes "electronic communication," which is defined as "any transfer of signs, signals, writing, images, sound, data, or intelligence of any nature transmitted in whole or in part by a wire, radio, electromagnetic, photoelectric or photo-optical system."

The Act was designed to protect the contents of stored electronic mail, voicemail, and remote computing services. The law was also intended to prohibit providers of the electronic communication services from disclosing the contents of communication that had been stored electronically without the lawful consent of the person who originated the communication. Prior to ECPA, Title III privacy protection had been limited to surveillance of the "common carrier" facilities available to the general public. ECPA extends protection to the use of all carriers, including private telephone systems and branch exchanges, and local area networks.

Furthermore, ECPA amended the Title III definition of protected "wire communication" to "include communications utilizing wires, cables, or other line connections within a switching office … regardless of whether the communications are between two cellular telephones or between a cellular telephone and a 'landline' telephone." It provides protection for the wire portion of cordless phone conversations, but specifically notes that "wire communication" protected under Title III "does not include the radio portion of a telephone that is transmitted between the cordless telephone handset and the base unit."

ECPA clarified privacy protection related to the use of radio paging devices. The Department of Justice defined voice and digital display pagers as "a continuation of an original wire communication" that should therefore be subject to Title III protection. The law also identified "tone-only" pagers as devices whose use is not protected under Title III. The law further identified the Cable Communications Policy Act of 1984 as the exclusive source of protection policy governing home reception of unencrypted cable satellite programming. That 1984 law had established a set of policies to address cable satellite reception issues that pertained more to the conduct of commercial enterprise than to privacy issues. ECPA also increased criminal penalties for malicious or intentional interference that impedes the delivery of satellite transmissions.

One of the most important provisions in ECPA is that it restricts government access to subscriber and customer records belonging to electronic service providers. It states that government agencies must first secure a search warrant, court order, or an authorized administrative or grand jury subpoena to access service provider records without first notifying a subscriber or customer

The implications of ECPA could play an important role in your information security program. Under ECPA an employer cannot monitor employee telephone calls or electronic mail when employees have a reasonable expectation of privacy. However, the Act does allow employer eavesdropping if employees are notified in advance or if the employer has reason to believe the company's interests are in jeopardy.

CAUTION The most important thing to take from this is that if you think you will *ever* have need to monitor employee electronic communication for *any* reason you *must* inform them that they have *no* expectation of privacy. This is why it will be stressed later that system users should be provided with an acceptable use policy that they must read and sign prior to receiving any system access.

CHALLENGE

Balancing the need for security policy enforcement and compliance with federal, state, and local privacy laws can be tedious. Security professionals must be cautious to ensure that they do not overstep their bounds when performing their duties. For example, you must be careful not to target individuals when logging system actions without express consent by that person. Obviously, if you suspect a user of violating security policy, you are not going to run up to them and say, "Hey, can we monitor your activity on the network?" However, you do have to inform them that they might be monitored.

CHALLENGE (continued)

So how is this done? One of the most effective ways is to use the acceptable use policy form mentioned in Chapter 4. This form must summarize what is and is not acceptable use of IT systems and must inform the user that they should have no expectation of privacy on the network. Additionally, this form must make it clear to employees that their signature on the form indicates their express consent to monitoring.

Another important component of making users aware that their activity is subject to monitoring is to display a warning banner prior to each logon. The banner should require that the user actually click on a button to acknowledge they have read the warning banner. The banner text should be consistent with the acceptable use policy form. Having this express consent is an important component of avoiding future problems with privacy laws if you do, in fact, have to monitor the activity of a user. Also, make sure the language in your banner is not "welcoming" those who are connected but clearly states that the system is for authorized users only.

Assuming you do have this express consent you can monitor the activity of an individual user who is suspected of violating policy. It is still very important to follow careful procedure when monitoring a user's activity. Make sure you get all the right people involved. At a minimum you should have the user's manager, human resources, and the legal department involved. As a security professional don't ever take it upon yourself to track a user's activity unless specifically instructed to do so by one or more of those persons just mentioned.

With one of our previous employers, we went through a period of "staff reduction" when it was discovered by a member of the executive board that users were violating a policy on acceptable use of the Internet. In a one-month period at least four people were very publicly escorted to the door after their violations were confirmed through detailed keystroke monitoring. The policy was clear. Users were made aware. They signed the form. After those four cases, the instances of policy violation stopped almost completely. Word got out.

In this case all the right steps were followed. The tracking software was in place on the Internet proxy server. Daily reports were generated that identified the sites users were visiting and the information they were downloading. When violations were identified in the report the senior executive would gather the user's manager, a representative from human resources, and members of the information security staff. Using some network tools, the team would turn on keystroke monitoring for the suspected violator. Once it was witnessed and confirmed by all parties, the violator was immediately escorted to the door.

Computer Security Act of 1987

Oddly enough, Robert Morris' father was an employee of the National Security Agency (NSA), whose job it was at that time to develop computer security standards for government systems. In 1984, National Security Decision Directive (NSDD) 145 established the NSA as the controlling agency for all government computer systems containing "sensitive but unclassified" information. This was followed by a second directive issued by National Security Advisor John Poindexter that extended NSA authority over non-government computer systems.

In 1987, the U.S. Congress enacted Public Law 100-235, The Computer Security Act of 1987, reaffirming that the National Institute for Standards and Technology (NIST), a division of the Department of Commerce, was responsible for the security of unclassified, non-military government computer systems. Under the law, the role of the NSA was limited to providing technical assistance in the civilian security realm. Congress rightly felt that it was inappropriate for a military intelligence agency to have control over the dissemination of unclassified information.

The battle over who would be setting the standards for protecting government and government interest information systems was underway. The lines were pretty clear. The NSA would set the standards for all systems processing classified information and NIST would set them for all unclassified systems. The language in the act stated that NIST would have

... responsibility for developing standards and guidelines for Federal computer systems, including responsibility for developing standards and guidelines needed to assure the cost-effective security and privacy of sensitive information in Federal computer systems, drawing on the technical advice and assistance (including work products) of the National Security Agency, where appropriate.

National Information Infrastructure Protection Act of 1996

Let's jump ahead to more current legislation. Without a doubt the Computer Fraud and Abuse Act of 1986 is the groundwork for much of the legislation related to breaches of computer security controls. In fact, as you will see, it has become the core of all computer security-related works.

In 1996 the National Information Infrastructure Protection Act, part of public law 104-294, made specific amendments to the Computer Fraud and Abuse Act of 1986. The U.S. Government decided that it would be more practical to focus on making amendments to the Computer Fraud and Abuse Act to address new abuses that spring from the misuse of new technologies than to go through the entire U.S. Code and make changes to every law that pertained to computer and electronic security and privacy. The amendments to the Act are summarized in Table 2-1.

Section	Description of Change
1030(a)(1)	The language of § 1030(a)(1) should track the language of 18 U.S.C. § 793(e), which also provides a maximum penalty of ten years imprisonment for obtaining from any source certain information connected with the national defense and thereafter communicating or attempting to communicate it in an unauthorized manner.
1030(a)(2)	The new subsection § 1030(a)(2) is designed to insure that it is punishable to misuse computers to obtain government information and, where appropriate, information held by the private sector. Moreover, the provision has been restructured so that different paragraphs protect different types of information, thus allowing easy additions or modifications to offenses if events require.
1030(a)(3)	Three substantive changes were made to § 1030(a)(3): First, the word "adversely" has been deleted because including this term suggests, inappropriately, that trespassing in a government computer may be benign. Second, for clarity, the term "the use of the Government's operation of such computer" has been replaced with the term "that use by or for the Government of the United States." Consistent with this change, a similar change was made to the definition of "federal interest computer" (redesignated as "protected computer") in § 1030(e)(2)(A). Third, Congress inserted "non-public" to modify "computer of a department or agency of the United States." This change is intended to reflect the growing use of the Internet by government agencies and, in particular, the establishment of World Wide Web home pages and other public services.
1030(a)(4)	Amended to insure that felony-level sanctions apply when unauthorized use of the computer (or use exceeding authorization) is significant.
1030(a)(5)	Completely restructured in 1994, but the 1994 law may have had some unintended consequences. Most notably, certain government and financial institution computers may have been denied previously existing federal protection; some hacking activities may have been inappropriately decriminalized; and certain insider conduct may have been inappropriately criminalized. To remedy this situation in the 1996 Act, 18 U.S.C. § 1030(a)(5) was redrafted to cover any "protected computer," a new term defined in § 1030(e)(2) and used throughout the new statute—in § 1030(a)(5), as well as in §§ 1030(a)(2), (a)(4), and the new (a)(7). The definition of "protected computer" includes government computers, financial institution computers, and any computer "which is used in interstate or foreign commerce or communications."
1030(a)(7)	Covers any interstate or international transmission of threats against computers, computer networks, and their data and programs, whether the threat is received by mail, a telephone call, electronic mail, or through a computerized message service. The provision is worded broadly to cover threats to interfere in any way with the normal operation of the computer or system in question, such as denying access to authorized users, erasing or corrupting data or programs, or slowing down the operation of the computer or system.

Table 2-1. Summary of Changes to Public 100-235 as Made by the National Information Infrastructure Protection Act of 1996

Gramm-Leach-Bliley Financial Services Modernization Act

The GLBA was signed into law on November 12, 1999. The GLBA eliminates certain restrictions on affiliations among banks, insurance companies, and securities firms. To accomplish this the GLBA provides for "financial holding companies" (FHCs) under which these affiliations can be achieved. FHCs are subject to regulation by the Board of Governors of the Federal Reserve. In addition, FHCs are subject to regulation by functional financial regulators. Under the GLBA, FHCs may be established by filing notice with the Board of Governors of the Federal Reserve. A good summary of the entire law can be found on the U.S. Senate Web site at www.senate.gov/~banking/conf/grmleach.htm.

To ensure the privacy of customer information, Subtitle A of Title V of the Act imposes certain privacy disclosures and "opt out" requirements. Subtitle A of Title V imposes on "financial institutions" an affirmative duty to protect the private information of the institutions' customers. Section 502 of the GLBA specifically prohibits a financial institution from disclosing a consumer's private information to a "nonaffiliated third party" unless the institution has provided the consumer with specific disclosures and has given the consumer the ability to opt out of such information sharing. "Financial institution" is very broadly defined to include any institution "the business of which is engaging in any activities" that are "financial in nature or incidental to such financial activities," including insurance, merchant banking, and securities underwriting activities.

Financial institutions were quick to comply with this provision before July 1, 2001. You probably received several pieces of mail from your bank, broker, and other institutions with which you have affiliations and accounts. Those mail notices provided you the ability to "opt out" of any information sharing that the organization might conduct with its affiliates. In other words, if you chose to "opt out," then the organization would not be allowed to share your information with anyone else. Additionally, the Act requires financial institutions to tell its customers how it protects their information at the beginning of their relationship with the customer and annually.

Title V, Subsection A also requires that financial institutions protect the confidentiality and privacy of customer records and information, protect against any anticipated threats or hazards to the security or integrity of such records, and protect against unauthorized access to or use of such records or information that could result in substantial harm or inconvenience to any customer. Specifically, the Act requires the protection of customer "non-public" information. Customer non-public information is defined as:

Personally identifiable financial information provided by a customer to a financial institution resulting from any transaction with the customer or any service performed for the customer; or otherwise obtained by the financial institution.

The Act pertains to "financial institutions" including those regulated by the Office of the Comptroller of the Currency (OCC), the Federal Reserve System (Fed), the Federal Deposit Insurance Corporation (FDIC), or the Office of Thrift Supervision (OTS). The Fed, OTS, OCC, and FDIC published a joint final rule entitled "Interagency

Guidelines Establishing Standards for Safeguarding Customer Information." You can find a copy of these guidelines on the FFIEC Web site at www.ffiec.gov/exam/InfoBase/ documents/02-joi-safeguard_customer_info_final_rule-010201.pdf. A summary of these guidelines is included in Table 2-2.

Topic Area	Safeguard Description
Information Security Program	Each bank shall implement a comprehensive written information security program that includes administrative, technical, and physical safeguards appropriate to the size and complexity of the bank and the nature and scope of its activities. While all parts of the bank are not required to implement a uniform set of policies, all elements of the information security program must be coordinated. **Objectives:** A bank's information security program shall be designed to: Ensure the security and confidentiality of customer information; Protect against any anticipated threats or hazards to the security or integrity of such information; and Protect against unauthorized access to or use of such information that could result in substantial harm or inconvenience to any customer.
Board Involvement	The board of directors or an appropriate committee of the board of each bank shall: Approve the bank's written information security program; and Oversee the development, implementation, and maintenance of the bank's information security program, including assigning specific responsibility for its implementation and reviewing reports from management.
Assessing Risk	Each bank shall: 1. Identify reasonably foreseeable internal and external threats that could result in unauthorized disclosure, misuse, alteration, or destruction of customer information or customer information systems. 2. Assess the likelihood and potential damage of these threats, taking into consideration the sensitivity of customer information. 3. Assess the sufficiency of policies, procedures, customer information systems, and other arrangements in place to control risks.

Table 2-2.   Summary of "Interagency Guidelines Establishing Standards for Safeguarding Customer Information"

Topic Area	Safeguard Description
Managing and Controlling Risk	
Controlling Identified Risks	1. Design its information security program to control the identified risks, commensurate with the sensitivity of the information as well as the complexity and scope of the bank's activities. Each bank must consider whether the following security measures are appropriate for the bank and, if so, adopt those measures the bank concludes are appropriate: **Access controls** Access controls on customer information systems, including controls to authenticate and permit access only to authorized individuals and controls to prevent employees from providing customer information to unauthorized individuals who may seek to obtain this information through fraudulent means. **Physical access restrictions** Access restrictions at physical locations containing customer information, such as buildings, computer facilities, and records storage facilities to permit access only to authorized individuals. **Encryption** Encryption of electronic customer information, including while in transit or in storage on networks or systems to which unauthorized individuals may have access. **System change procedures** Procedures designed to ensure that customer information system modifications are consistent with the bank's information security program. **Dual control procedures, segregation of duties, and background checks** For employees with responsibilities for or access to customer information. **Intrusion detection** Monitoring systems and procedures to detect actual and attempted attacks on or intrusions into customer information systems. **Incident response procedures** Response programs that specify actions to be taken when the bank suspects or detects that unauthorized individuals have gained access to customer information systems, including appropriate reports to regulatory and law enforcement agencies. **Environmental protection** Measures to protect against destruction, loss, or damage of customer information due to potential environmental hazards, such as fire and water damage or technological failures.
Training Staff	2. Train staff to implement the bank's information security program.
Regularly Testing Controls	3. Regularly test the key controls, systems, and procedures of the information security program. The frequency and nature of such tests should be determined by the bank's risk assessment. Tests should be conducted or reviewed by independent third parties or staff independent of those that develop or maintain the security programs.

Table 2-2. Summary of "Interagency Guidelines Establishing Standards for Safeguarding Customer Information" *(continued)*

Topic Area	Safeguard Description
Overseeing Service Provider Arrangements	
Due Diligence in Selecting Service Providers	1. Exercise appropriate due diligence in selecting its service providers.
Requiring Service Providers to Implement Security	2. Require its service providers by contract to implement appropriate measures designed to meet the objectives of these guidelines.
Monitoring Service Providers	3. Where indicated by the bank's risk assessment, monitor its service providers to confirm that they have satisfied their obligations as required by section D.2. As part of this monitoring, a bank should review audits, summaries of test results, or other equivalent evaluations of its service providers.
Adjusting the Program	4. Each bank shall monitor, evaluate, and adjust, as appropriate, the information security program in light of any relevant changes in technology, the sensitivity of its customer information, internal or external threats to information, and the bank's own changing business arrangements, such as mergers and acquisitions, alliances and joint ventures, outsourcing arrangements, and changes to customer information systems.
Reporting to the Board	5. Each bank shall report to its board or an appropriate committee of the board at least annually. This report should describe the overall status of the information security program and the bank's compliance with these guidelines. The reports should discuss material matters related to its program, addressing issues such as: risk assessment; risk management and control decisions; service provider arrangements; results of testing; security breaches or violations and management's responses; and recommendations for changes in the information security program.
Implementing the Standards	
Effective Date	1. Each bank must implement an information security program pursuant to these guidelines by July 1, 2001.
Two-Year Grandfathering for Servicers	2. Until July 1, 2003, a contract that a bank has entered into with a service provider to perform services for it or functions on its behalf satisfies the provisions of section III.D., even if the contract does not include a requirement that the servicer maintain the security and confidentiality of customer information, as long as the bank entered into the contract on or before March 5, 2001.

Table 2-2. Summary of "Interagency Guidelines Establishing Standards for Safeguarding Customer Information" *(continued)*

The provisions and requirements in the GLBA are not all that spectacular. They call for common sense security controls that, hopefully, most financial institutions already have in place. Probably the most critical component of the new statute and the supporting guidelines is that the board of the institution must be involved in establishing and overseeing the program. This, essentially, obtains buy-in from the highest level.

Health Insurance Portability and Accountability Act (HIPAA)

The Health Insurance Portability and Accountability Act (HIPAA) of 1996 was signed into law by President Clinton on August 21, 1996. This broad legislation deals with a wide set of health policy issues ranging from health insurance access to healthcare reimbursement fraud and abuse to simplification of a variety of administrative tasks associated with healthcare services.

One of the major purposes of the legislation is to adopt a national electronic standard for automated transfers of certain healthcare data between healthcare payers, plans, and providers. Once these standards are in place, a healthcare provider will be able to submit a standard transaction for eligibility, authorization, referrals, claims, or attachments containing the same standard data content to any health plan. This is supposed to simplify clinical, billing, and other financial applications and reduce costs.

There are several good Web sites that provide information on HIPAA. This list highlights a few of those sites:

- **The Health Care Financing Administration**   www.hcfa.gov/medicaid/hipaa/content/more.asp

- **The American Hospital Association**   www.aha.org/hipaa/advocacy.asp

- **U.S. Department of Health and Human Services**   www.hhs.gov/ocr/hipaa/genoverview.html

For those of us in the information security field, one of the most critical components of this legislation is the section on administrative simplification and privacy. It is within this portion of the law that standards are set for protecting sensitive information. These standards have begun to have a major effect on healthcare-delivery organizations and health plans. This is especially true of organizations that deal with medical records, member and patient accounting, enrollment, personnel and information technology. The bottom line is that HIPAA applies to virtually any entity that handles Protected Health Information.

As you can imagine, the thought of simplifying the myriad of information that is passed from one organization to another in the medical industry is a pleasing thought. By the same token, it is a bit scary to think of how much more private medical information will be floating around computer networks and undoubtedly the Internet. Thus the law has specific guidelines for protecting the privacy of patient information. For organizations that participate in this electronic processing of such information, compliance with this law may be costly.

The Security Standards are comprised of four areas: administrative procedures, physical safeguards, technical security services, and technical security mechanisms. All of these are being designed to protect the confidentiality, integrity, and availability of health information. Each of these areas are listed and described in the following section.

HIPAA Administrative Security and Privacy Standards

In the category of administrative procedures are mainly policies and procedures. Table 2-3 lists each requirement with methods to implement. It is important to note that, according to the Standard, all implementation features must be in place to satisfy the requirement.

Requirement	Description
Certification	Each entity will have to evaluate its system(s) and/or network(s) to certify the appropriate security has been implemented. This certification can be done internally or externally through an accrediting agency.
Chain of Trust Partner Agreement	If data is processed through another entity, then both entities will have to agree to electronically exchange data and protect that transmitted data. There may be several of these types of agreements depending on the organization. A healthcare clearing house, for example, will more than likely have several of these agreements in place. Both entities therefore depend upon and are required to maintain the integrity and confidentiality of the data.
Contingency Plan	This is for systems emergencies, and one of the most critical parts of the standard is the requirement that an entity have " … available critical facilities for continuing operations in the event of an emergency …". This would be covered in the Emergency Mode Plan.
Formal Mechanism for Processing Records	This is an information classification policy that pertains to health information. It deals with the creation, dissemination, destruction, storage, and/or transmission of health data.
Information Access Control	These are policies and procedures that govern who can authorize access, what levels of access are established, and who can modify the access levels. Access controls are mentioned in all other sections as well.
Internal Audit	This is a requirement for an ongoing internal auditing process to be in place.
Personnel Security	All personnel with access to health information must be authorized to do so after receiving the appropriate clearance. One of the most critical statements is that systems maintenance personnel will have to be supervised by knowledgeable persons. So contractors, or internal staff, doing system maintenance (or patches, installations, etc.) will have to be supervised.
Security Configuration Management	This involves establishing policies and procedures to maintain the systems in a secure manner.
Security Incident Procedures	This involves having a plan and procedures for reporting on and responding to security-related incidents.

Table 2-3.   HIPAA Administrative Security Standards

Requirement	Description
Security Management Process	This is the establishment of a formal security management process to address all security issues/functions. Keep in mind that the standard does not state that a specific office/staff be created but that the management process is established. It requires that the process include risk analysis, risk management, a sanction policy, and a security policy.
Termination Procedures	These are formal policies and procedures for dealing with the termination of employees.
Training & Awareness	User awareness training. One of the most critical statements is that all personnel, including management, are to be trained.

Table 2-3. HIPAA Administrative Security Standards *(continued)*

HIPAA Physical Security and Privacy Standards

This category deals mainly with policies and procedures as they relate to physical security. Table 2-4 lists each requirement with methods to implement. It is important to note that, according to the Standard, all implementation features must be in place to satisfy the requirement.

Requirement	Description
Assigned Security	The formal, documented designation of security responsibility to either a person or an organization.
Media Controls	Policies and procedures that pertain to the access, storage, dissemination, and disposal of media (tapes, diskettes, etc.) that contain health information. This could be part of the information classification policy.
Physical Access Controls	These are required to limit access not only to health information but to the entity itself. Some of the key features are the "equipment control," "verifying access authorizations," and "need-to-know procedures."
Policy on Workstation Use	This is similar to an acceptable use policy.
Secure Workstation Location	Entities are required to implement physical safeguards to minimize the possibility of unauthorized access to health information. This could be anywhere in the organization. This is especially important in public buildings, provider locations, or other heavy pedestrian areas. This could range from access to doctor's offices to the claims department in a hospital setting.
Awareness Training	This is required for all employees, agents, and contractors.

Table 2-4. HIPAA Physical Security Standards

HIPAA Technical and Privacy Security Standards

This category deals mainly with controls that authenticate and allow access to users. Table 2-5 lists each requirement with methods to implement. It is important to note that, according to the Standard, not all implementation features must be in place to satisfy the requirement.

HIPAA is much more than a regulation that specifies information protection standards. That is only one part of the regulation. Compliance with HIPAA will be, for most, a large and costly effort. For organizations that have a well-established information security program already in place, compliance with the privacy portion of the regulation will be easier.

HIPAA Gap Analysis

If you decide to have a HIPAA gap analysis or assessment done to help you prepare for the inevitable government audits and reviews that are coming, it is suggested that you make sure it is a comprehensive assessment. The company that does your assessment should be looking at more than just your information security program. They should be doing a complete HIPAA gap analysis including looking at your business processes and the entire organization to ensure that you comply with all parts of the regulation.

Requirement	Description
Access Control	Required portion is the "procedure for emergency access," which may be covered in the DRP but will need to be reviewed. These controls are aimed at only allowing access to those personnel with a "business need-to-know."
Audit Controls	Basically the methods that an entity has that allows for the recording and examining of system activity.
Authorization Control	This is the mechanism that is used to obtain the consent for the use and disclosure of health information. This may be part of the information classification policy for some organizations.
Data Authentication	Organizations are required to prove that data in their possession has not been tampered with or destroyed in an unauthorized manner. Possible methods are checksums, digital signatures, etc.
Entity Authentication	Most organizations already have this in place, although it may be incorrectly implemented. For example, most places have usernames and passwords but the user is not required to logoff at night nor do they have auto-logoff enabled at the server.

Table 2-5.   HIPAA Technical Security Standards

In many cases the company you choose to conduct the gap analysis will actually be a partnership of companies. This permits the team to be more effective since they will bring together expertise in core areas. Partnerships might include healthcare consulting specialists, legal firms, and information security companies. HIPAA assessments and gap analyses are being conducted by a wide range of companies including the "Big Five" accounting firms, large consulting firms, healthcare IT consulting firms, and information security consulting firms.

There is an interesting "HIPAA Gap Analysis and Implementation Guide" on the IGCN Web site at www.igcn.com/solutions/healthcare/hipaa.pdf. Similarly, EMSI has information on its HIPAA Assessment at www.emsi-inc.net/hipassess.html. Another great resource for HIPAA information is on the Phoenix Health Systems HIPAA Advisory Web site located at www.hipaadvisory.com/.

Most organizations have 24 months from the effective date of the final rules to achieve compliance. Normally, the effective date is 60 days after a rule is published. The Privacy Rule was published on December 28, 2000, but didn't become effective until April 14, 2001. Compliance for the Privacy Rule is required by April 14, 2003. (Exception: small health plans, that is, those with an annual revenue of $5 million or less, aren't required to comply with the privacy regulations until April 14, 2004 according to 45 CFR 164.534.) The Security Rule final standards are not yet published but are expected in the summer of 2002. Some organizations are not proceeding in their security assessments for HIPAA compliance until this rule is final. This might be a mistake since everyone will be scrambling to become compliant at that time and the cost of those assessments may skyrocket.

RESOURCES

There are numerous resources on the Internet to find out more about the laws that may pertain to your information security program. Make sure you consult with your legal counsel to ensure you understand and interpret these laws properly.

- **FEDLAW**   GSA's web site that offers a summary of information technology laws, fedlaw.gsa.gov/legal8.htm
- **The "Patriot Act"**   packetstormsecurity.nl/papers/legal/patriot.doc. This site provides an overview of the "Patriot Act," passed in 2001. This law makes changes to some of the laws discussed in this chapter.
- **U.S. Department of Justice Computer Crime and Intellectual Property Section (CCIPS) link page**   www.cybercrime.gov/links.html

CHECKLIST: KEY POINTS IN INFORMATION SECURITY LEGAL ISSUES

Remember that laws and regulations can really play two roles in your information security program. They can drive your program by specifying what you must protect and how you must protect it. Other laws protect you from cyber-crimes. The checklist below will be useful in your information security program.

☐ Establish good working relationships with the legal, compliance and human resources departments to ensure you share important legal and compliance information.

☐ Make sure you are aware of all laws and regulations with which you must comply and incorporate them into your security program—especially policy.

☐ Be aware of the cyber-crime laws that are designed to protect you from breaches in computer security.

☐ Establish a relationship with law enforcement including local, state, and federal organizations in your area.

☐ Review changes in laws and make sure your program remains compliant and that policies and procedures are current.

☐ If your organization is a financial services firm read the interagency guidelines for GLBA and make your program compliant.

☐ If you are involved in the healthcare industry in any way get familiar with the HIPAA regulation and be prepared to be compliant soon.

CHAPTER 3

Assessments

We spend a great deal of time assessing things. We assess our financial worth, our health and fitness, our spiritual well-being, our placement in the hierarchy at work, the size of our real estate, the type of car we drive, along with many other facets of our lives and work. In our assessments we compare ourselves to standards, some well defined, such as dietary guidelines for healthy eating or weight and fitness levels, and some simply set as de facto standards, such as "keeping up with the Joneses." In the information security arena, we assess risk to information and information technology. As with any assessment, it is valid for only a short period of time. Risk assessments are a "snapshot" in time and must be continually redone.

A typical dictionary definition of *assessment* is "the act of assessing; appraisal." Following this definition to its root we find *appraisal* defined as "an expert or official valuation." An assessment is an act of measuring and comparing. In an information security risk assessment we are determining the level of risk. In its simplest form, an information security risk assessment tells us how likely we are to have critical information exposed to compromise, unauthorized access, alteration, or denial of service.

Assessments come in several flavors. There are self-assessments where you attempt to take an objective look at how well your security countermeasures are defending your environment. At the next level, there are more formal assessments, often conducted by third-party teams such as large accounting firms or specialty organizations.

These third-party assessments can range from vulnerability assessments that primarily identify known vulnerabilities in operating systems and system-level software, to full risk assessments that are more comprehensive because they consider more than just technical vulnerabilities and include a look at the threat environment as well. Another type of assessment is the penetration test. Penetration tests focus on attempts to exploit known vulnerabilities. This type of testing should only be done by professional, specialty organizations.

Other types of activities that are similar to assessments are audits, both internal and external. Audits are typically less technical than risk assessments or penetration tests. They generally involve reviews and checklists. Audits are an effective tool for ensuring compliance with policies and regulations.

In our role as consultants we often get asked which type of assessment is appropriate. Our answer is always—"It depends." It depends on your objective. In Table 3-1 we present our views of which type of assessment is most appropriate to achieve various objectives.

In the remainder of this chapter we go into more detail about each type of assessment. Specifically, we describe what to expect from each assessment, how they are conducted, what they produce, and how often to conduct each.

INTERNAL AUDITS

Not all organizations have an internal audit department. Generally, internal audit departments are found in large organizations and those that have some government oversight, such as financial service companies and those that deal with financial data. In most cases, internal audit departments have at least one IT auditor. These folks have the

Assessment Type	Uses	What You Get
Internal audit	You don't usually get to choose when these are done. Internal audits are usually done on a cycle that the audit department selects and they periodically review security controls for specific systems. May precede an external audit. The results of internal audits are usually shared with the system owners and appropriate business unit managers.	A set of findings to which you must respond, explaining how you are going to fix.
External audit	You also don't usually get to choose when these will be done. These are the major audits often conducted by your accounting firm. The results of these audits are usually viewed by senior executives and possibly even the board of directors.	A set of findings to which you must respond, explaining how you are going to fix.
Self-assessment	You should use a self-assessment when you have major modifications to your environment, just after an incident, or when you expect an audit.	A better sense of your security posture. May be a bit biased since you've done it yourself.
Vulnerability assessment	You should have vulnerability assessments done rather frequently—at least quarterly and after changes to the environment.	A list of all found, known vulnerabilities for each type of technology with a list of ways to correct these vulnerabilities.
Penetration assessment	You should have a penetration assessment done at least annually or when new, critical systems and applications come online or change drastically.	A confirmation that vulnerabilities are actually exploitable. This indicates risk.
Risk assessment	You should have a full risk assessment conducted approximately every 18–24 months (assuming you are doing quarterly vulnerability assessments). Effective tool to determine current security posture. Can be useful in winning new customers if security is an important evaluation factor for them (assumes your risk assessment results are good).	A detailed report identifying areas where information security is weak and listing specific ways to improve security. Does not focus exclusively on technical risks. Includes administrative and environmental risks as well.

Table 3-1.   Uses of Different Assessment Types

proper training and certifications to understand IT security controls. Their primary role is to ensure that the IT infrastructure is compliant with any specific regulations to which the organization is bound.

Internal auditors often plan which systems they will audit in a given year. When they conduct their audits they will usually start by interviewing the system owner, the system developer, and any other persons who understand the way the system functions. Auditors will try to determine how sensitive the information is that this system processes, how critical the system is to business operations, and what types of security controls are in place. Finally, they will inspect security controls to ensure they are sufficient.

If the auditor has knowledge of the system controls they will usually develop a series of tests to validate that security controls are properly implemented. If they have limited or no knowledge of the system controls they will generally rely on the answers of system administrators and other personnel. They should ask to see security controls demonstrated while they watch. They may walk through a checklist of items and ask specific questions to help them identify ways that the system security may be weak.

It has been our experience that internal auditors are not the most highly respected bunch. In fact, even in our profession, they garner little respect. This is unfortunate because their services are an important part of an effective information security program. They help monitor and control compliance and keep the IT department out of hot water. Internal auditors form a unique bridge between the business units and the IT department. They usually have a pretty good understanding of the business functions of the company and therefore can better explain why a particular weakness in a system control could be dangerous to the business. Unfortunately, internal auditors are often under-trained and over-worked. This results in the lack of respect from the IT department.

We've heard the joke among security and IT personnel that the internal auditors usually have negative findings based on the latest information that appears in industry trade magazines. For example, auditors will suddenly audit the anti-virus capability of the mail gateway shortly after the release of a new mail-borne virus. The auditors will read an article in an information security trade magazine that describes, usually at a high level, the types of security controls that should be in place. The auditors will call the IT or security folks and say, "Are we blocking attachments of type xyz?" for example. The response is often condescendingly, "Of course we are."

This is an unfair categorization of internal IT auditors. Organizations should be thankful for the auditors and the role they play, and should work more closely with auditors to keep them educated and up-to-date on the latest technology. This assumes, of course, that you have nothing to hide from the auditors. It has been our experience that this is sometimes the case. We have seen attempts to keep the internal auditors in the dark so they won't find the problems that are known to exist. This is a bad ploy and could result in serious ramifications if the weakness is discovered by external auditors, or worse yet, hackers.

You can make the internal audit department more valuable to you if you cooperate more closely with them. The best way to do this is contact them early and often. Keep them involved in new system development activities. Make them aware of changes in the environment. Educate them. If you get them involved early in system development projects they can help guide you and ensure that the final product is compliant and will easily pass audits.

You can expect internal IT auditors to check each system no more than once a year or maybe even once every 18 months. They are usually understaffed and can't get to every system as often as they should. After they visit you will usually get a written report that identifies their findings. For negative findings they will generally expect a response within some specified time frame that describes how you plan to mitigate the risk uncovered in the audit.

If an organization properly utilizes their internal audit team they will track these outstanding findings and hold each department accountable for mitigating the risks associated with those findings. Unfortunately, in some cases, the internal auditors have no teeth and their negative findings are ignored and brushed under the carpet.

One of our clients, a sizeable bank, had a pretty active internal audit department. Throughout our engagement with this client, over more than two years, we were provided with internal audit findings for a number of systems. One of the more recent findings related to router configurations. There were several negative findings for router settings that were expected to be addressed by the network department. We were asked by the information security department to provide the network department with guidelines for securely configuring routers. We developed a configuration standard that was adopted and put into use. This response to the internal audit finding was considered sufficient and mitigated the risk identified.

EXTERNAL AUDITS

External audits are usually conducted by accounting firms or regulators. They are often done annually. Unlike internal audits that usually focus on a single system, external audits are often comprehensive, lengthy, and costly. External audits may be required by laws and regulations or may be requested by your business partners. For example, if you are a specialized processor of data from a bank partner you may be requested by the bank to have an external audit conducted.

One of the more popular audit types is known as the SAS-70. This audit report format was established by the American Institute of Certified Public Accountants (AICPA) and is widely accepted as the most definitive audit. They are costly and lengthy. They are done for organizations that process or facilitate transactions on behalf of another institution (that is, third-party processors or vendors). Copies of the SAS-70 report are delivered to your client institution, your regulators, and your client's regulators.

A typical SAS-70 audit is comprehensive in its scope and the auditors will review all aspects of your operation to include physical security, logical access controls, change management, disaster recovery, and policy/procedures. Table 3-2 shows all the areas that are considered in an SAS-70 audit.

Physical Security	Personnel Management	Logical Access Controls
Environmental conditions	Change management (system development lifecycle)	Policies and procedures
Business continuity and disaster recovery planning	Problem reporting and management	Event monitoring

Table 3-2.   Areas Considered in a SAS-70 Audit

In addition to accounting firms and depending on your type of business, you may be audited by federal regulators such as the Federal Depositors Insurance Corporation (FDIC), the Federal Financial Institutions Examination Council (FFIEC), the Office of Treasury Services (OTS), or others. Without a doubt, financial services firms are the most frequently audited organizations. One of our clients recently underwent an internal audit followed by an SAS-70 and then a federal audit all within a six-month period. Needless to say, they were happy when all the auditors left. Appendix A describes these external audits in more detail.

The results of an external audit are usually lengthy documents with specific findings. These findings are usually shared with senior management including, possibly, the executive board. As explained earlier, if the audit is an SAS-70 report, the findings go to your client, their regulators, and your regulators. These findings are sometimes provided with recommendations to mitigate the risks described in the findings. Very often, senior management will expect the technical findings to be reviewed by the IT department. The IT department is expected to provide a plan with a schedule to mitigate the risks described in the findings report.

External audits are almost always viewed as a headache by IT personnel. This is probably because the auditors are often underfoot, on-site for several weeks, digging and asking numerous questions. They usually leave and then produce negative findings that result in more work for the IT department. Like the internal audits, this notion that external audits are a nuisance is unfortunate. They are still valuable to the business and are an objective look at the system controls.

ASSESSMENTS

The previous two sections described types of audits, which are designed to measure compliance to some policy or regulation. They don't always provide the complete picture of where your information security program is at any given time. Assessments are designed for this type of result. There are guides within specific industries that help auditors. For example, the FFIEC has guides for auditors to use when examining IT systems in financial organizations. In addition to the FFIEC guidelines there are guides from many other organizations. Unfortunately, there are not as many guides for assessments. There are a few, but there are no set standards for conducting assessments. In fact, there is no guarantee that any two audits or assessments will reveal the same results because they may have been conducted with very different methodologies. The next several sections focus on various assessment types.

Self-Assessments

If you have the time and resources to conduct a self-assessment it may prove to be a cost-effective way to ensure that information security is working properly for your organization. The difficult part of this is finding objectivity and being disciplined enough to complete the work. If you don't have the time or the appropriate staff to conduct a self-assessment, then you should not consider doing it at all. If you do conduct the assessment without the proper time and appropriate staff, you are fooling yourself and will end up with the proverbial false sense of security.

For the sake of argument, let's assume you do have the resources necessary to conduct a self-assessment. Self-assessments can be narrowly focused. For example, you could simply assess the security of a single application or server. Self-assessments are good to use when a new system is about to come online or a major change has occurred in your network. It can be a sanity check to confirm that security is working as planned.

One of the difficulties of assessing yourself is being objective. You obviously have prior knowledge of the systems you are assessing. This makes it difficult to determine how likely a complete outsider would be at skirting your defenses. Additionally, it is difficult to remain focused and thorough with self-assessments because day-to-day operations often overshadow plans to assess your own security. This means that self-assessments end up being done in pieces.

If you do decide to conduct self-assessments you should be careful to document your plans. Save yourself aggravation and time by tracking progress against specific assessment objectives. Tackle one system or gateway at a time and document the steps you are taking. This will make it easier if you have to stop and start testing. It will also make it easier to re-test the same system later and be consistent with your testing.

Don't rely on self-assessments as the only source of testing for your security controls. As the old proverb states, "you can't see the forest for the trees." In self-assessments you may well be overlooking some obvious and not-so-obvious weaknesses in your network and system defenses. It would be much wiser to periodically engage the services of a professional information security team to assess your security countermeasures. This will ensure a more objective and unbiased evaluation.

Vulnerability Assessments

Probably the most popular of all assessment types is the vulnerability assessment. This has become especially true in the past few years with the advent and maturation of automated vulnerability scanning tools. These tools, if run properly, can help you identify known vulnerabilities in a multitude of operating systems and applications. Table 3-3 identifies some of the more popular scanning tools, both commercial and open source.

Unfortunately, automated vulnerability scanners are not foolproof and generate a fair percentage of false positives. Without careful analysis of the results of these scanners, the

Product	Vendor	Purpose	Notes
Internet Scanner	Internet Security Systems (ISS)	Scans network devices for known vulnerabilities. Reports findings with recommendations to fix.	Runs on Microsoft Windows NT/2000; scans Unix, Microsoft Windows NT/2000, and network devices.
CyberCop Scanner	Network Associates (NAI)	Scans network devices for known vulnerabilities. Reports findings with recommendations to fix.	Runs on Microsoft Windows NT/2000; scans Unix, Microsoft Windows NT/2000, and network devices.

Table 3-3. Popular Vulnerability Scanning Tools

Product	Vendor	Purpose	Notes
NetRecon	Symantec	Scans network devices for known vulnerabilities. Reports findings with recommendations to fix.	Runs on Microsoft Windows NT/2000; scans Unix, Microsoft Windows NT/2000, and network devices.
Nessus	Freeware	Scans systems for known vulnerabilities, reports findings, and suggests ways to fix.	Client/server configuration. Server must run on Unix host. Scans Microsoft Windows NT/2000, Unix, and network devices.

Table 3-3. Popular Vulnerability Scanning Tools *(continued)*

output is not of significant value. Too often organizations accept the raw output of these scanners as a final analysis when, in fact, no analysis has been done. To be effective, the output of a vulnerability scanning tool should be analyzed by a security professional to help weed out false positives. The analyzed results of a vulnerability scan show possible weaknesses in the IT infrastructure. A good vulnerability assessment will also provide recommendations for eliminating or reducing these vulnerabilities.

Vulnerability assessments should be conducted quarterly, especially if you have a number of systems that are exposed to the Internet. Because of the relative ease of use and availability of open source automated vulnerability scanning tools, many organizations are choosing to let their IT staff members conduct these scans on their own. However, we still strongly recommend that organizations engage third-party security professionals to conduct quarterly vulnerability assessments using commercial scanning products. These professionals have experience with conducting these scans and can isolate the false positives and help you interpret the results.

CAUTION Open source vulnerability tools can cause system problems and are not always reputable. There is always the danger that open source security tools can be malicious or contain malicious code. Make sure you research the tools you intend to use. Check to see if they are mentioned in information and IT industry trade magazines. If you cannot find enough information about them, then you should test them on non-production systems before ever considering their use in your production environment.

Penetration Tests

The most intrusive of all assessment types is the penetration test. These tests are designed to attempt exploitations against known vulnerabilities usually uncovered through the use of vulnerability scanning tools. Penetration tests are what some people refer to as "ethical hacking." Using commercial and open source tools, the testers will attempt to penetrate systems and gain access to critical system files, functions, and information in an effort to validate the security measures in place. Penetration tests take vulnerability scanning to the next level by attempting exploits against found vulnerabilities.

We have had clients approach us with requests to perform penetration tests. After a few moments of discussion with the client we usually discover that what they really want is a vulnerability assessment. The moment we mention conducting exploits that could "break" systems, they usually back down and say "No, don't do that." They just want to find the holes. We quickly correct their usage of the term "penetration test" and then conduct a vulnerability assessment.

A true penetration test should follow a methodical approach and be clearly documented in a plan. The first step in conducting a penetration test is planning. Like any testing, you must decide what it is you hope to accomplish. Once you've established your objectives the testing coordinator should obtain a complete description of the target of the attack. The target description should include such information as location of target, operating systems in use, applications in use, types of remote access permitted, and any other information that provides a detailed description for the tester. Thirdly, the test plan should spell out the methodology to be used. At least at a high level, the plan should state the procedures to be used when testing. For example, the plan should state which systems are to be tested at what times and in which order.

Penetration testing can be conducted with or without specific knowledge of the target. In some cases it might make sense to conduct the penetration tests "blind" (meaning that the penetration test team is given as little information about the target as possible). This is typically only done in two cases. The first case is when a system or network is going to be tested for the very first time. The second case is when you have a new penetration test team and you want to see what they can find out on their own.

In "blind" penetration tests, the test team is usually given some very vague information about the target. This can be as little as a domain name or even a company name. In this scenario the penetration test team must first conduct a great deal of reconnaissance to establish the scope of the target. This is usually done using Internet searches and tools such as ARIN, WHOIS, and other registries of domain names and IP address ranges.

Once the penetration test team believes they have established the scope of the target they should confirm their findings with the client. Once the client confirms that the target is correctly identified the second phase of testing can begin. The second phase is typically comprised of low-level stealth scans. These are attempts to identify specific information about the target(s). The objective of this phase is to establish a catalog of data about the targets without letting the client know they are being reconnoitered. In some cases, penetration testing has the objective of determining the client's ability to detect attempts to gather information. In these cases the client will not let the IT department know they are the target of attack and wait to see if they detect the attempts.

Once the penetration test team has gathered all the information they can about the targets (information such as operating system type and revision, system patch levels, major applications running, ports opened, and so on), they typically will run heavier vulnerability scans specifically configured for the types of targets identified. The results of the vulnerability scans are then used to select specific exploits to be attempted. For example, let's assume the reconnaissance revealed a system running Microsoft Windows NT and Microsoft IIS 5.0. Let's also assume that a vulnerability scan of that host revealed the possibility that the Microsoft FrontPage Server extensions had the wrong permission set, possibly allowing an authorized user to edit content on the Web server. Using Microsoft FrontPage, the penetration test team might try to publish content to the server. If they were successful then they would have proven that the vulnerability both existed and was exploitable. The previous scenario was precisely the case with a recent penetration test we conducted from the Fortrex lab.

Because penetration tests can exploit vulnerabilities and leave systems exposed, it is critical to trust the team conducting the test and completely understand the test plan. It is strongly recommended that you check the references of any organization you are considering for penetration testing. You should ask for the résumés of the test team members and consider having background checks conducted on those individuals. Make sure the rules of engagement are clearly spelled out and that you agree to them. Finally, make sure your test report specifies all activities that were conducted by the test team and the results of each test.

You should employ the use of penetration testing at least once a year. This will give you a good sense of just how exploitable your IT infrastructure is. It is also wise to have penetration tests done against new systems that face public networks such as the Internet, or when your IT infrastructure undergoes major changes or upgrades.

Penetration tests, as you might expect, are more expensive and time consuming than vulnerability assessments. This is largely because they pick up where vulnerability assessments leave off.

Be careful when engaging a third-party organization to conduct a penetration test. It is critically important to select a reputable organization. Make sure you check references carefully and find out what types of tools they intend to employ. Review their methodology and ensure that you understand exactly what they intend to do. Also, beware of companies that will send their superstars to the pre-sales meeting, but will only send their junior staffers to the actual penetration testing. Agree in advance who the specific penetration testers will be.

One effective vehicle that we employ with all of our penetration test clients is the use of a penetration test plan that includes a "rules of engagement" section, an outline of which follows. The document clarifies exactly what is and is not to be done during the testing. It includes dates and times that testing may be conducted and specifies contact information and what to do in case of a problem.

- **Objective**   Describe what the test is to determine
- **Description of the target**   A brief description of the target systems and networks
- **Methodology**   Describe how the tests will be conducted, in what order and with what tools
- **Roles and resonsibilities**   State who does what before, during and after the testing
- **Deliverables**   Describe what will be provided to the customer at the end of the testing

- **Rules of engagement**   Agree to these specific test parameters:
    - *Dates of test*   Including test time windows
    - *Site primary POC*   A person at the client site who can speak authoritatively about the testing
    - *Site alternative POCs*   Personnel who can be contacted for specific parts of the testing
    - *Scope*   IP address range of systems and networks included in the testing
    - *Permission to exploit*   Establish a procedure for exploiting vulnerabilities. Client may want to be contacted prior to any exploits being conducted. Establish what markers should be used (such as placing a file on exploited system or capturing a file).
    - *Acceptance of rules*   Get a signature from a senior decision authority accepting the terms of the testing and ROE

Remember that penetration testing is, by its very definition, intrusive. It can have a negative impact on operations. Therefore, penetration testing should usually be conducted during non-peak business hours unless a recovery plan is in place. It would be quite a problem if, during a penetration test, the testers executed an exploit that caused a main Web server to crash during the middle of the business day.

The results of a penetration test should be detailed in a report that shows what was done, what tools were used, the results of the vulnerability scanning, the specific exploits used, the results of those exploit attempts, and a list of recommendations to close any vulnerabilities found to be exploitable. If, during testing, a specific vulnerability is determined to be exploitable, the testing team should contact you immediately to close the hole and not wait until the written report is delivered.

Risk Assessments

The most comprehensive of all assessment types is the risk assessment. The risk assessment considers not only vulnerabilities but also threats and consequences—the core components that make up risk. The risk assessment looks at all aspects of information security including physical, environmental, administrative, and technical measures. It provides a complete evaluation of the risk at which an organization's IT infrastructure operates and puts the vulnerabilities in perspective for the business. For example, rather than simply stating that a vulnerability exists in system X—as done with the vulnerability assessment—the risk assessment describes why this particular vulnerability coupled with a known threat poses a risk to the organization.

It is important to make a distinction about different types of risk assessments. There are at least two risk assessment types to consider separately—information security risk assessments and business risk assessments. Information security risk assessments focus exclusively on the risk to information and information systems. Business risk assessments consider risks to business operations. Information security risks are a subset of business risk. Information security risk assessments should only be performed by information security professionals. This is in contrast to business risk assessments that should be performed by organizations such as accounting firms who have a strong understanding of business risks. For the remainder of the book, when we refer to risk assessments we are speaking of information security risk assessments.

Risk assessments are done very methodically and should be performed nearly the same way each time. This provides for consistency. Risk assessments are conducted using a combination of interviews, observations, audit methods, questionnaires, and automated vulnerability scans. They take longer than vulnerability assessments and are more costly. During a risk assessment, the assessment team will collect a significant amount of information that must be carefully reviewed and analyzed.

In a typical risk assessment the assessment project leader should provide you with a project plan that identifies what will take place during each phase of the assessment, the estimated dates of each activity, and the required resources. Prior to on-site visits the assessment team will likely request some or all of the following:

- Company overview documentation
- Organization charts
- Policy and procedure documents
- Network diagrams
- System descriptions
- IP address ranges
- Physical locations of all relevant sites

If the assessment team receives all of this information prior to their on-site visits they can save a great deal of time and focus their interviews. At Fortrex we start with a questionnaire that is to be completed by the person responsible for information security. The questionnaire, when completed, provides us with a great deal of information about the organization and how important information security is in their company.

On-site work conducted by the assessment team will usually consist of interviews with key personnel, site surveys, observation, and audits. A good assessment team begins their work the moment they arrive on site for the first meeting. A little snooping around, a peek here and there, and some social engineering are the typical modus operandi when the assessment team members enter the facility.

Interviews are the first order of business. The assessment project leader should provide you with a list of persons or position titles they wish to interview based on the organization chart you provided. They will usually expect you to coordinate these interviews. On average you should expect the assessment team to interview eight to ten people over a two- to three-day period. This number will vary depending on the size of your organization. The interviews should last approximately one hour per person. The team will most likely want to interview the following persons:

- Person responsible for information security
- Physical security manager
- Human resources manager
- IT manager
- Network manager
- Server manager
- Application development manager
- Compliance officer
- Internal audit manager
- Heads of major business units

CHALLENGE

Let's look, for example, at an assessment we conducted when we first joined Fortrex. As soon as we arrived on site, we began our work. The receptionist was on the second floor. This gave us an opportunity to snoop around the first floor. We found we were able to get into training rooms with computers. Once on the second floor we were greeted by the receptionist. We introduced ourselves and asked for our contact person. While we waited we asked many questions about the company. While one of us kept the receptionist busy, the other walked up an unblocked, spiral staircase that lead to the executive offices. In later visits we walked around the building and found that we could gain entrance through the door propped open for smokers. We noted there were no cameras. This is the type of information that an assessment team can gain by simply walking around.

In another assessment, we conducted some "social engineering" by calling numbers we found in the company phone directory. Pretending to be from the "network shop" we told users we were troubleshooting issues with the file server and needed them to log off briefly. While still on the line we explained that we were watching the network traffic from their system and we needed them to log back on to the network. We'd say something like; "Okay, it's a little jumbled on the wire here; what userID are you using?" In most cases they'd provide this without question. We'd continue, "Alright, the userID looks fine, but slow down and state each character of the password as you enter it so we can track it on the wire and make sure this is working properly." Not every person fell for this; some started asking questions, and a few would give us the passwords as they entered them. If we got the userID and password we'd say, "Thanks, we've got the issue solved."

After interviews are completed the assessment team will most likely want to conduct a formal site survey of each major location to be included in the assessment. This is separate from the informal snooping mentioned earlier. In these visits the team will be escorted through the data center and other areas requested by the assessment project leader. This might include a review of the alternative power sources (such as diesel generator or battery backup), file storage areas, application development areas, tape backup storage facility, and other locations they specify.

During these visits, the assessment team is looking for physical and environmental security countermeasures. They should be looking for door locks, identification badges, fire suppression systems, power sources, visitor logs, and many other physical and environmental controls. They may be using checklists to ensure that all aspects of security are considered. This portion of the assessment is more like an audit.

In addition to the visual inspection of these facilities, the assessment team members will also be closely observing the way personnel conduct their day-to-day business. The team will note whether personnel are following policies and procedures they reviewed previously. They may be looking for things such as:

- People holding automatic doors open for others (often referred to as *piggy-backing*, which causes individual electronic badge accounting to be rendered useless)
- Unlabelled media
- Unclaimed printer and facsimile output
- People leaving consoles logged on and unattended
- People sharing user accounts

The last activities conducted on site are system audits and vulnerability scans. The assessment team should want to see how user accounts are established. This may mean that they want to see the domain controller (in a Microsoft Windows environment) or the user registry. They are looking to see how certain parameters such as the following are configured:

- UserID schema
- Password length
- Password expiration period
- Number of allowed authentication attempts
- Type of logging conducted
- Types of user groups or profiles

The internal vulnerability scans must be conducted from a connection to the network. The assessment project leader will ask for your internal IP address scheme (this is especially true if they have to obtain license keys for commercial scanners) prior to arriving on site. They will expect you to provide a list of IP addresses to be scanned and dates and times that the scans can be conducted. As stated previously, the vulnerability scans are intrusive and can cause network congestions and latency. You should consider having these scans run at non-peak times. Note that some organizations may charge you more money to conduct scans during non-peak times.

In addition to internal scans, the assessment team will probably conduct external vulnerability scans. These can be done at almost any time during the assessment. Like the internal scans, these can cause network and system congestion and you may want to have these done during non-peak times.

As you can imagine by the description of the assessment, a substantial amount of information is gathered. The assessment team will take this information back to their office where they will begin collating and evaluating it. During this time the assessment team may grow to include others from their organization. The results of the assessment should be presented in a formal document with all findings clearly explained, and include recommendations for mitigating any risks identified. Some organizations, including Fortrex, offer an oral presentation of their findings. Depending on the size and scope of your assessment, you should expect to see the first draft of your assessment report about two weeks after the assessment team leaves your site.

CHECKLIST: KEY POINTS IN ASSESSMENTS

The following is a checklist of steps to follow when considering an assessment of your network and systems:

- ☐ Determine your objective(s) (for example, find vulnerabilities only, determine risk, prepare for external audit, and so on).
- ☐ Identify the appropriate assessment type (refer to Table 3-1 earlier in the chapter).
- ☐ Determine if the assessment will be conducted in-house or by a third-party organization
- ☐ Develop and agree to a firm assessment plan.
- ☐ Conduct the assessment.
- ☐ Review findings and recommendations.
- ☐ Implement corrections as specified in recommendations.

PART II

Plan Implementation

CHAPTER 4

Establishing Policies and Procedures

In a perfect world every information security program would begin with a strategic plan followed by a security policy and procedure manual. That's a pleasant dream for information security professionals such as ourselves. In fact, it's downright blissful—but unreal. However, one thing is certain: Without a clear set of guidelines that specify what is and is not allowed concerning the use of information and information processing resources, the organization will never have a solid information security program. If you don't have a well-defined information security policy then you are fooling yourself if you think you have security in place. In this chapter we discuss the critical importance of having well-defined information security policies and procedures.

Think about a sports game—baseball, for example. What would it be like if there were no rules? Umpires help ensure the game is played according to the rules. Umpires must attend annual training. The training focuses almost exclusively on the rules and changes in the rulebook. The rules help make the game playable. Without the rules, an understanding of them, and someone to enforce them, the game might not be able to be played at all. Running an information system infrastructure securely is not much different. There must be a set of rules, people must understand them, and someone must have the authority to enforce them.

During our risk assessments we often discover that organizations have an incomplete set of information security policies. Usually, we find some outdated policies that are not sufficient along with some more recently documented policies that were quickly written to handle specific systems or technology such as e-mail, Internet access, or PDA usage. We rarely find a controlling, central document that is the core of the information security program. Although not always essential to every security program, this type of a document can be very helpful in establishing the theme for a program.

In our many years of experience in the information security business we have come across folks who state they understand the importance of policy and procedures but it always gets pushed to the wayside because implementing countermeasures is more important. The problem with this philosophy is that without a well-documented reason for implementing countermeasures, you are likely to be guilty of a shotgun approach to mitigating risks. We realize that all information security programs don't start with a policy development exercise. Nonetheless, it is never too late to develop policy and procedures. Consider sexual harassment, for example. It is very likely that your organization has a policy against such harassment because if you don't there is legally no reasonable expectation that the employees should be expected to conform to any code of behavior. So too with information security. If there are no policies, there can be no real expectation of security.

PURPOSE OF POLICIES

Information security policy serves several purposes. Primarily, it establishes what is and is not allowed. It should be closely aligned with business goals. It also serves to protect the business. For example, an Acceptable Use of IT Resources Policy establishes how company employees may use IT resources. In general, such a policy tells employees that they may only use company IT resources to conduct company business. Without such a policy the company would have a hard time terminating an employee they catch running a small business from the Web server they built on their company desktop computer.

Policy statements should be made as broad and generic as possible so as not to have to change too frequently and yet be specific enough to not be ambiguous. You don't want to have policy statements that are so specific that they have to be re-written each time a new technology is deployed. For example, a policy that states "All user accounts must have a password of six characters" is too specific for a policy statement. It would become obsolete as soon as a system that does not support this policy is implemented. Additionally, if the company decided to implement a system that used a different type of authentication mechanism such as PINs, biometrics, or smartcards the policy would be useless and have to change.

Instead of writing such specific policy statements it is better to be broad. In the previous example it would have been better to state "All user accounts must use an authentication mechanism." This establishes that all users must be authenticated but does not specify a technology. This policy should be supported by a standard or guideline that specifies the allowable authentication mechanisms. The standard or the guideline would be the appropriate place to specify that when passwords are used as the authenticator they must be at least six characters in length. A good rule of thumb to use when writing policy statements is to consider whether the statement specifies a particular solution. If it does, it is probably too specific and needs to be taken up a level.

If you follow the principle of not making policies too specific then you must support policies with clear guidance in the form of procedures and standards. If you only state what can and cannot be done, then users will be asking how they are to comply with these policies. You must not leave too much room for interpretation. You must make it clear how to comply with policies through well-documented procedures and standards. Over time procedures and standards may change, but policies should remain constant.

Information security policies are targeted at users in all levels of the organization. They should be written with this in mind. Anyone who handles information and information technology is covered by these policies. This means that the policy must be written so that it is relevant to the average system user, management, executives, and system administrators. The policies apply to everyone. It is the procedures that pertain to each policy that might be different for various types of personnel in the organization.

POLICIES TO CREATE

In our work with various organizations including government and private industry we have seen a range of policy documents. In some organizations we have seen voluminous policy manuals in three-ring binders. In other organizations we've seen a single sheet of paper with a few bulleted items making up the corporate information security policy. As with most things in life, moderation is best. The problem with huge policy manuals that take up several binders is that they never get read. The single sheet policy is likely to be insufficient in its scope, leaving too much unprotected.

To answer the question "What policies do I need?" we need to first ask ourselves what it is that we need to (or want to) protect. Additionally, we must consider other policy drivers such as laws, regulations and industry requirements. At a minimum there are a few policies that every organization should consider. They include an acceptable use policy, information security policy, and a data classification guide. There are plenty of other policy topics that should be covered, but we lump them all into the information security policy. We'll discuss each of the major policy areas next.

Acceptable Use Policy

In some industries employees are required to read and sign a confidentiality or non-disclosure agreement. Typically, this agreement is a covenant between the company and the employee stating that the employee will not reveal confidential information that he or she may learn as a result of employment.

Its intent is two-fold. First it is a tool for the company to protect itself and its secrets. If employees sign this document they agree not to reveal the secrets. Since employees explicitly agree not to do this by signing the document the company has leverage in any administrative or legal actions that might result. The second purpose of such an agreement is to educate employees about the sensitive nature of the information they may handle in the day-to-day work they do.

An acceptable use policy—affectionately known in the industry as the "AUP"—is somewhat like a confidentiality agreement. Its purpose is to explain how IT resources are to be used. If employees violate the acceptable use policy, the company has a signed copy of the document that they can use as leverage in administrative or legal action. It is an important component of the overall protection of information. It focuses on protecting the confidentiality of information.

The acceptable use policy usually highlights and re-emphasizes the major points of the information security policy. Specifically, the acceptable use policy should explain that IT resources are for business purposes only. It should define what is and is not acceptable use. Unacceptable use might be described to be such things as running your own business, sending or receiving inappropriate material such as pornography, sending chain e-mail, and reading other users' files. It should also help define what is acceptable use. If non-business use is permitted, it should be made clear when, where, and how this is permitted.

The truth is that most companies allow IT services to be used for incidental employee use, similar to using the company telephone. Companies don't mind if an employee uses the telephone for incidental calls that are secondary to their job. So too with Internet and other AUP uses. The company can protect itself even if they allow Internet and other IT use for incidental purposes, but this can only be done in the framework of the AUP.

Additionally, the AUP should also discuss the user's expectation of privacy. It must be made very clear to the users that they should have no expectation of privacy when using company information technology if that is your policy. If you do provide employees an expectation of privacy then you should likewise let them know this. It depends on your environment. It might be safer to let them know they have no expectation of privacy to protect yourself from potential litigation.

You should explain that the company reserves the right to monitor activity on all corporate IT resources and that users grant this right to the company when they sign the acceptable use policy. The AUP should also cover the company policy on the use of software. It should explain that business software must be properly licensed and that no unauthorized or unlicensed software may be installed on corporate systems. Finally, the AUP should cover the company policy on using only authorized communications and network connections.

We have developed a pretty standard AUP template that we include in our Information Security Policy Manual that we develop for our clients. It takes up about two full pages and is included in a section entitled "IT Code of Conduct." Additionally, we replicate this entire policy section in the appendix of the policy manual and add a space for employees to sign and acknowledge that they have read and understand it. We encourage organizations to adopt the practice of having all new users read and sign this document prior to issuing them any accounts. We recommend the signed document be kept by either the human resources or IT security department.

For legacy users who may have been issued accounts prior to adoption of this policy we recommend they receive a copy, sign it, and return it within a pre-defined period of time (usually 30 days). If they do not return the signed form their accounts should be suspended. The form should be revisited and signed annually. This serves to both remind users of their responsibility and to draw attention to any changes that may have been made in information security policy or procedure over the previous year.

Recently we've introduced a Privileged User Acceptable Use Policy that is designed for any users who have accounts with special privileges such as those associated with system and network administrator accounts. We encourage organizations to have these policy documents and corresponding forms read and signed when such users receive their new, special privileges. This Privileged User AUP reminds administrators that they are being entrusted with accounts that provide special and dangerous capabilities for which they must be extra cautious. Like the standard AUP, the Privileged User AUP should be signed and returned to either the human resources or IT security department. Additionally, this document should be reviewed and signed annually.

Information Security Policy

As far as we're concerned this is the mother of all policies. This is where the organization puts all of its key policies and procedures pertaining to the protection of information. It is the one place that anyone in the organization can go to find out what is and is not allowed. It is also the policy that is referenced in the AUP. It can be put together in any number of ways. The form is less important than the function. However, the form does play a role in the readability of the document.

For many years now we have been involved in the development of security policies for organizations ranging from huge government intelligence agencies to small "dot.coms." Over that time we have been able to see several policy formats and pick out what we considered to be the best of each. Our goal, when writing an information security policy manual, is to make it as comprehensive and complete as possible. We also strive to make the policy as timeless as well as practical. This means that policy statements have to be at the proper level—not too specific but not too ambiguous.

To provide a glimpse of what should typically be included in an information security policy manual, we have included an outline:

- **Introduction**

    Purpose
    Scope
    Roles and Responsibilities

- **Compliance**

- **Acceptable Use of IT Resources**

    Computing Code of Conduct
    Expectation of Privacy
    Use of Software
    Unauthorized Communications Methods

- **Information Sensitivity and Classification**

- **Administrative Security Controls**

    Authorization to Use Company IT Resources
    Privileged User Authority
    Account Management
    Log Review
    Data Backup and Restoration
    Incident Response

- **Physical and Environmental Controls**

    Facility Access Controls
    Power
    Temperature and Humidity Control

- **Technical Security Controls**

    User Identification and Authentication
    Malicious Code Protection
    Host (Desktop, Workstation, and Server) Security
    Portable Computing Technology Security
    Network Security

This is a lot of information to include in a policy manual, but it makes the manual comprehensive. As we mentioned previously, we have seen many different variations of policies from large manuals that fit into several binders to single-page documents. Some organizations choose to publish all of their policies in a single volume and others like to publish individual policies for each policy area. The format you choose will probably depend on corporate culture, existing policy document formats, and the individual style of the person(s) writing the policy.

Our personal and professional preference is to develop a policy manual that follows the outline shown in this section. What this creates is a central repository for all policies and procedures related to information security. It also creates a more comprehensive approach to information security and makes the policies more cohesive. When policies are created one at a time they can contradict one another and sometimes overlap, making them confusing for users.

Expanding the Outline

Probably the best way to explain the various sections of the information security policy is to describe each section shown in the outline. Regardless of whether you choose to put all the policies into a manual as we do or publish individual policies for various topic areas as the need arises, we suggest you cover, at a minimum, the topic areas shown in the outline.

Introduction   As with any formal corporate document there should be an introduction section that describes the purpose and scope of the document. The information security policy is no exception to this rule. Also included in this section of the policy manual is a definition of the roles and responsibilities of various positions in the organization including the IT director, security manager, executive board, and many others.

The introduction section should make it clear that the policies and procedures in the manual are blessed by the organization at the highest level and that information and the resources on which information is processed are important and critical to business operations. To send a powerful message, include on the first page of the information security policy binder a memo from the president/CEO stating the importance of information security, how committed he or she is to information security, and how he or she expects every employee to be 100 percent committed to information security. Additionally, it is a good idea to relate the policy manual to any other relevant corporate policies in existence, such as an employee handbook or corporate standards manual.

The purpose of the policy manual is to ensure that information is provided an appropriate level of protection in the form of confidentiality, integrity, and availability. It is also in this section that we usually describe the difference between policies, procedures, standards, and guidelines. *Policies* are statements of security rules identified by management as ways to achieve objectives. Policies must be followed. Any deviations from or exceptions to policy compliance should be required to be in writing to management. You might want to provide an example of a policy statement. The one we typically use states "All system and application accounts require users to identify and authenticate themselves."

Similarly, *standards* are corporate-accepted methods, products, or technology for implementing security. Standards identified within the manual must be followed. Requests for deviations from standards should be required to be made in writing to management. An example of a standard (specifically related to the policy example given previously) is, "All passwords will be a minimum of eight characters in length and will contain a mixture of alphabetic and numeric characters."

Guidelines are very much like standards but might not have to be followed as strictly. The difference between standards and guidelines is small and you may choose to simply have policies, standards, and procedures.

Finally, *procedures* are defined as the specific ways in which users can comply with policies and standards. An example of a procedure, also related to the policy example given earlier, is "If users forget their password, or think it has been compromised, they should contact the Help Desk." The procedures help clarify policies and standards.

It should be apparent from the examples given that policies can be written to be enduring. Standards and procedures that support policies are more likely to change over time. For this reason some organizations choose to only include policy statements in the main body of the policy manual and include all the standards and procedures in the appendices. This way the appendices can be replaced with updated material while the main body remains intact.

The scope subsection of the introduction should make it clear what portions of the organization are under the purview of the policy. Generally, the scope includes all forms of information technology including computers, workstations, servers, network devices, portable computing technology (laptops and PDAs), printers, facsimile machines, and possibly even telephone equipment.

The last subsection of the introduction is roles and responsibilities. It is important to make sure that everyone in the organization understands their responsibilities pertaining to protecting information. The major roles described in this section should include the CIO or CTO, the HR manager, managers in general, system administrators, and users. If you have an information security manager, then that role should certainly be included. There may be others you want to include. It depends on your organization's structure.

Compliance   This is a short section and primarily states that everyone in the organization is required to comply with the policies put forth in the manual. This section should include a policy statement making it mandatory to comply with all information security policies. It should also provide procedures for requesting waivers to policies and/or standards. This is also the section to let users know what the penalties are for not complying with the information security policies of the organization.

Make sure you check with the human resources and legal departments before you publish this section. In fact, the human resources and legal departments should have been acutely involved with the initial design and construction of these policies. Ensuring that the human resources and legal departments are brought in early in the development process ensures that they will be more likely to be on your side. Bringing them in too late creates a potential clash. You don't want to state that employees will be terminated if they violate information security policies if HR and legal don't approve or support this.

Information Sensitivity and Classification   Data classification is an important policy topic to cover. Without a clear policy that describes what data/information is sensitive and requires protection, users may not understand the purpose of the rest of the information security policies. The policy should define what levels of classification exist in the organization and how to determine the classification level of data. Additionally, this policy should explain who may determine the classification of data.

This policy section should include a statement requiring all information repositories to have a designated data steward. The data steward is a person who can speak to the sensitivity of the information under their purview, decide who may have access to that data, and what types of access those persons may have (for example, read-only, edit, execute programs, and so on). The data steward should be the signature authority on access request forms for users requiring access to the data under their control. Data stewards should be located in each major business unit.

In addition to the policy statements pertaining to data classification, there should be clearly explained procedures on how to determine the classification of data. In fact, a data classification guide is a great tool to refer to in this section and can be included in the appendix. You should define at least two levels of data classification, such as *confidential* and *open* or *public*. Some organizations choose to expand to three levels of classification. However, if you get too granular in your classification levels it becomes increasingly more difficult to determine the actual classification level of your data.

Table 4-1 is an example of a tool that you can use as a data classification guide. The first column defines the name of the class of sensitivity levels. The second column is necessary to help individuals in your organization to make a classification determination. For the purposes of this book the Examples column is rather generic. In your data classification guide you should be as specific as possible to ensure no confusion on behalf of the guide's user. Column 3 provides information on how this type of data is to be protected while it is in its various forms during processing, storing, transmitting, and printing. The last column identifies the person or the title with the responsibility and authority to make classification determinations. You should be specific in this column and name individuals and or titles. If the individual is a senior executive it is likely he or she will name a "designee" to make decisions on his or her behalf.

Administrative Security Controls   The policies in this section of the manual pertain to the non-technical controls, such as authorization to use systems, account management, privileged user authority, data backup and recovery, log review, and incident response.

Authorization to use systems is an administrative control often overlooked by organizations. It is, however, an important control gate at the beginning of the account management life cycle. Accounts must be initially created, modified over time, and eventually removed.

User accounts should only be created after a specific authority approves them. In a well-defined account management process managers request that accounts be created

Sensitivity Level	Examples	Protection Requirements	Data Steward
Restricted	Strategic business plans such as mergers or acquisitions and sensitive human resources information such as employee investigations	Must be labeled. Printed copies must be numbered and accounted for. Computer files must be password-protected and/or encrypted. Documents must be shredded when discarded.	Senior executives or designees
Confidential	Employee, payroll, financial, pricing, and customer information	Should be labeled. Paper copies should be limited to only those with specific need to know. Computer files should be protected with proper access controls. Should be shredded when discarded.	Department heads or designees
Public	All other information	None.	Legal or public relations department

Table 4-1.   Data Classification Guide Example

for their staff. Usually, some type of a form, electronic or paper, is completed by the manager requesting that the IT department create a new account. Since users often access data owned by other groups in the organization, we suggest that the data owners of any systems or applications to which the user requires access be part of the approval chain.

Having the data owners or data stewards approve access requests to the data for which they are responsible is another important control gate that too many organizations forget to implement. In many of the organizations we have worked with or consulted, the IT department or the security department is the approval authority for access requests. Since the IT department does not actually own the data on the systems they administer, it is definitely not the right authority.

Assuming that a request form is used, once all the approvals are obtained the IT department can establish the user's initial account. Over time this user may change job duties, transfer, or get promoted. In these cases this user will likely need different access than originally granted. The same form and same process should be used to request modification of the account access privileges.

If the user leaves the organization altogether their account must be removed. In cases where the user is involuntarily terminated (a nice way of saying "fired"), the account access is usually removed instantly based on a phone call or e-mail from the human resources department or the user's manager. It is imperative that accounts be disabled or deleted upon an employee's departure from the company. In many companies, accounts have stayed dormant for years. This is a huge danger when dealing with disgruntled employees.

We recommend that follow-up paper work be submitted and filed to ensure a record of the event is maintained. For voluntary separations the standard process should be followed—the manager submits a form and the account access is removed on the user's last day.

Data backup and recovery are sometimes considered technical security controls related to system availability and data integrity. We include them in the administrative security section of the policy manual because they refer to the procedures of backing up and recovering data, not the tools that do the backups and restores.

The backup policy and procedures should define what data must be backed up, how often it must be backed up, where it should be stored (off site is best), who may conduct backups, and when to restore data.

Reviewing event logs for security purposes is an important part of security management. Unfortunately, we know almost no organizations that consistently review logs. They usually only look at logs when they suspect something bad has happened. Best practices, however, dictate that logs be reviewed frequently. The problem is, log review is tedious. This is due in a large part to the fact that companies don't know what specifically to log. They therefore log far too much data, most of it being irrelevant. But this logging creates scores of gigabytes of logs that somehow must be analyzed.

The security policy should specify what events are to be recorded in event logs and when those logs are to be reviewed. The frequency of log review depends on the size of your organization, the criticality of the data and systems, and the exposure of those systems to threats. Weekly log review is probably sufficient for most organizations.

Finally, incident response policy and procedures should be included in the administrative security section of the policy manual. Since an incident response plan and procedures can be large, some organizations may choose to include this as a separate document.

Incident response plans should, at a minimum, define what constitutes an incident, identify who is to be contacted when an incident is suspected, define specific roles and responsibilities for the incident responders, and provide specific guidance for actions to take in the event of more frequently occurring incidents such as malicious code attacks.

Physical and Environmental Security Controls   This section of the policy manual should address the major areas of physically protecting IT resources. At a minimum you should include policies and procedures that address controls for the data center (for some that means an entire facility, for others that might mean the room in which the servers reside).

This section of the manual might be less policy-centric and more a set of standards and guidelines about how the physical and environmental controls protecting the IT resources are to be configured. Guidance should address minimum requirements for physical access controls, power conditioning (surge protection), AC power sources, battery backup, power generation, air temperature, humidity, water censors, and fire suppression.

Technical Security Controls   The technical security section of the information security policy manual should define policy for several key technical security controls and provide guidance and standards for using these controls. Areas to cover should include at least user identification and authentication, file level access controls, network security controls, malicious code protection, host security, portable technology and remote access controls. Rather than describe each of these areas we will pick one, user identification and authentication, and dissect it for you.

Keep in mind our philosophy on policy. We prefer policy to be at the highest level possible yet still be focused, clear, and unambiguous. We like to use procedures, standards, and guidelines to support policy statements. Keep it short and sweet and make sure the supporting guidance is as detailed as it needs to be.

For user identification and authentication the policy should be similarly high level and straightforward. It is important to remember the purpose of identification and authentication. We have to be able to uniquely identify each user for the purpose of accountability. We authenticate users as a way of verifying their identity. For most systems passwords are the method of authentication.

Generally speaking, we include the following policy in our policy templates for user identification and authentication:

- "All user accounts shall utilize a unique user identifier."

- "Each user shall be held accountable for actions conducted under his or her user identifier."

- "All systems must require users to be authenticated prior to allowing access to any system resources."

You may have additional policies related to user identification and authentication. But be careful that you are not making procedural matters into policy statements. We typically support these policy statements with guidance on selecting passwords, creating user identifiers, and other account management procedures such as how and when to remove user accounts.

For each of the other technical security controls you currently use or plan to use, include a section in the policy manual.

DEALING WITH EXISTING DOCUMENTS

In the previous section we discussed, at great length, what we consider an industry best-practice policy manual. This assumes that you have not written a single policy document or that no policy exists in your organization. We realize this is rarely the case. Some security-related documentation is likely to exist. We'll take an educated guess and say that it is probably outdated and insufficient. Nonetheless, it does exist; people probably know about it and it may have even been "blessed" by senior management. The question is what do you do with such documents?

There is no single, correct answer to that question. It really depends on several factors, including how much existing documentation is lying around, how dated the material is, how strong the information security program is, and whether or not the

---

CHALLENGE

One of our clients had a fairly well-established information security program. Their policies were largely driven by regulations at several levels including government and industry. They also had a pretty decent set of policies. Some were old as dirt and had not been revised in years. Of those very old policies, some were still relevant and perfectly fine just the way they were. Others were outdated and some were just plain missing. We worked with them, reviewing and suggesting updates, revisions, and additions to their policies.

This particular client had all of their policies located on their intranet. For this reason we did not suggest putting them into one, big manual. Having all the policies located on their intranet allowed them to update one policy at a time, submitting them for senior management approval, and then publishing them. If you do revise, add, or remove any information security policies, make sure you inform your user population of the change through an awareness program. Placing the polices on the corporate intranet is an excellent way to ensure that the policies are always easily accessible. Also, having them on the intranet ensures that the latest version is available.

---

existing policies and procedures have been reviewed and approved by anyone. The answers to those issues will help you determine your best course of action with respect to existing policy documentation.

If you have very little documentation, it is mostly outdated, and it has never really been reviewed and approved by senior management, the choice is easy. Write an entirely new manual and encompass the concepts from the previous documentation that make sense. If, however, you have a substantial amount of policy and procedure documentation, some old and some new, and it has made its way up the chain and has been approved, then re-writing it might not make the best sense.

GETTING BUY-IN

If there is one thing we have learned in all our years of formal and informal management training it is that people oppose change. We become very comfortable with the current state. Unfortunately, this means the information security program manager will not be everyone's favorite person because he or she must be an agent for change. Let us illustrate.

In more than one case we have consulted clients who have lax user account management policies and procedures. Generally, they allow accounts to have non-expiring passwords, they have short passwords, and they may even allow sharing of accounts. In some cases, when we make the suggestion that they tighten up the account management, we get a grimace from the security manager. Very often we get a response similar to this one: "Well, we've always allowed it to be this way and I don't think we'd get senior management to go for it."

We understand the reluctance of the security manager to be the bearer of bad news but it needs to be done. The best way is to convince management of the importance of such policies and procedures. We've learned that a hammer rarely works. Don't try the "scare management to death" tactic. Instead, show them the cost of not making the change. Management needs to understand that it is not a matter of *if*, but rather *when*. It is no different from physical security. Physical security breeches *will* occur. The point is to have policies and procedures in place to deal with them when they do occur. Make it clear to senior management that there is the potential of a loss of revenue and customer trust if a serious infraction occurs. Dollars speak volumes to senior management.

In some cases the security manager is still too afraid to make the call or they feel they don't have complete credibility with senior management. In such cases we recommend a third party. We can tell you that in several instances we have made presentations to senior management on our findings and recommendations from a risk assessment. In almost every case we end up recommending stronger policy. Usually, senior management nod their heads in agreements. After the presentation we hear from both the security manager and senior management that the concept of better policy had been previously presented but it was usually shot down. Suddenly, when management hears it from an outsider they think it's the greatest idea since the ballpoint pen.

However you do it, gaining senior management buy-in is critical to the success of your program and the acceptance of policies. In fact, once policies have been approved by senior management, there should be some statement from them making it clear that everyone is expected to adhere to the new policies and that they will be held accountable.

In addition to getting senior management buy-in, you must get your general user population to bite the bait. It is true that by its very nature policy must be adhered to. However, policies are better followed when the population finds them understandable and rational. If they think that a policy is just another obstacle to completing their jobs, they will do their darndest to find a way around it. So getting their buy-in is also important for policy success. Success of a policy is measured by the effect it has on reducing the risk it was intended to reduce.

General user population buy-in can be achieved through senior management support (they've got to follow the new policy or else) and training and awareness. Help them to understand why the success of this policy is necessary and how it helps the company and ultimately themselves. Try to get them to say, "I get it." Whether it is for an entire information security policy manual or just one new policy, corporate buy-in is essential to making the security program successful.

POLICY REVIEW

Although we have repeatedly said you need to write policy at a high level to give it longevity, it still must be reviewed to ensure it is current and accurate. Procedures and guidelines require even more frequent review. There are several factors that drive the need to review policy. They include changes in laws and regulations that affect you, changes in your business, and changes in your technology. Let's take a quick look at each.

As we stated previously, laws and regulations are important policy drivers. Your industry may be regulated by federal, state, and/or local governments. Additionally, there may be some industry oversight organizations that drive some of your policies. As these regulations change your policies may have to reflect these changes. For example, the recent passage of the Gramm-Leach-Bliley Act has put pressure on a number of financial institutions to formalize their information security program and get the written program manual to be approved by the board of directors. This is a significant change for most banks.

Secondly, changes in your business may affect your current policies. If you acquire or merge with a company this may be a driver. Other changes include going public or restructuring your company. There are a multitude of company changes that affect your current information security policies. This is why it is important for the security manager to be at a significant level in the company and be tuned in to company plans.

Finally, policies may have to change as your use of technology changes. Think about how migrating to client-server environments has changed your policy. Where once all the data was housed on the mainframe, it is now distributed in small databases that hold a chunk of the data that used to be stored on the mainframe. The use of portable computers and PDAs, remote access, Internet connectivity, e-mail, and wireless technology all may require that new policies be written to ensure that the risk these news technologies bring to the business are kept at an acceptable level.

CHECKLIST: KEY POINTS IN ESTABLISHING POLICIES AND PROCEDURES

The following checklist will be helpful when you start developing your security policies:

- ☐ Make sure policy is based on company goals, laws and regulations, and industry standards.

- ☐ Keep policy at a high level—detailed enough to be unambiguous but not so specific that it becomes obsolete too fast.

- ☐ Be comprehensive—cover administrative, environmental/physical, and technical security measures.

- ☐ Get buy-in from senior management and the general use population.

- ☐ Review, revise, and update policy as often as necessary.

Additionally, consider these resources:

- *Information Security Policies Made Easy,* by Charles Cresson Wood (Baseline Software, 2001).

- *Writing Information Security Policies,* by Scott Barman (New Riders Publishing, 2001).

- *Establish a policy and procedures that prepare your organization to detect signs of intrusion* at www.cert.org/security-improvement/practices/p090.html.

CHAPTER 5

Implementing the
Security Plan

The primary goal of any information security program must be to manage the risks to information and information systems. The program's plan is to develop ways to lower current risks through administrative, environmental/physical, and technical measures. The challenge is identifying risks, ranking them by severity, and deciding on a way to manage them. This is exactly what an information security program manager must do.

The security plan must incorporate the company's objectives for protecting information and consider the risk tolerance level of the business. Remember that the information security team does not own the data or systems. Likewise, the IT department does not own the data or systems; they just manage them. It is the business that owns it all and they must establish the requirements for protecting information.

There is a multiphased approach to an information security program. We discuss it in more detail later in this chapter. In brief, it includes assessing risk, establishing policies, deploying countermeasures to risk, educating the population regarding the risks and solutions, and monitoring and reporting on the progress of the program. This process is, by design, circular and repeatable.

The first phase involves identifying the corporate objectives for protecting information and identifying the businesses' tolerance for risk. Additionally, in this phase you will assess the level of risk in your environment. Once you know what risks you have and the level of risk the corporation can live with, you can develop a risk reduction plan aimed at lowering those risks to acceptable levels.

The next phase of the process requires that you develop and deploy clear policies and guidelines for protecting information. This becomes a tool for managing risk. Policies are a countermeasure. They tell everyone what they are expected to do with respect to information security.

Once policies have been established it is time to act upon them and enforce them by deploying and implementing security solutions. Solutions are not always technology-based. For example, you may incorporate new processes for user account management as a means of controlling who gets system accounts. Technology will certainly be part of your strategy and you may deploy anti-virus software, firewalls, and intrusion detection systems in an effort to lower risk to the level that the business said they could tolerate.

Educating the population and making them aware of threats, vulnerabilities, risks, and solutions is another key element in the security process. We must make users aware of the policies with which we expect them to comply as well as educate them as to the ways in which they can comply. Managers and those who will implement and manage security solutions also need to be educated through your security training and awareness program.

Lastly, you must monitor and audit your program to ensure it is achieving its goals. To ensure that security controls are functioning properly, you will deploy auditing and logging tools that report back to you how well security is functioning. You will have to track progress administratively as well use things such as security training attendance records and visitor sign-in logs. The primary object of this phase of the process is to make you aware of how well you are doing at lowering risk. You must report this information to the business units to show return on investment.

Figure 5-1 depicts this information security process "wheel." You can see that it is continuous and really has no start or end. You can get into the process at any stage.

This process sounds simple enough but, for most organizations, this is truly a difficult thing to accomplish. Developing and implementing a security program plan takes a great deal of work. To help you get started and keep your program focused on the risks that are important to the business, you may wish to consider creating a panel consisting of business representatives to help you establish your priorities. This is the panel to whom you will report progress and show return on investment.

Remember that there are several audiences for and participants in the information security program. Management, system administrators, and the general user population all will read the plan and play a role in program execution. In fact, you may divide the plan up with a version for each of those groups. This is not a trivial effort so unless you have a lot of free time on your hands we'd suggest you just create a single manual aimed at all audiences.

In the sections that follow we will explain how to begin implementing the plan you have created on paper. We will describe how each of the three audiences mentioned above relate to the plan slightly differently.

WHERE TO START

Let's begin with a scenario. You've been the director of information security for ACME Widgets, Inc. for three months. Although new at this company, you have extensive experience managing information security programs. You realize you have to get the "lay of the land" here at ACME before you commit to any projects. You were left with a few policy documents that are outdated and seem incomplete. There is a dusty audit report

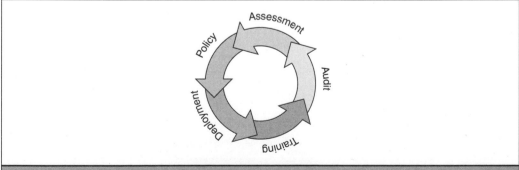

Figure 5-1.   Information security process wheel

from one of the big accounting firms that has some IT security control findings. You've been told that there is a huge project about to kick off to Web-enable most of the organization's major applications using some fancy portal technology and there is another major IT audit coming in six months.

Establish the Plan

In Chapter 1 we discussed the role of the information security program and described how the security department relates to other parts of the company. It was clear in that chapter that we must get off on the right foot with the rest of the organization by first learning about how the organization functions. This is critical to establishing a successful program.

For example, let's say that as the new director for information security at ACME Widgets, Inc., you have been asked to create a panel with representatives from each business unit, human resources, legal/compliance, physical security/plant maintenance, and any others you see fit to include. Figure 5-2 shows the typical makeup of the information security panel. The objective of the panel is to help you establish the information protection requirements for the company and quantify the company's risk tolerance level. These two critical pieces of information will establish the target objectives of your plan and create vital buy-in from the organization.

You will have to facilitate this panel and guide them. You must extract requirements from them in much the same way a project manager for a new software system would collect requirements.

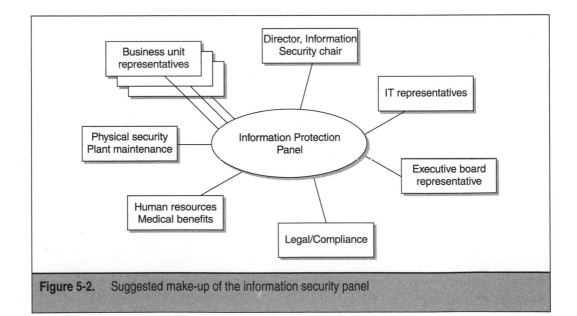

Figure 5-2.   Suggested make-up of the information security panel

---

CAUTION   Make sure when you are doing this that you pull all the requirements up to the proper level. Don't allow the panel to specify solutions. For example, you don't want the panel stating that one of their requirements is to put in a firewall between branch offices. What they should be saying is; "We need to protect the networks and systems at branch offices from external threats."

This is where the information security program manager will have to use diplomatic skills and do the translation of business requirements into security program plan requirements. Try to get the business units to honestly tell you what level of protection they require. Find out what their most sensitive information is and which are their most critical systems. When you first engage your panel it will be very helpful to explain to them what your objectives are and how the information security program will enhance the business by lowering the likelihood of bad things happening to their systems and data. This becomes crystal clear to business unit representatives when you describe how a compromised system may cost them money.

Next, either as a group or individually, have each business unit representative tell you how they operate and what systems and data they own and use. These are two different things. For example, a business unit might own System X and Database X but they also use System 2 and Database 2. The objective of this exercise is to find out their critical systems and data. This is basically a business impact analysis, which is the first stage of disaster recovery planning. It will reveal to you their "pain points."

As you gather this information from each business unit you should be asking them questions such as the following:

- If this system were unavailable for one hour, how would this impact your ability to conduct business? Would it cost you money? (Ask this question several times with the unavailable time incremented from one hour to four hours, to one day to several days.)

- How much would it affect your business operations if the database became corrupted?

- What is the worst thing that could happen that has the potential to seriously impact operations on your business unit?

The objective of the questions above is to get the panel members to begin thinking about how dependent they are on IT resources, which of those resources are most critical, and ultimately what is their tolerance for risk. All of the answers to those questions will provide you with the information you need to complete the plan.

After you draft the plan, share it with the panel members before you submit it to senior management for approval. Make sure that you accurately captured the business unit security requirements and risk tolerances. Make any needed adjustments after the panel members have reviewed it. Next, submit it to senior management for approval.

This plan is a fundamental building block for your information security program. No one in the business units can argue with it because they, in essence, developed the plan. Once it is approved, all of your individual information security projects should be directly tied back to the overall plan.

If, after establishing the plan, someone approaches you about a project not in the plan, you can simply bring the requirement before the whole panel and ask them to help you re-prioritize the current plan to integrate the new requirement. This lifts the burden off of your shoulders and keeps the business units in the loop. For example, if the plan has been established and then suddenly, mid-year, one of the business units approaches you and says they need a secure mail capability to support a new system, you can simply assemble the panel and bring them the new requirement. You must ask the panel to decide just where in the current prioritized list of information security projects they want you to place this new requirement. Hopefully, you are beginning to see the value of establishing this panel.

Risk Assessment

So, now that you have this snappy plan all documented and approved by the panel and senior management has blessed it, you have to get it moving. Bring this plan to life. One of the best first things to do, especially in brand new programs, is to conduct a security risk assessment of the entire IT operation. This is the best way to find out where the big risks are. Surely you are aware of some of the bigger gaps you have, but hearing from an objective third party will be helpful to you. In Chapter 3 we covered the different types of assessments in detail. In this case we'd recommend that you have a full-blown risk assessment of the environment done. Make sure the assessment includes a look at the administrative, environmental/physical, and technical environments.

You need a complete risk picture so you will know what the highest risks are and where you should spend your time initially. Armed with the business unit priorities for protecting information, you can help the risk assessment team focus on major areas of concern. Put out an RFP to have a risk assessment of your IT environment conducted. Select an appropriate vendor and get started. Clearly set out your expectations and work with the assessment team to ensure you get a comprehensive assessment. Once the results are in you should be presented with a set of findings and recommendations. The company doing the assessment should provide you with a high-level plan for tackling the risks they identified during the assessment. This risk reduction plan should become your operating plan for the next several months to a year.

Risk Reduction Plan

Once you get your risk assessment report you should have a list of findings. Go through the list and rank them with your business panel representatives. Remember that you don't own the data or the systems. The business units are the owners and they are the right people to make the call as to which risks most concern them. You can help them rank the risks using your experience and knowledge over which vulnerabilities are the most dangerous and which threats are most prevalent. Once you have ranked the risks, then you can develop a risk remediation plan. This is a plan that spells out how you will reduce the risks.

Armed with the risk reduction plan you may have to develop a budget if you don't already have one or if the one you do have is too small. Let's assume that as the new director of information security you have managed to acquire a small staff of three or four personnel. If you do not have staff then you will have to consider this in your budget calculations. You will have to matrix in people from other parts of the company, hire staff, or outsource the work. In either case you must determine the level of effort required for each project on the risk remediation plan in order to determine your budgetary requirements. Let's further assume that your budget is sufficiently large enough to begin tackling some of the projects on your risk reduction plan. The next step is to start the first project. Based on our experience most organizations end up with a risk reduction plan after a risk assessment that includes some or all of the projects shown in Table 5-1. It is a sanitized plan from an actual assessment we conducted in 2002.

Low Hanging Fruit

There will be some items in your risk reduction plan that you can tackle with little effort even if they won't make a huge difference in lowering risk. These are sometimes referred to as the *low hanging fruit*. This category includes things that might have been detected during the risk assessment such as dormant accounts, accounts without passwords, accounts with the same password as the userID, systems missing critical security patches, and systems running dangerous and unnecessary services. Other things, like implementing the use of a sign-in log sheet at the entrance to the data center and locking certain doors, also fall into this category.

You can take care of these things relatively quickly without too much planning or time. Assign these tasks to the appropriate persons and provide an expected completion date. Once these things have been completed you can check them off of your risk reduction plan. You may wish to re-evaluate systems that have been remediated to ensure that the vulnerabilities have been properly removed and that the proposed correction was done correctly and is effective. Eliminating these simple things gets them off your "to do" list and begins lowering risk, even if just a little bit.

Moderately Sized Projects

Once you have eliminated some of the more simple projects it is time to plan and complete slightly larger projects. In this category are such things as an anti-virus audit (although for some organizations this might be a large project) and creating a DMZ. These projects will require some amount of planning, such as research, design, or engineering. Completing these projects should have a bigger impact on lowering your risk profile. These may require changes in your budget and may even require some outside help.

Project Name	Description	Estimated Level of Effort
Eliminate high and medium risk host vulnerabilities.	This project will eliminate the high- and medium-level vulnerabilities identified by the vulnerability scans. The scans identified 19 high-level and 57 medium-level vulnerabilities. COMPANY XYZ IT staff should mitigate the high-level vulnerabilities immediately and develop a schedule for eliminating the medium-level vulnerabilities over the next several weeks.	8 hours for high-level vulnerabilities, 40 hours for medium-level vulnerabilities.
Develop a disaster recovery plan for LAN servers, applications, and supporting infrastructure.	The project will result in a formal, written DRP for the non-AS/400 servers that host critical applications. This is not a trivial project and will require a significant amount of time.	160 hours to develop and exercise the plan.
Change user account password settings.	Completion of this project will eliminate the risks identified in the report related to accounts having non-expiring passwords. This project assumes that a policy will be approved that requires all accounts to have expiring passwords. COMPANY XYZ will need to develop a schedule for expiring passwords so that not all user accounts expire simultaneously as the new policy is implemented. All accounts that allow expiration should be set to expire every 60-90 days. The setting should be consistent with the policy.	40 hours to identify all systems that support password expiration, develop an expiration schedule, and implement the change.
Create a DMZ segment at Internet gateway.	This project will involve the installation of a third interface on the current firewall and the relocation of certain publicly accessible servers such as the e-mail relay, Web servers, and RAS servers.	2 weeks to plan and execute.
Control visitor access to facility.	At a minimum, this project will involve possibly locking the side entrance to the lobby, creating a visitor sign-in log book, issuing visitor identification badges, and requiring escorts. A total employee badge system for the entire facility may be considered. The badge system could be used to control access to various portions of the data center.	1 week to plan (implementation time dependent on the solution selected).
Develop and implement an organization-wide information security training and awareness program.	This project will dovetail with the development of the formal information security program identified previously. The security training and awareness program will, at a minimum, provide the organization with ongoing awareness of the risks inherent in using IT resources and steps that they can take to ensure they are compliant with company policy and that they are reducing the overall risk.	4 weeks to plan. Implementation will vary depending on the program developed.
Research fire suppression alternatives for server room.	This project will initially involve research and cost/benefit analysis for replacing the current liquid-based fire suppression system with non-liquid in the server room. The results of this project may lead to a project to implement changes to the fire suppression system.	1 week to plan and research.
Conduct anti-virus audit.	This project involves the complete audit of the anti-virus protection currently in place. All hosts should be reviewed to ensure they are current and properly configured. The results of the audit should be documented and any corrections needed should be completed in a timely manner.	2 weeks to conduct the audit.

Table 5-1.   Sample Risk Reduction Plan

Larger Projects

The final category of risk reducing projects includes the ones that will take a significant amount of resources including time, planning, and probably money. From the risk reduction plan shown in Table 5-1 this would include such projects as the creation of a training and awareness program, researching alternatives for the fire suppression system in the data center, and developing a disaster recovery plan. These can be very large projects and would require formal project management.

It is suggested that projects of this size be formally documented and presented to a senior management board for approval since they will likely result in a requirement for more funding. As you can see from the level of effort estimates in the risk reduction plan in Table 5-1, the development of a corporate-wide information security training and awareness program could take four weeks just to plan. This does not include the time to develop materials for the program and actually execute the program. Likewise, developing a disaster recovery plan for IT components can be a lengthy and costly project, but it's essential if your IT infrastructure is required for the business to operate effectively.

The larger projects may be too big and time consuming for you and your staff to tackle by yourselves. You may want to consider consulting with a security services organization to come in and help you manage these projects or even to take them on completely. If your company has a department that provides IT project management you may also want to consider using their services to help plan and manage these larger projects. Be honest with yourself when you scope these projects. If you even think they might be too much to handle, then seek help.

Develop Policies

Following along with the information security process introduced at the beginning of the chapter, the next step after the assessment is the development of policies and procedures. If this is a start-up information security program you will need a complete set of policies and procedures that establish what is and is not allowed in your environment. Chapter 4 is devoted exclusively to the policy development process.

Remember to get the policies approved by senior management. Also, don't create policies in a vacuum. You may establish a policy that you think is just great but then come to find out that it makes no sense at all for certain business units. This is another very good use of the information security panel with the business unit representatives. Allow them to help you develop practical policies that will ultimately reduce the risk to information but at the same time make sense with the way the business is conducted. Having the panel involved with the policy development will also gain buy-in since they will have had a hand in developing the policies.

Solution Deployment

The next step in the information security plan must be to deploy solutions that allow you to implement and enforce your policies. It is nice to say in a policy document that passwords must be a combination of upper- and lower-case letters and include at least one non-alphabetic character. It is quite another thing to enforce this policy with technology.

The risk reduction plan, as part of the larger information security program plan, will specify solutions sometimes based on the recommendations that came out of the risk assessment. The assessment report may have pointed out that the lack of anti-virus at the e-mail gateway posed a high risk of being infected with e-mail-borne malicious code. The risk reduction plan may recommend a project to identify candidate gateway anti-virus solutions and to select and deploy the best solution. It is the information security program manager's job to make this happen in accordance with that plan and the priorities set by the business unit panel representatives.

Training

The information security process wheel that was shown in Figure 5-1 specifies security awareness training as the next phase. As described in other chapters in more detail, the goal of the security training and awareness program must be to make users aware of the risks to information systems, the policies in place to protect those systems, and the solutions that have been deployed that will help with policy compliance.

Training is an important and cost-effective part of the security process. When members of your entire company are aware of the risks to their data and their systems they are less likely to conduct any intentional system misuse and are more likely to properly use security controls. Systems administrators will be better able to manage the security of the systems for which they are responsible and managers will be better equipped to enforce policies.

Audit and Reporting

The final phase in the information security process and likewise part of your plan implementation must be to monitor your program. This is done to ensure that security controls are operating as planned and to help determine the level of compliance. Monitoring is done both administratively and through technology.

Manual audits can be conducted to ensure that administrative security policies and procedures put in place are actually being followed. Technology can be deployed to collect audit logs and to report security events to the security management team.

The manager of the information security program must use this information to determine if the program is successful. Additionally, reports concerning the plan's progress should be provided to the panel. This is a helpful way to measure return on security investment. For example, if we go back to the anti-virus gateway deployment mentioned previously, we might be able to show the panel that the number of virus infections dropped by some large percentage, thus easily demonstrating the return on investment.

Do It All Over Again

Let's assume now that you've completed all that was listed above. You developed the program manual with a strategic plan, policies, and procedures. You had the risk assessment completed and your team followed up on the risk reduction plan and did everything it suggested. You're finished now, right? Of course not! The cycle just begins all over again. This is not a once and done thing. Information security and risk management is a never-ending job. Risks will always exist. So let's go back to the beginning.

Do you conduct another full-blown risk assessment? Do you have a pending audit that might uncover some weaknesses and issues? How should you proceed? These are good questions and ones we suspect we may all have asked at one time or another. The answers to these questions vary depending on your specific environment. Nonetheless, there are some things that are common among all environments.

Here comes the soapbox. Security is a process not a thing. The objective of an information security program should be to manage risk. Since risk never completely goes away you must be constantly managing it. So, although you may have handled the first round of risks identified in that initial assessment, there are many more just waiting to show their ugly heads.

Since security management is continuous you should consider putting in place all the supporting processes as soon as you've gotten the initial list of risks under some modicum of control. Get a risk identification and quantification process in place that will allow you to identify and measure the risks to your information and systems. Develop a training and awareness program. Establish an incident response capability. Develop and continuously test a disaster recovery plan. These are a few of the more important ongoing processes you should establish as a key part of your information security program.

Now let's see how each different group plays a role or is affected by the program.

CHALLENGE

Okay, so in a perfect world there would be no risks for which you would have to even develop and implement a security plan. So let's shoot for as close to perfect as possible since we know there are risks. In that almost perfect world you would be named the information security manager of a just-forming company and have a clean slate from which to build your information security program. There would be no half-completed policy documents, no systems without security patches, and no dormant system accounts. Senior management would all think highly of information security and you'd have a budget approximately 10 percent of the total IT budget.

If you had this clean slate, then you would be able to start from the beginning of the security process as we just walked through in this chapter. Assess your environment, develop policy, deploy solutions, educate your users, and audit/monitor the solutions you've implemented to ensure they are effective. You should continually migrate through this process. We don't know too many information security professionals who haven't fantasized of this scenario.

In the real world, however, it is more likely that you were just brought in to a company that has been around for many years. They have a well-entrenched IT department, some really strong political undercurrents, a shrinking IT budget and enough security risks to go around. On top of all this you have been brought into the company because they are about to have an enormous audit in three months. Talk about a reality show. No pressure.

As consultants, we have been brought into such environments numerous times. Working closely with the security program manager, we always recommend a "don't rock the boat" approach in the beginning. Follow the steps outlined earlier in this chapter and you should get a good footing. Start by first getting a good "feel" of the organization. Walk around and meet as many people as you can at all levels in the organization. Say little. Listen a lot. You might not even have to tell them precisely who you are or what you are there to do. Once you start to understand how the organization operates and what level of awareness there is to information security matters you can begin to build your program.

Start with the security panel. Depending on your environment you may want to individually meet with each prospective panel member. You don't have to mention the panel right away. This might cause them to back away, especially if they think it will mean more work for them or a chance they could be seen in a bad light. Find out their "pain points," what their information security risk tolerances are, and which systems and information they depend upon. Once they've shared, you can feel more comfortable asking them to be part of the security panel.

Document your panel findings and then have a risk assessment conducted. Match up the risks identified in the assessment with the pain points specified by the panel members. Where the identified risk surpasses the risk tolerance specified by the panel you must then develop a risk reduction plan. In reality, this is how you get your information security projects prioritized. This may also be how you get your budget. "If you want the risk reduced to a level that you find acceptable, Mr./Ms. Business Unit Representative, then I will need X dollars." The business can decide if they are willing to pay $X to reduce the risk.

If this sounds more like the environment you're in, then join the crowd. You are the ones who need to follow the steps identified. The good news is that the information security process shown above is circular. There is really no beginning or end. This means you can jump into the process at any time.

WORKING WITH SYSTEM ADMINISTRATORS

System administrators do the bulk of plan implementation. These are the techno-geeks (and we mean that in the most respectful way because we wish we were as nimble on the keyboard as they) who do a multitude of tasks, such as hardening operating systems, managing user accounts, creating application environments, establishing system logs, installing software, and many other jobs.

When policies are approved it is the administrator who will most likely be responsible for implementing them. If you go through the recommended security policy outline from the previous chapter you will see that many of the policies are aimed at controlling how users get access to systems and the information those systems process. To a large extent the implementation of such policies is done through user account management. Establishing a user account, setting a password, putting the user into a pre-defined group, and establishing the access rights of those groups are all things that system administrators do.

In some organizations we have seen the role of user account management put exclusively in the hands of the information security team. This is not a bad idea for large organizations. For smaller organizations it might not be feasible to have system administrators and another full set of security administrators.

System administrators have the proverbial "keys to the kingdom." Due to the nature of their role they must have significant privileges in order to do their job. This means, of course, they must be trusted. However, trust only extends so far. In addition to trusting these individuals you must monitor their actions closely. In some industries, monitoring the actions of the administrators is mandatory and specified by regulations. In fact, it is a good idea to run credit checks against employees who will be system administrators, especially on critical systems such as money transfer, and so on.

You will find that good system administrators are already security-conscious. They don't like to have a bunch of users tromping around on "their" systems. This is a comforting factor. However, our experience also shows that administrators can be bribed. A few snacks, a nice lunch, and some flirting will go a long way with this breed of IT professional. This, unfortunately, means that they tend to get suckered into doing "favors" for "friends," such as giving permissions that have not necessarily been approved through the proper channels. We are guilty of having used friendships with system managers and administrators to get special access and privileges.

For this precise reason we recommend that you set boundaries for your system administrators. As mentioned in the previous chapter, you may want to consider having all system administrators read and sign a "privileged user acceptable use policy" form. Such a policy reminds system administrators that they have special privileges that can be dangerous and that they are therefore held to a higher standard of trust. Additionally, we would make sure that system administrator actions are closely monitored and their activities reviewed by either the information security or the internal audit department.

Finally, if you don't already do this with all of your IT staff, you may want to have a criminal background check done on all of your system administrators.

We realize this all sounds rather "big brother-ish" but think about just how much power these individuals have. They can create users, give those users access and privileges, alter files, delete files, alter and delete data, and worst of all—they can alter log data to make all they have done disappear.

System administrators are users too. Not only do they have to help you implement the security policies but they must abide by them as well. Although they are usually security-conscious they may have their own opinions about how security should be implemented. If their ideas differ from yours then you may be in for a surprise when your first audit occurs. It is therefore important to get their buy-in to the policies you create. The best way to do this is to get them involved in the policy development process. If they see that you value their input into the security policy development process then they will be more inclined to be consistent with that policy during implementation.

There are some technical measures you can implement to help you keep system administrators in check. One of the biggest issues with system administrator accounts is that they are shared by more than one person and they do not allow for individual accountability. This means that the actions of the system administrator cannot be directly linked to a person. These accounts are usually identified as "administrator," "root," or "admin."

For some Unix systems you can keep users from logging in directly as the root (superuser) account by implementing the wheel group. This feature requires that all users log in as their general user account and then execute the "su" command to become the root user. This allows for individual accountability.

To use the illustration we started in the introduction to this chapter, let's see how the implementation of the new user account management policy affects the system administrators. First, system administrators are users too. So, their accounts must be approved by management and their system administrator accounts must conform to the new password standards. Secondly, as the most likely implementers of the new policy, the system administrators will be the ones who build user accounts that conform to the new policy standard. They will activate the security features of each operating system that requires passwords to be six characters in length, use at least one numeral, and expire every 60 days. If the systems for which they are responsible do not have the ability to enforce such a policy they must inform the information security manager so a decision can be made to either waive the policy or find a suitable solution, such as a third-party product or a home-grown solution.

An effective countermeasure is to give the system administrators two accounts, one for their system administration duties and the other for non-system administration duties. Require that they use the non-system administration username when doing general purpose computing.

WORKING WITH MANAGEMENT

Management plays several roles in policy implementation. Using the policy template provided in the previous chapter, you will see that management must approve policy and enforce policy. It is management that must help develop and approve the written security policies. Once policy has been approved they are the ones that must help ensure policy is understood by their staff, participate in following the procedures for each policy, and enforce the policies when necessary.

Managers are sometimes the bottleneck in getting policy approved because they are likely to have the most work to do once policies are approved and implemented. If you think about this it makes sense. It is management that must review and approve the policy annually. It is management that must participate in the daily processes created as a result of policy implementation. And it is management that has the headache of enforcing policy that may include terminating otherwise perfectly good employees.

Like system administrators, managers must be made part of policy development. This will gain their acceptance and better understanding of the need for such policies. It has been our experience that managers usually understand the rationale behind most policies. Their reluctance to develop new policies is just what we stated previously: it creates more work and problems for them.

If managers are made part of the policy development process then they will certainly be actively involved in the implementation of those policies, if for no other reason than to make sure it is done in such a way to minimize the additional work they may encounter. Managers want to protect the company assets and they understand the importance of reducing information security risks. In certain organizations within the company you might find that managers have already implemented department-level policies designed to protect the information for which they are responsible.

In fact, during most risk assessments, even when we find that there are no comprehensive, corporate-wide information security policies we still find at least one or two departments that have stringent polices (not always documented but de facto) that are aimed at limiting access to sensitive information and systems. This is typically found in departments that handle financial, customer, and employee data such as payroll, human resources, accounts payable, accounts receivable, and others.

Continuing with the policy implementation example of a new account management policy, let's see how management's role is vital to implementing this new policy. We must remember, once again, that managers are users and they have accounts that must follow this new policy. More importantly, managers must be the ones who review and approve the access requests for users under their purview. They must carefully review each access request for employees in their organization and make sure they are only requesting access for systems and data they need to do their jobs effectively. If managers are not taking this responsibility seriously the system breaks down quickly and enforcement of policies is made more difficult.

We want to make the distinction clear about the manager's role in approving access requests versus the role of the data steward. The manager should be reviewing the access requests before they go to the data steward. For example, if Susan works for

Anne, Anne should be reviewing Susan's access request form to ensure that Susan is only requesting access to systems that she really needs to do her job. If Anne finds that Susan has requested access to a particular special capability on a system that had nothing to do with her job, Anne should be correcting this and changing the request form before it is submitted to the individual data stewards of the systems Susan has requested access approval for.

Finally, for this new policy implementation the management of the organization must be prepared to enforce this new policy. This might mean that a manager first makes each of his or her staff fully aware of this new policy and the need for the policy. Next the manager must be ready to reprimand policy violators. Remember, for the reprimand to be effective, it must have been clearly documented in the original policy. Otherwise, there may be no legal recourse to castigate the employee.

For example, if a manager were to discover that one of his or her staff had contacted a system administrator directly to build an account on a production system without going through the proper channels and without using a request form, the manager must follow the prescribed punishment for such a violation. This might be a verbal reprimand with a notation made in the employee's personnel file.

In any organization it is the management that sets the standards. They must live up to and exceed the standards themselves if they expect others to do so. This is true also with the implementation of information security policies. Management must make their staff aware of the policies, follow the policies themselves, and be prepared to enforce policy compliance. It is imperative that managers take this responsibility seriously for information security policy to be effective. Don't forget, effective information security must work from the top down.

EDUCATING USERS

New policies must be introduced to users not just to ensure that they know about them but also to protect the company from the counter-suit that might result from an employee being reprimanded or even terminated over violating a policy for which they were not made aware. As with any corporate policy you must make sure that every affected employee is made aware of the policy, how to comply, and the consequences of non-compliance.

Policy awareness training is vital also to gaining user acceptance and buy-in to new and changed information security policies. If, for example, you publish a policy that now requires user accounts to have expiring passwords when previously this was not required, then you must make the general user population aware of such a change. To forestall the almost instantaneous uproar from the masses, you must first get out on the road and help the users understand the importance and purpose of this new policy. As you may have already encountered, users will oppose almost anything that they perceive as a hindrance to their success.

Users are a hard lot to convince that information security policies and procedures are going to make their lives better. You must either convince them by making them see how information security makes their lives better or you must resort to having senior management say, "You will comply with these policies or else …". This is not the preferred method, but it sometimes works. Try the more gentle approach first, using training and awareness.

CHECKLIST: KEY POINTS IN IMPLEMENTING THE SECURITY PLAN

The following is a checklist for the key points in implementing the security plan:

☐ Establish a panel that includes members of each business unit.

☐ Gather each business unit's information protection requirements and risk tolerance levels.

☐ Create a security plan from the panel's input and allow them to prioritize the items in the plan.

☐ Conduct a risk assessment to identify and quantify current risks.

☐ Share the risks with the panel and re-visit the plan; revise the plan as required.

☐ Develop policies and procedures.

☐ Deploy solutions in accordance with the plan and to support the policies.

☐ Educate the users and make them aware of risks, policies, and solutions.

☐ Monitor and audit the program's success at lowering risks.

☐ Report progress to the panel.

☐ Start all over again.

CHAPTER 6

Deploying New Projects and Technologies

Every organization deploys new IT systems to enhance the productivity of the employees or to offer new services. Likewise, the security department will occasionally deploy new security systems to provide additional information or to better manage information security risk. Both situations offer opportunities and risks to the organization and to the security department.

This chapter will discuss a methodology that can be applied to both situations. The methodology is really nothing new as it is, very simply, good design methodology.

When we discuss the development and deployment of new systems from a security perspective, there are some additional concerns that must be dealt with. It is very rare that the security department will design and deploy a system without the assistance or cooperation of other departments. On the other hand, other departments (especially business units) may be able to design and deploy new systems without the involvement of the security department. While this may add additional risk to the organization, it can certainly happen. Preventing this is one reason why relationships are so important (see Chapter 1).

NEW BUSINESS PROJECTS

New systems are usually started in response to a business need. A department in the organization identifies a means of reducing costs or offering a new service. The system concept is developed and brought to the attention of the development or IT department. Once the cost is identified, a budget is drawn up and the project is either approved or not. If the project is approved a project manager is assigned and development begins.

Most development organizations have an approved development methodology. The project manager will assign appropriate resources to each step in the methodology. It is very important to remember that the job of the project manager is to complete the project within the projected budget and on schedule. Therefore, the project manager will not like surprises.

The biggest security mistake that most organizations make with regard to new projects and security is that they will examine the security of the system too late in the development cycle. Often, no one actually looks at the security issues surrounding the system until it is ready for production deployment. When this happens, the organization is put into a difficult position. If security risks are identified that are too large, the risks must be left in the system or expensive delays are incurred as the risks are reduced. Much of these delays and costs could be avoided if security got involved in the development process earlier.

 SECURITY ALERT!   Projects that expect security to be added on as the project goes into production are asking for failure. Security needs to be involved early on, not at the last minute.

A design methodology usually includes the following steps (see Figure 6-1):

- Requirements definition
- System design
- Development
- Test
- Pilot
- Full production deployment

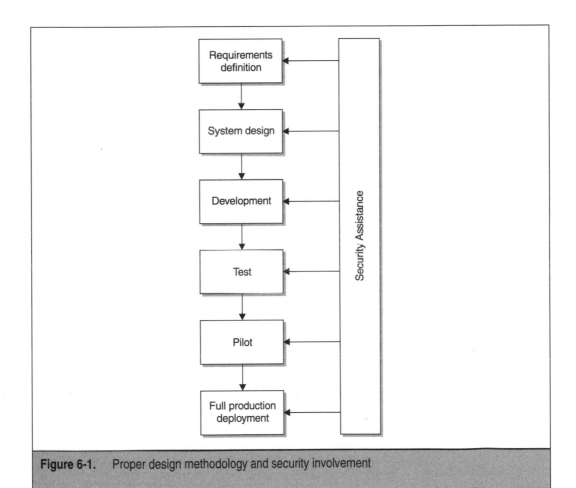

Figure 6-1.   Proper design methodology and security involvement

Security can and should provide input into each step in the design process. By doing so, risk can be managed throughout the process and in the final system when it is ready for deployment. The following sections go into detail about this involvement.

TIP The security manager should get to know the various development and business unit project managers. In so doing, the project managers are more likely to call upon the security department for help in their projects.

Requirements Definition

The identification of proper requirements is perhaps the most important phase of any project. If the requirements are not properly specified, the system will not do the job that is expected. The same is true for the security of the system. If the security issues and requirements are not properly identified at the beginning of the project, additional risk and expense will be incurred as the project gets ready for full production deployment.

The proper specification of the business requirements is beyond the scope of this book but the identification of security requirements is not. The specification of security requirements should fall into the four primary security services:

- Confidentiality
- Integrity
- Availability
- Accountability

The specific requirements for each service are derived from the security policies of the organization, the value of the service to be offered, the value of the information in the system, and the ramification of a policy violation. This information generally comes from a security risk assessment. In other words, what bad thing might happen to the system and how will it affect the organization.

During the requirements definition phase of the project, the security department should assign a resource to work with the project manager. This will allow security to be involved and make sure that the security requirements are properly identified. The importance of this cannot be overstated. Security must be part of new projects from the beginning. Adding security on after the project has been developed will add cost without really dealing with the security issues.

Confidentiality Requirements

Confidentiality requirements come about because information used in the new system will be sensitive and thus not everyone should be able to see or read it. Ideally, confidentiality requirements will come from the organization's information policy. However, not every organization has such a policy or the policy that exists may not be specific enough to quickly identify what information is sensitive.

To fully define the confidentiality requirements, all of the information in the system should be characterized. Some information may be public, some may be releasable to employees and other information may be releasable to a very limited number of employees. Information that comes from other systems may be required to have the same types of protections as in the other system. It is also possible that the confidentiality requirements of some information may change over time. For example, if a system were to manage acquisition information for an organization, the information would be very sensitive and access to it should be very limited until the acquisition is announced. At that point the information is public.

Closely related to the confidentiality of information is the restriction of certain system functions. For example, there may be capabilities of the system that only certain employees will be allowed to use. Some functions may require two employees. An example of this type of function is a funds transfer at many banks. A teller prepares the transaction. Then a supervisor reviews and approves the transaction in order to have it executed. If the supervisor finds an error, the transaction is referred back to a teller for correction. As with the information in the system, each function should thus be characterized.

Integrity Requirements

In many ways the integrity requirements of the system will be closely related to the confidentiality requirements. To properly define the integrity requirements, we must be able to identify the individuals or roles that will have the ability to modify information in the system. This information may come from the organization's information policy but more likely, it will come from the operating rules of the business unit. Many of the integrity requirements will actually be inferred from the manner in which the system operates. For example, an order is placed by a customer to be used by the system to fulfill and ship the merchandise. It can be inferred from this brief statement that the order must remain as the customer intended as it traverses the system. Clearly, the system would not properly fulfill its role if the customer received a blue shirt when green pants were ordered. As with confidentiality requirements, it is best to characterize information throughout the system as to the level of integrity protection that is required.

In addition to the information within the system, the system itself may have integrity requirements. These requirements usually come from the organization's configuration control policy or procedure. For example, what protections are required for the systems Web page or source code? These requirements, when added to the sensitivity or importance of the system, may dictate additional integrity requirements for system components. As an example, think of a Web-based ordering system. This system will provide a public image for the organization. Therefore, any unauthorized change to the front-end Web page may have serious repercussions to the organization. Such an unauthorized change does not have to be defacement by a hacker. Misspelled words may have a similar affect to the public image of the organization.

Finally, as with confidentiality, access to functions must be examined for the way in which this access will impact the integrity of information within the system. Access to certain modification functions may need to be restricted depending on the integrity requirements for various pieces of information in the system.

Availability Requirements

The requirements for the system, capabilities, and information associated with a new system fall under the category of availability. In some cases, the availability requirements will be very simple. For example, the employee time card system must be up and able to accept information between 8:00 A.M. and 6:00 P.M., Monday through Friday. In this case whatever components of the system are needed for the accepting of information from the employees must be up and available ten hours a day, five days a week.

Not every system is this simple. Many systems that are being installed into organizations are very complex and thus may have different availability requirements for different parts of the system. All of the availability requirements for all of the various components of the system should be specified. This includes the front-end servers, database servers, and communications medium. As the systems become more complex, the interactions between various components may be obscured. Care must be taken to understand the dependencies and interactions of system components.

In addition to the availability of the components of the new system, there may be requirements placed on existing infrastructure. For example, a new system will deliver information to distributors of a manufacturing company. This system will use the Internet to provide the communication system. If this new system needs to be up during normal business hours for distributors in all 50 states, that means that the Internet connection to the organization's site must also be up from 7:00 A.M. east coast time to 6:00 P.M. Hawaii time! If this is the case, the systems can only be down (and not affect this particular system) from 11:00 P.M. to 7:00 A.M. east coast time. Such a requirement may have implications for maintenance windows and on the Internet connection as well.

During the requirements definition phase, the potential cost of the system being down should also be identified, if possible. This will have implications for some of the trade-offs that will need to be performed during the design phase of the project.

 SECURITY ALERT!   Failure to properly set the availability requirements in this phase of the project will have ramifications as the system goes to production.

Accountability Requirements

The accountability requirements for any new system should come from the organization's security policies. These requirements include those for how users will be identified and authenticated and what information will be captured for auditing purposes. If there is a requirement for certain types of authentication due to the sensitivity of the information on the system, they should also be defined here.

Depending upon how the system is envisioned, it may be necessary to include the password length, content, and aging requirements from the security policy in the requirements document. The reason for this is that if the system will include its own password management system for authentication, it will have to conform to the password requirements of the security policy.

The input of security in the requirements definition phase is perhaps most important during the definition of the accountability requirements. The reason for this is that some requirements may need interpretation. For example, the organization's security policy requires that smart cards be used for access to sensitive information. The organization is developing a system to allow customers to view their own information online. Clearly the information that the customer is seeing is considered sensitive and yet it may be inappropriate to require that smart cards be used by all customers to view their own information. In this case, the security department can help the business unit define an appropriate requirement (and later system design) to meet the intent of the security policy (and manage the risk appropriately) without requiring a huge cost to the organization.

The same is true for auditing requirements. The security department should assist in the project by identifying which information would be useful during an investigation of a security incident. Some of the information that could be captured may not be useful and thus the requirement to capture the information may only lead to unnecessary cost and complexity.

TIP   Accountability requirements are often forgotten completely. In order to prevent this, the security person should enter the requirements phase of a project with a list of questions and issues to bring up.

System Design

System design is the interpretation of the requirements into a working system. Mixed into this process is the need to develop a system that fulfills the business requirements while still falling within the total allowable cost of the project. Designing for the security of the system has a reputation (in some cases deserved) for escalating the overall cost of the project without providing useful functionality.

Just to make our point here, we will provide a story from an organization for which we once worked. We designed systems for military use. As such, there were always security requirements to be met. Many of these designs had to be prepared for our responses to a government Request for Proposal (RFP). The RFP would specify system requirements and the engineers would begin working on them. At some point in the process, a security engineer was called in to determine if the design would meet the security requirements. It rarely would since the design engineers were not paying much attention to the security requirements of the system. The security engineer would make his determination and would depart. The design engineers would be sent back to the drawing board to try again. This is a stovepipe look at designing a system (see Figure 6-2). Clearly, this is not an efficient or effective way for security to participate in the design process.

It would have been much better if the security engineer were part of the design team. If this were the case, the security requirements could have been included in the

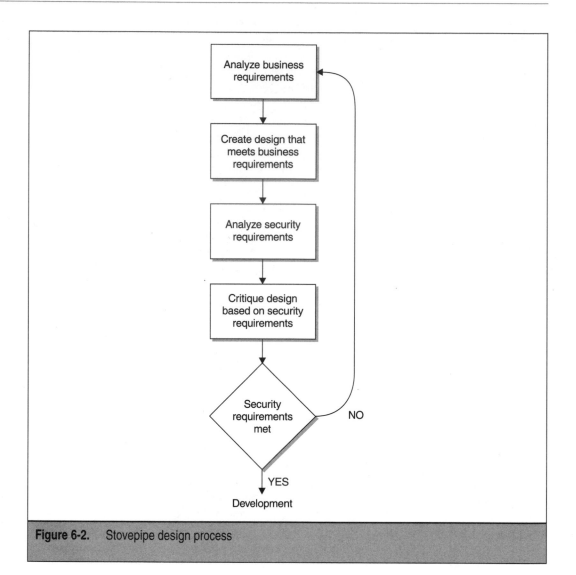

Figure 6-2.   Stovepipe design process

designs from the beginning and the various trade-offs could have been conducted during the design process rather than at the end of the process. This integrated approach (see Figure 6-3) is the method that will be discussed in the following sections. Security should be a full, equal partner in the design phase of a project. This is the best way to control costs and to make sure that all of the requirements of the project (both security and business) are met in the final system design.

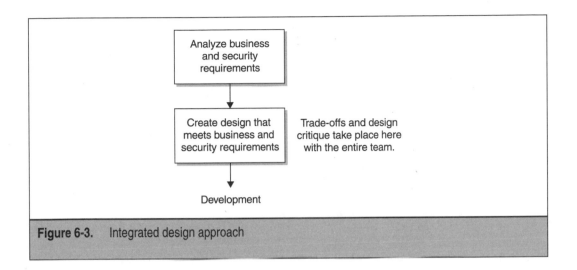

Figure 6-3.   Integrated design approach

Designing for Confidentiality

When we design a system to protect the confidentiality of information, we must be sure to examine all the places where information will exist and how that information may be compromised. Figure 6-4 shows a typical Web-based system and the various locations that must be examined for confidentiality.

Figure 6-4 shows a specific type of system and the confidentiality issues associated with it. However, we can generalize the issues as follows:

- Information may be compromised on the user's computer system.
- Information may be compromised in transit across an open network.
- Information may be compromised while on a front-end server.
- Information may be compromised while in transit across a closed network.
- Information may be compromised while in storage.

The User's Computer System   When designing a system, the most easily forgotten part is the end-user's computer system. Often, no design work is really required here since it is assumed that the end-user will be using a Web browser to access the system. If the system sends sensitive information to the end-user's system, the information must be protected while it is there. Some risk must be assumed to be beyond the technical design of a system, for example, the risk that the information may be examined while it is on the screen. This is not something that the security of the system is likely to prevent or manage. This risk must be managed by the end-user. However, the overall design

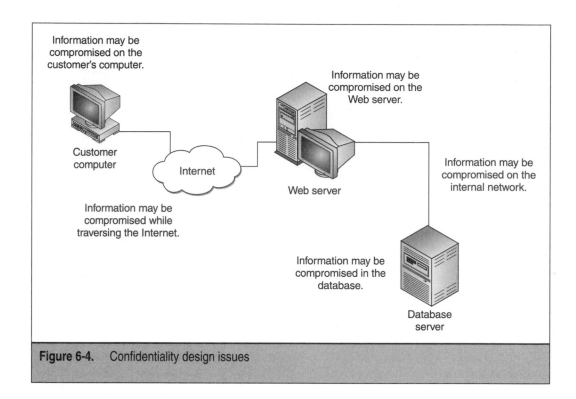

Information may be compromised on the customer's computer.

Information may be compromised on the Web server.

Customer computer

Internet

Web server

Information may be compromised on the internal network.

Information may be compromised while traversing the Internet.

Information may be compromised in the database.

Database server

Figure 6-4. Confidentiality design issues

of the system might note this risk and include a discussion of it in the documentation that is sent to the user.

Most of the confidentiality issues associated with the end-user's computer system can be eliminated if information is not stored on the system. If information must be stored on the end-user's computer system, every effort must be made to limit the sensitive nature of the information or to protect it in some other way. An example of the latter might be the use of encryption. Some systems use cookies that are sent to a Web browser to track the end-user's session. These cookies could be encrypted to protect them and they may even become non-persistent so that they are not written to disk but stored in memory. In both cases the security requirement has modified a part of the system design.

Transit Across an Open Network   As the flow of information is mapped out during the design process, it may be that some information must transit over insecure networks. An insecure network is one that the organization does not have complete control over and thus may include individuals who are not authorized to see sensitive information. At the same time, the systems on the network are not under the control of the organization and thus may be configured to locate, identify, capture, and/or store some of this sensitive information.

The protection of sensitive information in an insecure environment has always been a problem for designers of security systems. At this point in time, there is really only one design solution to this problem: encryption. The placement and usage of the encryption is something that must be worked out in the design. In some cases, the solution becomes very easy. For example, in the system in Figure 6-4 a Web browser and Web server are used to exchange information across an insecure network. In order to use encryption, the system design need only specify the use of Secure Socket Layer (SSL) over the Web connection. The system can then make use of an already developed encryption system.

In other cases the solution is not as clear-cut. If the organization chooses to use a newly developed program on the end-user's computer and a newly developed server, the encryption piece may have to be developed or purchased. This may add cost and schedule delay to the entire system.

The third alternative is to use a separate link encryption device on the physical link itself. Unfortunately, this usually will not work across an insecure network like the Internet since the link encryptor would encrypt the packet header information as well as the data. The security engineers on the design team must work with the other engineers to develop the most cost-effective solution to this particular problem.

Front-End Servers   For the purpose of this discussion, front-end servers are any systems that are used between the information store and the end-user's computer. These may be systems such as Web servers or application servers. Generally, they are used to hide the syntax of the information store from the end-user and thus make the overall system easier to use.

By their very nature front-end servers are a location of potential exposure for sensitive information. Generally, they are open to some number of unauthorized individuals. This means that they may also be open to attack or compromise from such individuals. Take the example of the Web server in Figure 6-4. The Web server is attached to the Internet. In this example, we will assume that the Web server can be reached by any browser. This means that it is also a likely target of hackers and other criminals. If the system is not properly patched, any information stored on the Web server may be compromised. There have been far too many examples of this in the news recently. In some cases, the intruder was able to compromise credit card numbers.

Given this risk, how can the system design manage the risk? The easiest method is to prevent the storage of sensitive information on the front-end server. This is especially true if the front-end server is accessible from the Internet. Other methods include the use of such things as intrusion detection systems and vulnerability scanners. In fact, if the front-end server must store sensitive information, the overall system may impose a scanning and patching requirement on the system administration staff. Again, we have an example of a technical problem being solved through procedures and policies rather than through technology.

Transit Across a Closed Network   Sensitive information will also transit across closed networks or networks that are completely under the control of the organization.

Often, these are considered to be safe networks in that there is little risk of exposure outside the organization and in some cases this is absolutely correct. However, what if not all employees are authorized to see the sensitive information in the system? This will be the case with new regulations such as HIPAA (see Chapter 2). This may mean that internal networks may have to be considered as dangerous as open networks like the Internet.

The same design solutions and alternatives that are available for open networks apply for closed networks. There is still no silver bullet, and encryption is still one of the easiest solutions. The only difference is that a closed network does make it possible to limit access to whole segments of the network. For example, if we take the system shown in Figure 6-4, the network between the Web server and the database server could be segregated from the rest of the internal network of the organization. In this way, access to the information would be limited without the use of encryption. However, the cost in equipment for doing this may be more than the cost of using encryption.

In Storage   Information in storage may be the most difficult and hardest to appropriately and effectively secure. The reason for this is that much information with different sensitivities may be stored together and thus different employees may be allowed different levels of access. Access controls based on identity or roles must be designed into the database.

The storage system itself must also be designed to protect sensitive information from unauthorized individuals. This means that special configuration requirements may be placed on the system. These requirements must be defined in a configuration procedure for the system so that administrators understand what is expected when the system goes into full production.

Designing for Integrity

Designing a system for integrity is much the same as designing a system for confidentiality. The same general issues must be examined: where information is potentially vulnerable and where information resides for any length of time. Figure 6-5 shows the same system that we used for the discussion of confidentiality, however, the potential integrity issues are now highlighted.

Again, we can generalize the integrity issues shown in Figure 6-5 as follows:

- Information may be modified by the user.
- Information may be modified in transit across an open network.
- Transaction information may be modified while on a front-end server.
- Static information or system software may be modified on a front-end server.
- Information may be modified while in transit across a closed network.
- Information may be modified while in storage.

Information May Be Modified by the User   In many systems, the user will be allowed to provide information to create a transaction. This information must be stored as the transaction is created and finally approved. In some Web applications, the information

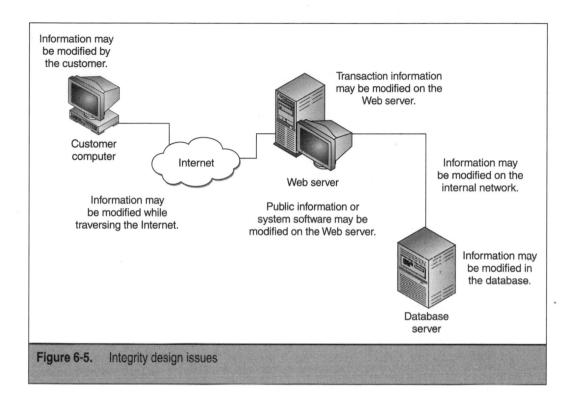

Figure 6-5. Integrity design issues

that the user enters is stored in a user modifiable location (the URL, for example). If this is the case, the user may modify the transaction information in such a way as to create a transaction that should not happen. For example, a Web site that allows users to order merchandise must store the item number, the price, and the quantity. Some systems stored this information in the URL. The user could modify the URL before the final commit on the transaction and change the price.

Clearly, information that is provided by the user must be checked to make sure that the information that is processed is actually appropriate for the transaction. This type of integrity check can be designed into the back-end processing of the system so that the price of the item (for example) that is part of the transaction is checked against the real item price that is stored in the database.

Another issue with information supplied by the user is that there should be a way to prove that the user provided the information or that the user initiated the transaction. This part of the system design ties in with the accountability portion of the design (see the upcoming section, "Designing for Accountability") but it goes to the integrity of the transaction information and thus must be addressed during the integrity design as well.

Transit Across an Insecure Network   As information crosses an insecure network, it may be modified on purpose (through some type of attack) or by accident (perhaps an error in transmission). Unlike unauthorized access to this information, the modification of the information as it traverses the network cannot be prevented.

If a modification of information in transit cannot be prevented, the best option is to be able to identify when a change has been made. There are several mechanisms that can detect such changes. The most commonly used choice is encryption. If the information is encrypted and some information is changed, the decryption will not work properly and thus the modification will be detected. In this case, if the confidentiality problem is solved for information transiting a public network, the integrity problem is likely also solved.

If encryption is not used, some type of checksum must be used so that any change to the information is noticed. Unfortunately, most such mechanisms (CRC checks, cryptographic checksums, and so on) can detect accidental changes but may not detect all intentional changes. If an intruder can intercept the information, make the change, and also change the checksum, the modification will pass unnoticed. Thus the best way to solve the problem of modification while in transit is to use some type of encryption.

Transaction Information on a Front-End Server   In the same way that sensitive information that is stored on a front-end server can be compromised, the integrity of transaction information can also be compromised. If the front-end server is successfully compromised (as opposed to simply defaced), the intruder may have access to any information on the system. Therefore, one option open to such an attacker is to modify transaction information. This could be a modification of a shipping address or the addition of a money transfer.

As was mentioned when we discussed designing systems for confidentiality, transaction information can be protected from such an attack by not storing it on a front-end server. The information should be moved off the front-end server as quickly as possible.

As an alternative to moving the information off the front-end server, take, for example, the idea of putting checksums on information that is stored on the front-end server to detect a change. Since the transaction information is created during operations, the checksums must also be created during operations. Then as the transaction is processed, the checksum must be checked at every step. Since the checksum and the information are both stored on the front-end server, an intruder may also be able to change the checksum when the information is modified. The addition of the checksum processing will also add load to the server. All in all, it is best to move the information off the front-end server as quickly as possible.

Static Information or System Software on a Front-End Server   The front-end server is likely to be the location of static information and the application software itself. The static information may be sensitive (with limited distribution) or it may be public information (an organization Web page or catalog). Since the information is not always confidential, encrypting it is not an option. The same is true for the application software. This information must still be protected from modification.

There are two primary dangers to static information and application programs: intentional attack and accident modification. An intruder who gains access to the system may be able to modify static information just as they could transactional information.

However, there is a difference in how the static information can be protected. Since the information is static, a checksum can be created and stored in a location that is write-protected or off the server. Periodically, the static information or software can have a checksum recalculated and compared to the original. The checksums can be computed at a time that is appropriate according to the load of the system.

The primary cause of accidental modification is an employee (developer or administrator) making a change to the system that has not complied with the organization's configuration control procedures. The change is normally intended to correct a problem in the software or to update the static information. The fact that the configuration control procedure was not followed makes the change a violation. The accidental modification of information can be detected in the same manner as an intentional attack.

Transit Across a Closed Network   It is possible (though unlikely) that information integrity may be compromised while moving across a closed network. The same detection mechanisms that are used over an insecure network can be used to great effect in a closed network. Since all of the systems on a closed network are under the control of the organization, it is much more difficult for an intruder to gain access to the traffic and thus it is less likely that the integrity of the information may be intentionally attacked.

In Storage   Information in storage is perhaps the most vulnerable to modification. This is due to the fact that some information in storage may not be accessed for long periods of time. When it is accessed, small modifications, additions, or deletions may not be obvious. Such changes may be made by authorized users or by intruders who have gained access to the system.

The protection of information in storage is not an easy task and thus it is best done using multiple mechanisms. The system must be protected from intrusion. Thus a procedure for the vulnerability testing and patching of the system must be used. The system must have strong authentication mechanisms to prevent an unauthorized user from guessing passwords and thus gaining access to the system. An access control policy must be enforced to prevent unauthorized users from making changes to the information. For those users who are authorized to make changes, an audit record must be kept and reviewed so that the original information can be re-created if necessary. In some cases, it may be appropriate to require two employees to authorize a change to any information.

In some cases, it may be possible to perform a cryptographic checksum on the information and have the system alarm if the information is modified. This solution is best used with small sets of information that do not change or that change very rarely. Large databases or stores of information that change frequently are not good candidates for the use of cryptographic checksums.

Designing for Availability

When we design a system to meet availability requirements we are actually playing the odds with our design. The reason for this is that (even more so than with any other part of security design) we cannot predict when an outage may occur. Outages are caused by any number of different things. Bad hardware can cause an outage as can a backhoe.

Therefore, when we design a system to meet certain availability requirements we are trading off cost (equipment, redundant communications, and so on) for the reduced chance that a single failure will cause an outage. As part of the design process, each single point of failure should be identified and the costs associated with its removal computed. We must also realize that multiple failures do sometimes occur. If multiple failures were to occur simultaneously, there is a high likelihood that the system will be unavailable.

Figure 6-6 shows the same typical system that we have used to analyze security designs for confidentiality and integrity. This time, it shows the various single points of failure and indicates what the potential problems might be. The following sections will provide more detail on each of these failure points.

Communications Availability   For the purposes of this discussion the communications system will include all networks and hardware used to communicate outside of the

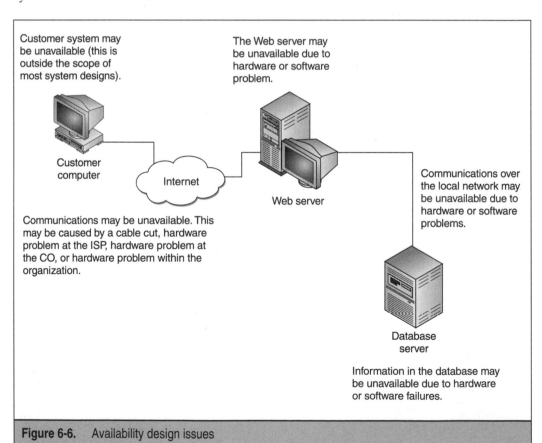

Figure 6-6.   Availability design issues

organization. Therefore, whenever we design for a high availability system or to limit our single points of failure in the communications system, we must consider the physical communication cables as well as the routers and firewalls and the demands of organization on the communications systems provider. Generally speaking, the physical communication plant is very robust. However, backhoes do exist and construction crews can accidentally cut cables. The question for the system designer at this point is whether the possibility of such a cable cut is an acceptable risk to the organization. If not, redundancy in the communication links may provide the necessary insurance, however, this will significantly increase the cost of the project.

The routers and firewalls that the organization uses to route traffic to the external communications systems can also be made redundant. The configurations can be an automatic fail-over so that new equipment takes over from the failed piece of equipment automatically and instantaneously. Alternatively, equipment could be stored nearby and installed if the primary systems fail. Any such redundancy requires the organization to increase the cost of equipment. It should be noted here that the equipment that we are talking about is generally used by the organization as a whole and not specifically for one project. If high availability is required for this one project, this project may drive the equipment requirements for the entire organization's Internet link, for example.

It should also be noted here that many of the failures that may occur to the external communications system are far beyond the control of the organization. It is possible that the failure may actually be an attack against the organization. For example, a denial-of-service attack may be launched against the organization to prevent traffic from getting to or from the organization's systems. In this case redundancy either of communications systems or equipment may be insufficient to allow the systems to continue to operate as they should. The potential for such attacks must be considered and included in the design process for a new system.

Front-End Server Availability   The front-end server is generally one or more pieces of computer equipment that are performing a task for the system. When considering the availability of a piece of computer equipment we must evaluate the availability of hardware as well as the availability of the software processes running on the system.

The hardware availability of the system is often the easiest to understand. Motherboards, hard drives, and network interface cards can fail. For some of these failures the solutions are relatively simple. For example, if the failure of a hard drive were a concern, the use of a RAID-5 system would be appropriate. Through the use of RAID-5, we would prevent a single hard drive failure from taking down the entire system and causing the loss of information. Other hardware failures will necessarily take down the entire system. For example, it is difficult for a system to continue operation when the motherboard fails.

The more complete the failure of the hardware system, the more expensive the solution becomes. If the loss of the entire system is a subject of concern, multiple systems could be used to provide the same functionality. The multiple systems could be front-ended by a load balancer so that incoming communication is balanced between the multiple systems. The loss of one hardware system then does not cause the loss of the entire system's functionality.

While hardware failures do in fact occur, software failures tend to be more common. While there are methods and mechanisms that can be used to restart software processes that fail, it is often best to design the availability of the system overall by identifying the failure of a particular computer system as opposed to differentiating between a hardware or software failure. Therefore, if the failure of a computer system is a significant risk to the project, the design should include multiple systems providing redundant services.

Local Network Availability   The internal local area network is not often considered a source of availability problems. Unfortunately, while the local area network cabling system is often very robust and very difficult to completely bring down, the other services that are necessary for the network to function are not as robust. For example, the internal DNS must function properly in order to resolve internal system names. If the DNS system is not functioning, then it may be difficult for the communications between the front-end server and the database server to function. If this is the case, then the entire system has an availability problem since transactions cannot be completed.

Communications hardware can also fail. Even more likely is a hardware configuration error. For example, internal routers may be misconfigured so that a route to the database server (as shown in Figure 6-6) is no longer available. In this case, it does not matter if the router hardware has failed, the router is failing in its function.

It is very possible, therefore, for a new project that requires high availability to place availability requirements on many computer systems within the organization. The costs of these changes must be considered as the system is designed. We will discuss this in greater detail later in this section.

Information Storage Availability   In Figure 6-6 information is shown stored in a database server. Generally, the system that stores information is hard to make redundant. The reason for this is that you cannot simply duplicate the system as you would the front-end server. Unfortunately, it is still vulnerable to the same hardware failures as any other computer system. In order to provide high availability for the information storage system, we normally provide a clustered system that operates on one source of information.

As part of the design process the availability of the information storage system must be defined. It is possible that the information availability requirements of the system may not require that the system be available 100 percent of the time. In such cases it may be more appropriate to back up the information on a regular basis (perhaps daily) and restore the information if the failure does occur.

TIP   Again it becomes very evident that the higher the availability requirements of the overall system the more cost that must be incurred. The design of the system for availability is probably the area in which cost trade-offs come into play the most. It is therefore extremely helpful if the business unit can clearly define the costs of the system being unavailable for various lengths of time.

Designing for Accountability

Designing a system to meet the accountability requirements of the project is perhaps the most difficult and most often forgotten portion of the security design. This is because the accountability portion of the security design does not necessarily meet any of the functional requirements of the system. However, the accountability design helps other portions of the security design (namely the confidentiality and integrity designs) meet their requirements.

The two primary components of accountability are identification and authentication (I&A) and audit. I&A is a proactive component while auditing is a reactive component. The following sections provide more detail on these two components.

Identification and Authentication   The proper authentication of an individual is a key component in providing proper access to information by authorized individuals. It is also very important for the protection of the confidentiality and integrity of any information in the system. Without properly identifying an individual, confidentiality controls and integrity controls in fact cannot work. To illustrate our point, let's examine the system shown in Figure 6-6. For the purposes of this discussion, we will assume that the information being provided to the customer needs to be kept confidential. In order to provide the confidentiality of the information, it will be encrypted as it crosses the Internet. By doing this information is protected from an unauthorized individual who might be monitoring information as it flows from the Web server to the customer. However, for true confidentiality, the system must also keep the information from an individual who is not authorized to see it. The question becomes, is the customer really authorized to see the information and at the same time is the customer really who he says he is. One condition for access to information is for the customer to identify himself before he is given access to the confidential information. In order to determine that the customer is in fact who he says he is, some form of authentication must occur. It is clear from this example that without proper authentication the confidentiality design of the system is not complete.

As noted above, I&A requirements fall from a number of places including the security policy of the organization. It is up to system designers to develop a proper authentication mechanism to meet the requirements and at the same time allow the system to function properly. The selection of an inappropriate mechanism will increase the overall cost and complexity of the system. The choice of a proper mechanism is influenced by several characteristics of the overall system. These include:

- The number of users
- The control the organization has over the users
- The sensitivity of the information in the system

Another aspect of the authentication design of the system is the fact that the choice of the authentication mechanism will affect the way the users interact with the system. This means that the technical aspects of the authentication mechanism may also influence the policies, procedures, and training required for the users when the system is finally employed.

Up to this point we have discussed the issues associated with how the authentication mechanism is designed for the system, but we have not discussed any particular mechanisms. Authentication can be accomplished through one of three things:

- Something the user knows
- Something the user has
- Something the user is

Passwords are an example of something the user knows. A smart card or credit card is an example of something the user has. Biometrics such as fingerprints or retina scans are examples of something the user is. It is obvious that each of these methods of authentication mechanisms have specific characteristics that may make them more suitable or less suitable for particular systems. For example, a Web-based ordering system for a clothing retailer is unlikely to have success using biometrics as an authentication mechanism for its customers. On the other hand, authenticating its customers by something they have (a credit card) is very appropriate.

 SECURITY ALERT!   The authentication mechanism will touch every user of the system. Choosing the wrong mechanism (that is, a mechanism that is inappropriate for the project) can cause the project to fail, as the users will not use an authentication mechanism that they consider to be too intrusive.

Audit   Auditing is a mechanism for identifying what has happened to the system in the past. Because of this fact, the audit mechanism does not in and of itself prevent bad things from happening. The audit trail of the system is however, extremely important for its ability to determine the events that occurred and thus help to reconstruct the events of a security breach if one does occur.

The design of the auditing system should be based completely upon the requirements set forth by policy or other regulations. These requirements will define how and what information about events must be recorded. What these requirements may not tell you, however, is where the audit information must be stored. Since the audit trail becomes very sensitive and important information, it must be protected from unauthorized modification. It is therefore best to move this information off the system where it is captured as quickly as possible to a protected storage location.

Design Trade-offs

Throughout the discussion of the security design of the system we have mentioned costs as a major factor in the choice of mechanisms. In truth, every portion of the security design of the system will be a trade-off between cost and risk. Since it is impossible to completely remove risk, the organization needs to be able to define the level of risk that is acceptable. The easiest and most obvious design trade-off that shows this concept is the trade-off for availability. When the availability portion of the design is developed, the organization must identify how much money can be spent on redundant equipment. This amount will affect the potential of the system to suffer an outage.

Another key design trade-off will be between the usability of the system and the overall risk. Customers of retail operations want a quick and easy way to order merchandise. The design of an online ordering system needs to take this into account. For this reason, most online ordering systems will accept a name and credit card for payment. The usability of the system would be seriously compromised if every single user were required to create an account and receive a strong password for an order to be placed. Would the use of a strong password provide any additional security? Perhaps. However, the usability of the system would be significantly compromised and the retailer would likely see significantly less business. In this case, the decrease in usability does not outweigh the small reduction in risk.

Internal Development

Once the design of the system has been completed, the design is turned over to development. During the actual coding of the software, the security department will provide guidance to the developers. The reason why guidance is important during this phase of the project is that many security vulnerabilities can be introduced during the coding phase of the project. The two primary issues the developers need to be aware of are problems with user input and the insecure copying and manipulation of string variables.

User Input

When a user is asked for input, there is no guarantee that the input that is expected will be what is provided. The reason for the unexpected input may be accidental or malicious. In either case, the software must understand what type of input is appropriate and discard input that is not appropriate. The developer who assumes that all user input will be exactly what is expected is asking for trouble and incorporating vulnerability into the system.

In order to prevent this, the security department should provide instruction to the developers on how to alleviate this problem. The easiest solution is simply to have all user input checked to make sure that it conforms to the expected input. If there is something wrong with the input, it should be discarded. Generally speaking, writing software that does not have major security problems is not hard (functionality problems are another issue, however). All it takes is attention to detail and good coding standards.

String Variables

The copying and manipulation of string variables is the primary reason for buffer overflow vulnerabilities in software. Unfortunately, many of the library routines included in standard C compilers do not check the length of variables before they are copied. This means that is very easy to insert the potential for a buffer overflow vulnerability into software if the developer does not check the size of the variables before copying.

TIP   The role of the security department here is again education. Developers should be shown how buffer overflows come to exist and how they can be prevented.

Third-Party Products

Not all new systems are designed and developed internally. Often an organization will choose to purchase all or part of a new system. If this occurs, the security department must still play a role in the project. Just because the system will be made up of purchased components, does not mean that the system does not have to conform to the security requirements.

The security department should be involved in the evaluation of the components to be purchased. If there are any security requirements that the product does not completely meet, these requirements should be noted and workarounds developed before the system moves into the testing phase. It should be noted that many of these workarounds might be procedural in nature.

There are often significant trade-offs when products are purchased rather than designed internally. If a product is chosen that does not fully meet the security requirements it is rare when the organization will pay for modifications to the product. Anytime that this occurs the security department should provide a risk analysis to the project manager. This risk analysis will identify the product's failing, potential workarounds that may alleviate the risk, and a final recommendation as to how the risk should be managed. In some cases, if the product does not meet significant security requirements, the recommendation may be to forego the use of that product.

Test

After a new system is developed or the components of the system purchased, the system must enter the testing phase. During the testing phase the functionality requirements of the business unit will be tested. At the same time the stated security requirements should also be tested.

During the testing phase the security department should provide a set of test procedures to verify that the security requirements are being met. It may also fall to the security department to actually perform the security tests. Bear in mind that it is impossible to test for all possible failure modes. What we mean by this is that positive requirements can be tested. For example, if the requirement is that the system accept a minimum of eight-character passwords, a test can be conducted to see if a seven-character password will work. However, a negative requirement is very difficult to test. For example, the negative requirement that states "no unauthorized user input shall be accepted" cannot be proved through testing. The reason for this is that it is nearly impossible to construct every possible variation of user input in order to prove that the system does not accept unauthorized input.

Pilot

Before a new large system moves into full production, a pilot phase is often used to provide the final testing and validation of the system. During the pilot phase, scalability issues are the primary focus. One of the most difficult things to test is how a system will perform with real-world users. At this point in the project, all security requirements should be met. This may mean that the system actually meets the requirement or a workaround has been developed in order to manage the risk to the organization effectively.

When the system is in the pilot phase, the security department should be analyzing any such workarounds to determine if they do in fact manage the risk effectively. Many procedural workarounds may be found to be ineffective given the way in which users are actually using the system. These types of issues are extremely difficult to identify prior to the pilot phase of the project. If a level of unacceptable risk is identified, additional changes to procedures or the system itself must be made.

CHALLENGE

On a late summer Wednesday afternoon, a project manager in the software development department of your organization stops by your office. He casually sits down to have a chat about a project he is working. He tells you that he has a small problem with the design of the system and wants to get your take on the issue.

The project he is speaking about is in the final stages of testing and is getting ready to go into pilot on Monday morning so he needs to deal with this issue. You have no idea what project he is talking about but you quickly run through the projects you know about and you cannot remember one that is going into pilot on Monday.

The project manager describes the problem he is having. It has to do with the storage of the database ID and password so that a web application, running on a publicly available Web server, can query and write to a production database on the internal network. Surprised, you say that the Web server should not be storing the ID and password at all. The project manager stops for a moment and then says that this system has to go into pilot on Monday because it has been promised to customers. This is the way the system is designed and if it cannot work that way, the project will have to be delayed and you will have to explain why to the CEO.

Now what do you do? You have two full business days and two days of a weekend before the project goes into pilot. Should you stop the project? Could you even if you tried?

This case serves to show why it is so important to get security involved early in the project. If this had occurred, this issue could have been identified much earlier and dealt with. At this point, you need to make management aware of the risks and take steps to manage the risk. What can you do? One option is to find a solution to the problem before full production but allow the pilot to occur. In the time before pilot, you can attempt to identify vulnerabilities on the Web server so that they can be fixed and thus reduce some of the risk involved. It may also be possible to restrict access to the Web server so that only members of the pilot group can gain access.

Full Production

Once the pilot phase has been completed, the system is ready to move into full production. Keep in mind that the pilot phase is not finished until any issues that have been discovered have been corrected. There are two security issues as a system moves into full production: the turnover documentation and the ongoing operation of the system.

Turnover Documentation

Up to this point, it is possible that the system is being operated by the employees who built it. As a system moves into production, it will be operated by the production staff. This means that the administrators and operators who manage the production systems must understand how the system works, how to troubleshoot it, and how to operate it.

As part of the turnover documentation, the security mechanisms of the system must be defined. The security department (specifically the security staff who worked on the project) should develop the portion of the turnover documentation that defines the security mechanisms, how they work, and how they must be operated.

Ongoing Operation

Depending upon the organization, the security department may have the responsibility for the ongoing operation of security mechanisms. If this is the case, the encryption, authentication, and audit mechanisms will now be the responsibility of the security department. Appropriate resources to properly manage the systems must be identified and trained on the new system.

If the security department does not actually operate the security mechanisms of the new system, the system administrators must be trained on their operation. This training should come from the security department (and again, specifically from individuals who worked on the project).

CHECKLIST: KEY POINTS IN DEPLOYING BUSINESS PROJECTS

The following is a checklist of key steps in working with business units to deploy new business-related projects:

- ☐ Identify project development methodology used within the organization.
- ☐ Develop a relationship with business project managers so that security is notified of new projects early in the development cycle.
- ☐ Identify the security tasks for each development phase.
- ☐ Identify security requirements for the project in the areas of confidentiality, integrity, availability, and accountability.

- ☐ During the system design, work with the business team to develop a design that meets security requirements.
- ☐ Conduct proper risk analysis/trade-off studies during the system design phase.
- ☐ Identify procedural issues that will not be covered by the technical design.
- ☐ Train the development team on how to avoid security vulnerabilities.
- ☐ If the system is to be purchased, assist the project team in the evaluation of vendor products.
- ☐ Develop a security test plan to test the system against the security requirements.
- ☐ Analyze the system during the pilot phase and modify procedures accordingly.
- ☐ Develop turnover documentation and training regarding the security mechanisms of the system for the administration staff.
- ☐ Determine the necessary level of security support during operation.

CHAPTER 7

Security Training and Awareness

Security awareness training is the best and most cost-effective measure to reducing your internal security risk. Users who are aware of the inherent risks of the information systems they use during the course of doing their jobs each day are less likely to allow exposures. If a user is unaware of the fact that e-mail, even internal e-mail, can expose sensitive information to unauthorized viewers, they are less likely to put sensitive information in e-mail.

Many years ago, during a risk assessment for a government agency, we discovered that the legal team was under the impression that their e-mail contents were automatically secured. We were shocked. These were the lawyers, for goodness sakes. Shouldn't they have known that the highly sensitive information they were putting into e-mail content was unsecured over the network? After thinking about it for a while we realized that we were making a huge assumption. These were not technical people.

Many of us take for granted that the people in our organizations are all technically savvy. We assume that the general user understands the risk of using certain applications. Our assumptions are wrong and we must consider that users utilize the technology to conduct their business. They rely on the systems and networks to provide them with information for making decisions and transacting business. They look to us to make the systems secure and to protect their data.

There are several forms of security training that must take place in any organization. One type of training is awareness training. Its purpose is exactly what its title indicates. It is intended to make users aware of the risks of using information systems and to make them aware of the policies and procedures for reducing that risk. Another type of training is security solution-specific. This type of training is usually reserved for the information security professionals in your organization who have the responsibility for managing and administering the security solutions that are integrated throughout your IT enterprise.

Awareness training comes in many forms and mediums as well. There is the traditional classroom training. This is usually reserved for specific security product training. You can also use less formal seminars. These are usually shorter in duration and less formal than the classroom setting. Other vehicles for awareness training include brown-bag sessions (similar to seminars), newsletters, awareness days, and Web sites. The best method is to use a combination of these vehicles for making users aware.

Training does not come without a cost. There is the time and effort to develop material and deliver the training, and the time users attend the training and are not doing their specific jobs. If training is outsourced or users go to a formal training course there is a cost associated with that as well. Nonetheless, awareness training is still one of the best values for the organization.

There are numerous benefits to security awareness training. First and foremost, users become knowledgeable about the vulnerabilities in the technology they use, the threats to the information they handle, the policies they must follow, and the tools at their disposal to help them comply with policies. Another benefit to awareness training, not always considered, is the deterrent factor. If users are made aware of the policies they must follow and then told of the company's ability to monitor compliance, they are less likely to conduct mischief.

One of the reasons that security awareness training falls off the radar for most companies is not that it costs a lot of money but requires a great deal of time. When you read on in this chapter and see what we prescribe just for general user awareness training, you might just choke. There is quite a bit to do. The time commitment for larger organizations is likely to be a full-time person or two. If you are a small shop, then you should adjust accordingly but never eliminate awareness training altogether.

In the remainder of this chapter we will discuss the different types of training each group of users requires and then describe some effective ways to conduct training.

USER AWARENESS

As mentioned previously in the book, the general user population sees policy differently than management and system administrators. It is true that even management and system administrators are users too. However, these two groups see policy as something they must enforce. Users see policy as something with which they must comply. They must be made aware of their role specific to compliance with policy and general risk reduction.

Users are the key to a successful information security program. If they do not follow sound information protection principles then the risk of a serious security breach is significantly higher. So, users will make or break your program. You must get them to do things that may lower your overall risk. If users are thumb-tacking slips of paper with their passwords on their wall, re-using the same passwords all the time, leaving their systems logged on while unattended, leaving sensitive documents in the printer and fax machines, then you are in for trouble.

One of the main elements of security awareness for users is getting them to understand why security is important. We said previously that almost all users see security controls as barriers to getting their jobs done. When they see security in this light they usually try to find ways around it. This, of course, defeats the whole purpose of having security controls. If, instead, they understand the reasons for security controls and you make the controls reasonable, then the likelihood that they will participate in security is much higher.

Don't get us wrong. There will always be some people in an organization that never get the purpose of security and simply refuse to cooperate. These are the folks that kick and moan when it is time to change their password and they scream when they learn they have to sign an acceptable use policy before they can receive their account. You must take these persons into consideration but also remember that you can never make everyone happy.

Information security should be treated with the same value as that of sexual harassment. The organization needs to have a low- to zero-tolerance policy for it. While it is true that we can never make everyone happy, regarding information security, all you can ask is that they be compliant, not necessarily happy.

Just the same, if you conduct your security awareness program in the proper way, you will gain the trust of the general user population and they will get it. Once they understand, the security bug is sometimes contagious. You may even find that there are folks on the complete opposite side of the spectrum from the security naysayers who become security gung-ho'ers. These folks can also cause you problems. Just keep them in check and make them part of your security evangelism program. Maybe you can even deputize them.

Nonetheless, awareness training for the masses must be effective. There are several topics that you have to provide to users. You don't want to beat them over the head with policy. This is a surefire way of putting them to sleep and getting no value or buy-in. Once again, they will see this as a hurdle not a help. So start by helping them understand the threat. It's juicy stuff. Tell them about hackers and viruses and denial-of-service attacks. This is James Bond stuff and will get their attention. Next, explain just how vulnerable the systems are that they use each day. After that you should describe how valuable and sensitive certain information is to the company's success. Show how bad it would be if that information were to fall into the wrong hands, be altered, or become unavailable. If they see that poor security habits can affect the company's ability to pay them, they will sit up straight and listen. Finally, you tell them about the policies and procedures they can follow to help reduce the likelihood of those bad things happening.

It sounds so easy but surely it is not. Users tend to forget quickly. For this reason you have to get in front of them frequently. However, you can't appear to be hounding them. So you must utilize all the tools at your disposal. An effective way to train is also to show the comparisons between information security and security in the real world. Take some of the abstract ideas of information security and show how they are consistent and similar to physical security and the end-users will have a much higher retention rate. We suggest that user awareness training follow the method we prescribe later in this chapter.

MANAGEMENT AWARENESS

Previously, we mentioned that management must be made an integral part of creating and enforcing information security policy. This will create buy-in and support for the program. If this actually happens within your organization then you will have half of your management awareness problem solved. Managers will already be aware of the importance and purpose of the information security program. However, regardless of whether or not management is supportive of the program, they must also be reminded of the importance of information security and their role in reducing risk.

Awareness training for management takes on a slightly different flavor than for the general user population. Management can certainly attend the same training as the general users. It is actually encouraged that they do this because it shows support for the training program. If general users and employees know that managers are attending security awareness training they will automatically sign up so they don't look so bad. Sure, we'd like all users to come to training because they think it is great, but the truth is we just want them to show up.

Managers must be aware of the threats to the information for which their department is responsible. They should be fully aware of the policies of the entire company and any department-specific policies. They must also be aware of laws and regulations that affect their information protection requirements. One department may be affected by laws that have no effect on another department. Managers must also be aware of their environment. If they have a disgruntled employee, for example, this could increase the risk of a security violation.

How does management stay aware? If you are not providing awareness training specifically aimed at management then they must be told where to get the information they need to stay aware of the things just mentioned. One way is for the information security department to create a security interest group with managers from each major business unit represented. The group should meet approximately quarterly to share information, learn of policy and legal changes that may affect their departments' requirements for protecting information, and learn about projects in other parts of the company that might affect the security of the data for which they are responsible.

Managers should also be receiving security reporting from the information security department on a regular basis. This should include summaries of security incidents, policy violation reports, status reports on security projects, and any other things the information security department can share that might help the managers.

An information security program does not simply run by itself. It requires a significant amount of effort. When management is fully aware of the risks to their information, the policies and procedures in place to protect that information, and their role in enforcing that policy, they are more likely to be supportive of the information security program.

SECURITY TEAM TRAINING AND AWARENESS

Individuals within your organization who are responsible in one way or another for implementing the security policies also require security training. This group of individuals requires both awareness training and product/solution-specific training. They should be reminded annually of their roles and responsibilities and they should be trained on the technology and other solutions they must manage and administer.

The primary audience in this group is the system administrators. They are responsible for a number of security-related functions including user account management and administration of security devices and products such as firewalls, routers, and anti-virus software. This group must be fully aware of the policies and know specifically how to make the security products enforce those policies.

One problem we run into frequently with clients is that their system administrators are managing software and products for which they have never had any formal training. Note that many security problems stem from the fact that administrators are improperly trained.

We are advocates of learning through on-the-job training for some things, but certainly not for administering production systems. It is especially important for technical personnel to have product-specific training on security technologies. It is a really dangerous thing to have a person learning to administer your production firewall through the process of trial and error. Spend the money and get them formal training.

All members of your information security team, not just the technical folks, need to keep their awareness high. One real danger is that the security team, like almost everyone else at the company, becomes too busy to stay up on current issues. The threat and vulnerability environment is constantly changing. Security team members must stay abreast of those changes. There are several ways for them to do this.

Security team members can stay current with their knowledge and skills by attending conferences, reading industry magazines, visiting pertinent Web sites, and subscribing to mailing lists for security alerts and other important information. They can attend conferences, formal classroom training, or join local chapters of security organizations such as the ISSA (www.issa.org), the Computer Security Institute (www.gocsi.com), and the International Information Systems Security Certification Consortium (www.isc2.org). There are many ways for the security team to keep up their awareness of the information security landscape.

TRAINING METHODS

As we mentioned in the beginning of this chapter, there are many ways to educate members of your organization and make them aware of information security issues. You should take advantage of every possible method to keep users interested and engaged. A two-hour lecture on the entire security policy manual contents is a recipe for a sleeping pill. However, a game show-like seminar that rewards participants with candy bars for correct answers is a great way to educate users on the proper ways to protect sensitive information. Believe us, we've done it both ways. The game show idea works better.

We're not training professionals but we've worked with instructional system designers and have done enough classroom training that we've learned what works best for security awareness training. The secret to keeping users' awareness level high and reducing the likelihood that they will do something that compromises security is to stay in front of them. Don't give them a chance to forget the good habits.

Using this philosophy, we recommend a full range of security training methods and mediums. Table 7-1 shows the primary methods we recommend for a strong security training and awareness program. Larger organizations should be able to take advantage of all of these methods. Smaller shops might just use a few. It depends on your available time and budget.

Table 7-1 includes a column that identifies the method of training, another column that defines the preferred frequency of the method, and a column that provides a description of the method. A more detailed description of each follows the table.

Method/Medium	Frequency	Description/Purpose
Job description	N/A	Include statements in each person's job description that make it clear they are expected to protect sensitive information while performing their job duties.
New hire orientation	Once—upon hire	Explain key elements of information security policy and company expectations for each new employee.
Acceptable use policy	Annually	Users must read and sign this document before they receive any access to information systems. Clarifies their responsibilities and emphasizes policy highlights.
Formal training	As needed	Formal classroom training primarily for security technology such as firewall administration.
Awareness seminars	Annually (at least)	Require all users to sit through a brief session that reminds them of the threats, vulnerabilities, and risks to information and systems. Discuss recent incidents and highlight any policy or procedural changes. Have them re-sign the acceptable use form.
Brown bag sessions	Quarterly	Focus on a specific topic such as virus protection, e-mail content filtering, or other popular topics. These sessions are informational only, small, and offered more frequently.
Newsletter	Quarterly	Disseminate changes (in electronic or paper format) in policy, tips, alerts, and schedules of events. May be a section in another, established company newsletter.
Web site	Update frequently, at least bi-monthly	Post all existing policies and provide tips, tools, and schedule of events. If you have an intranet this can replace the newsletter. Keep it fresh.
Awareness campaigns	Every 18–24 months	For larger organizations. Several days dedicated to security awareness. Include speakers, games, and other interesting events.
Conferences	Annually	For technical staff responsible for managing and administering security technology and for those who architect security solutions for the enterprise.
Info security quiz	Periodic	Have pop quizzes on topics of information security. As an encouragement, raffle off a nice prize, such as a DVD player, PDA, etc.

Table 7-1.   Recommended Training Methods

Job Description

What better place to set an expectation for protecting sensitive information than right in the job description? You might think we're nuts to expect anyone to actually do this but it has to become our reality. When you start a new job the first thing you should expect to receive is a documented description of your job duties and responsibilities.

This is one of the clearest ways of specifying what is expected of your new employees. Tell them, in black and white, what their job duties are. It makes it easy to evaluate an employee's performance.

In today's high-tech environment we provide our new employees with the latest gadgets and toys to do their job. They have cell phones, laptops, wireless PDAs, and broadband access from home. We give them access to the corporate network through remote VPN connections. We say "Go and be productive!" But we don't always say "… and do it securely."

We strongly recommend that in every employee's job description organizations add several statements that are consistent with the information security policy. These statements should address the expectations of the company with respect to maintaining the privacy of sensitive information and for reporting suspected security incidents. The following points are examples of statements that you might want to consider putting into your employee job descriptions.

- Employees are expected to be aware of and comply with all information security policies and procedures.

- Employees should report suspected security incidents immediately to the information security department or their manager/supervisor.

- Employees are expected to use information technology in an acceptable manner in accordance with the acceptable use policy.

By placing information security requirements into each employee's job description you accomplish two tasks. You make them keenly aware of the importance the organization places on securing information. Secondly, you set clear expectations for the employee so they see that protecting information is everyone's job, not just the security department or the management.

New Hire Orientation

Many years ago we asked a co-worker where a new co-worker was. He said she was at "charm school." We laughed and asked what he meant. He explained that she was at new hire orientation and that he referred to it as "charm school." Since then we have always referred to it the same way.

Most organizations, large and small, conduct some form of new hire orientation. Larger organizations often have multi-day, formal classroom setting events where they cover everything from health insurance benefits to how to dress. In smaller organizations the orientation might only be a one-hour session with the office manager. Regardless of the size of your organization you should talk about information security with all new employees, temporary workers, consultants, and contractors.

At a minimum, the discussion should cover the organization's information security policies, procedures, and the acceptable use policy. This is the place to get employees to read and sign the acceptable use policy (AUP) and any other security-related documents such as non-disclosure and confidentiality agreements. Users should be told what is expected of them, how they get system access, and how they should report security incidents.

Don't let this once-in-a-lifetime opportunity pass you by. Whether the information security orientation is done by the security department or the classroom trainer, make sure information security is discussed with every new employee. Remember, it is not just the employees that need this training; it is also for contractors, temps, and consultants.

Acceptable Use Policy

In a previous chapter we talked extensively about the different kinds of policies an organization needs to have. You will recall that the AUP is a vehicle for summarizing the main points of the information security policy, providing examples of what is and is not acceptable when using IT, and obtaining the user's consent to monitor their actions on IT systems for compliance.

The AUP is a vital legal tool for the organization and acts as both a deterrent to system abuse and a reminder of the employee's responsibilities. Since this document is so critical to protecting the company it is required that the corporate legal counsel be directly involved in its creation.

It is an effective awareness tool. For this reason we recommend that the AUP be revisited annually as a reminder to employees. It should be first signed at the new hire orientation or when users first request system access. It should be subsequently signed each year, possibly at the annual information security awareness training.

Formal Classroom Training

We mentioned earlier that we have been instructors in a number of information security courses. We found out just how hard it is to challenge students and keep their attention. Formal classroom training can be very dry and boring. Even the best instructors can't make dry material too exciting. For this reason we recommend that formal classroom training be reserved for product-specific training.

The best use of classroom training is to educate technical personnel to manage and administer security technologies such as firewalls, intrusion detection systems, content filters, and many other security products. The primary audience for this type of security training includes personnel from the information security department, system administrators, and network administrators. Also included in this group might be system developers, network engineers, and operations personnel.

The type of training we are referring to here includes courses offered by product vendors such as ISS, Cisco, Checkpoint, and Pentasafe. These organizations have specific security products and technologies that require detailed and rigorous classroom and hands-on training in order to be proficient. Some of these vendors offer certifications for learning to manage their products. For example, Checkpoint provides a systems administrator and a systems engineer certification for their firewall product. To maintain your certification, you must periodically attend training and take certification exams.

In addition to product-specific classroom training, other learning organizations including business schools, colleges, universities, and private training companies offer a range of security training. These courses range from classes that provide a general understanding of the concepts of information security to those that teach specifics on how to administer user accounts on Unix, for example.

As with all training and awareness programs, we think this type of training is most essential. Your technical staff must be proficient at managing and operating the information security technology you have deployed. Poorly configured and administered security technology can be more dangerous and risky than having no security solutions deployed at all.

Make sure you allocate funds for product-specific training for your technical staff. For knowledge depth, ensure that you have at least two people trained for each security technology deployed. In addition to allocating funds for such training, give your IT staff sufficient time to attend these courses and to study for certification exams.

Seminars and Brown Bag Sessions

Seminars and brown bag sessions are by far the most fun to do. They take some planning but people usually like coming to these because they are not mandatory. Over our years in this industry we have done our fair share of these and they are always a pleasure. The objective of these types of training and awareness sessions is to provide attendees with new and interesting information that will be useful to them. For example, if you just deployed a new e-mail encryption capability you could hold a series of seminars to explain how to use the technology prior to putting it into production. This would be an alternative to formal classroom training.

Remember a few rules when creating seminars:

- Make them timely and relevant.
- Keep them short (about 20–30 minutes).
- Explain what the issue or problem is.
- Tell how they can help.
- Tell what the company is doing to help.
- Send them home with something.

If you follow these few simple rules and conduct your seminars every so often you will increase awareness among your general user population and ultimately lower your corporate information security risk.

CHALLENGE

Most likely you will use seminars and brown bag sessions to cover new threats, new tools, and changes in policy or procedures. With one of our previous employers, we worked with the information security department to conduct a series of lunch-time sessions on malicious code. It was during the height of the Melissa virus period and we were implementing anti-virus gateways and had just created an incident response capability. Since we were getting a number of calls to the help desk about viruses and we saw a great deal of e-mail flowing around the company spreading panic, we decided it would be a good time to educate the users on malicious code and anti-virus techniques.

We developed a short 20-minute presentation and took it on the road. We had the corporate training department set up sessions at various times and locations around the corporate campus and off we went. We advertised through e-mail and on the intranet and had people sign up in advance. Our attendance was great. People were interested and asked plenty of good questions. We rewarded their attendance by handing out candy and treats at the meetings.

The reason this set of seminars was successful was because the information was timely and relevant. Malicious code attacks were prevalent in the news and many people were aware of folks who had been negatively affected by viruses. We educated them about the problem and explained what they could do about it and what we were doing about it. Knowing that many of them were probably exchanging diskettes between work and home and dialing in for remote access, we even told them how to protect their home computers. We checked our anti-virus license agreement and were able to give them access to licensed anti-virus software to load on their home computers if they wanted to. We helped lower the company risk through a seminar series. That was cost-effective.

Newsletters and Web Sites

Almost every organization with which we've worked or consulted has had some type of written corporate communication such as a newsletter or bulletin. With the advent of corporate intranets and e-mail, paper newsletters are not as popular as they once were and are being replaced by e-zines or electronic newsletters. Regardless of their format, any periodic publication aimed at the corporate staff is a good vehicle for providing information security awareness.

If your organization is large and has a fair-sized information security staff you may decide to have a newsletter specifically for information security matters. Be aware, though, that although you may think information security is the most interesting thing since the Slinky, others may not find it quite as enticing. So, we suggest that you consider putting an information security section into another corporate periodical. This will probably be more effective and more likely to be read.

As with seminars and brown bag sessions, keep the content of your newsletter section timely and relevant. In each issue make sure you cover something new and exciting, such as new security alerts or hacker techniques. Also, cover one policy and its corresponding procedures. You can use the newsletter to advertise upcoming seminars or remind people of security awareness training. Always provide contact information to report security issues and concerns.

CSI has a service called the *FrontLine End-User Awareness Newsletter* (see https://wow.mfi.com/csi/order/frontline.html). It is a quarterly, four-page newsletter designed to increase awareness in every employee in the organization. Since it is pre-written, it saves a lot of time. It can be customized with your company's own logo.

If you are fortunate enough to have a corporate intranet then you should definitely have an information security home page. The content on this page should include a description of the information security department, its roles and responsibilities, and contact information. Additionally, the site should provide access to all security-related documentation including policies, procedures, standards, and guidelines. Keep these policies updated with the very latest version. This will minimize your need to print paper copies of the policy manual, and users are more likely to see the most current versions. This also ensures that there is a single authoritative location for policies.

An information security Web site provides so many opportunities. You can include online access request forms, incident response procedures, and security alerts. The site should allow users to provide feedback and you can even use it to survey users or provide online training and testing. One product we have seen that does a nice job of allowing you to publish security policies and even test users to ensure they know the policies is Pentasafe's VigilEnt Policy Center (www.Pentasafe.com). This Web-based product is easy to deploy and use. Intellitactics (www.intellitactics.com) also has a similar product called the LivingPolicy, and Conquest (www.conquest.com) has their e-Minder electronic policy manager products.

As we mentioned earlier, one key to keeping your users aware of information security matters is to stay in front of them frequently. Newsletters and intranet Web sites are a perfect tool to make that happen.

Campaigns

Campaigns are all-out blitzes intended to flood the organization with material about the information security program. Think of them as mini-conferences held right in your office spaces. They take a lot of time and money to prepare so you are not likely to want to do these too often. In more than 20 years we have only been involved in two of these. Both were successful and required a significant effort to pull off.

Your organization might not be of the size or have the budget of a large federal agency so we suspect you might not want to put on such a big production. However, you can consider things like a week-long set of displays and activities in the main lobby of your building or a single day of events throughout the entire day. One of our clients used to set up a security awareness game outside the lunchroom at each of their buildings over the course of a week. During lunch time they would have employees go through a short series of explanations of a security tip such as how to set the screen

CHALLENGE

Probably the best way to explain what we mean by a campaign is to describe one of the two in which we were involved. This particular one was done as part of an agency-wide security awareness campaign. It was done for a large intelligence agency. As part of some new federal regulations it was decreed that every single agency employee had to undergo security awareness training. This was no small feat.

We decided that since we had to train every single agency employee (we can't disclose the total number since it is a classified government secret) we needed to keep it as short and as entertaining as possible. We made it like a game show. The students were all seated in the auditorium. The trainer, acting more like an MC, was on the stage and showed a short video clip depicting an information security situation. Following the clip a series of questions were shown on the screen with multiple-choice answers. Students responded as to their choice with hand-held, wireless responder units. The receiver unit calculated the total number of answers for each choice and displayed the distribution on the screen. Next, the trainer revealed the correct answer and explained why it was correct. This went on for about an hour.

The video clips (which we produced and directed ourselves with paid actors) depicted a parody of a popular television show. One scene had Murphy Brown at a printer with other cast member look-alikes pulling off pages of a printout that was not hers but contained interesting classified information. The questions were related to policies and procedures for handling classified printer output.

As you can imagine, this was an enormous and expensive project. We had to buy the answer/query receiver and hand-held transponders, produce the video clips, develop the questions and slides, and then run the show several times a week. It took over a year to execute the entire program. The team that ran the project included over 10 people.

lock on a PC or how to run a virus scan. After going through the three or four stations, the employee was rewarded with a spin of a prize wheel. Everyone got a prize ranging from a plastic slinky with a security slogan to candy bars.

This is an opportunity to be creative and get information out to the masses in a fun way. It is more expensive and time consuming but it might be just the right way to get a lot of valuable information out to your entire organization at one time.

Conferences

The conference business is quite a money-maker. There are conferences for almost everything. We'd bet there is even a conference for conference companies. We were in Las Vegas recently speaking at the National Association of Credit Management (www.nacm.org) Loss Prevention Division's E-commerce Business Credit Fraud Symposium. Down the hall was a group of caterers attending a national catering and food presentation conference. One of us commented to a friend: "So who do you think caters a catering conference?"

We realize that conferences are sometimes considered boondoggles. They are a bit expensive by the time you factor in travel and meal expenses. However, we still think they are valuable if you know why you are going. It has been our experience that, at some conferences, we don't plan on learning a lot of new stuff. The sessions are often the same old stuff you've heard just packaged a bit differently. If you want detailed training, take a formal classroom course. If you want a good, general overview of certain topics, then attend conference sessions.

There are a bunch of good information security conferences. There are so many that it is hard to select the best ones. RSA (www.rsa.com/), MISTI (www.misti.com/), CSI (www.gocsi.com), and ISSA (www.issa.org/) all sponsor very good conferences across the globe. We suggest if you are in a cost-savings mode, pick a conference that is local to you so you eliminate the travel expenses. Find one with the best session tracks for your specific learning need and get to all the sessions you can.

Conferences are especially good if you are considering some new security solutions. Let's say, for example, that you are thinking about deploying some content filtering solution for e-mail. To get the most out of a conference, find some tracks that discuss this topic. While at the conference attend those sessions and then start your product search. Walk through the vendor showcase and collect literature. Ask specific questions and take notes.

One of the mistakes we've made in the past when going from booth to booth is not writing notes on the literature. By the time you get back to work you'll forget which products you thought were best suited. Jot some notes down as the vendors answer your questions.

If you are the information security manager we'd suggest you attend one or two conferences per year if your budget permits. For your staff, we'd only send folks with specific requirements in mind. Be cautious sending junior staff to conferences. They can be overwhelmed and might not gain any value from attending. For mid- to senior-level staff, make sure you know why they want to go, what they hope to accomplish and then have them summarize what they learned at the conference for you and the rest of your team.

CHECKLIST: KEY POINTS FOR SECURITY TRAINING AND AWARENESS

The following are some points to remember for your training and awareness program:

- ☐ Know your audience and make the material appropriate for them.
- ☐ Educate the organization when new policies and procedures are introduced.
- ☐ Use multiple training methods to keep it interesting.
- ☐ Be creative.
- ☐ Use all the tools at your disposal.
- ☐ At a minimum get security training into the new hire orientation and conduct annual awareness training for everyone.

CHAPTER 8

Monitoring Security

As an organization builds a security program, systems and networks must be monitored to assure that it is, in fact, a good program and that it is managing the organization's risk appropriately. What is monitored within the organization also determines what can be measured and reported (see Chapter 11).

Unfortunately, the monitoring of a security program can also affect the privacy of employees. This is one reason why it is so important to have good policies as the basis for your security program and to involve the organization's general counsel and the human resources department. Having a policy that clearly states that employees should not have an expectation of privacy easily and unmistakably obviates this.

In this chapter, we will identify the most common types of things to monitor and suggest methods to accomplish each one. This is not intended to be an all-inclusive list but it should provide a good starting point for any monitoring program.

POLICY MONITORING

Policy monitoring is perhaps the most far-reaching of the monitoring activities that any security department can undertake. Obviously, a policy or set of policies and procedures must exist for the department to be able to monitor policy. We can monitor policy in four general areas:

- Awareness
- Systems
- Employees
- Acceptable use

For each of these areas, the aim of the monitoring is to determine how effective our compliance with the policy is. In the following sections we will discuss what we are monitoring and how we can do this.

Awareness

Policy awareness is a necessary condition for policy compliance. If an employee does not know about a policy, how can he or she know to be in compliance with it or even how to be in compliance with it. When we attempt to monitor the awareness of the employees, we are trying to determine whether the employees know about the policy and whether they know what parts of the policy must be complied with.

For most employees, the key security policies that they need to be aware of include

- Information policy
- Computer security policy (at least the parts that pertain to passwords and the sharing of other such authentication information)
- Computer use policy

For developers and system administrators there will be other policies and procedures that are specific to their jobs. The exact number of these policies will depend upon your organization. The same techniques that we will suggest for the general employee population can be used for these other groups as well.

Policy knowledge and awareness is most easily monitored through the use of tests and quizzes. By giving an employee a short test on a policy you can quickly determine how much of the policy the employee is aware of.

 SECURITY ALERT!   Tests can also put off employees as they may see them as useless wastes of time. The tests need to be as unobtrusive as possible.

The tests can take the form of short interviews with a security staff member. This method can be fairly time consuming. Recently, products have come on the market that allow organizations to track the policy knowledge of their employees through the organization's intranet. The Pentasafe Vigilant Policy Center is a good example of such a product. The product allows the organization to put its policies on the organization's intranet and track how many of the employees read the policy. Each employee can then take a short quiz on the content of the policy. The results of the quiz provide good information for metrics (see Chapter 11).

TIP   Use small incentives as part of the monitoring program so that employees will be interested in taking the quiz.

Systems

The monitoring of policy on computer systems is the monitoring of system configurations. We are looking at the system configuration to determine if the system has been configured in accordance with the organization's policy.

When we examine a system for policy compliance we may look at:

- Authentication mechanisms (length of passwords and so on)
- File permission defaults
- Services that are enabled on the system

Depending on the type of system that is being monitored, there are other items that may be examined as well.

To monitor system policy compliance, a security staff member might physically inspect each system. During this inspection, the staff member would have a list of configuration issues for each type of system. Then the staff member would manually check each system for each compliance issue. While it is possible to monitor policy compliance in this way, it is inefficient and also prone to mistakes. If a staff member will be performing this task, systems should be randomly selected. Performing a complete check of all systems is likely to be costly without significantly changing the risk of the organization.

A better (and usually more cost-effective and efficient) alternative is to use any of a number of different products that are on the market. Products such as Symantec's Enterprise Security Manager, Internet Security Systems' System Scanner, or Pentasafe Vigilant Policy Manager allow a central system to monitor the policy compliance of other systems within the organization (see Figure 8-1).

This type of monitoring provides a much more efficient use of security staff time and is far less prone to error. In addition, the use of these products allows the security department to conduct tests on a weekly or daily basis, thus keeping much better track of violations.

Employees

The monitoring of employee policy adherence is a complicated problem for security. This is due to two reasons. First, it is difficult to determine exactly how well an employee is following policy and second, it is often a management issue rather than a security issue. Let's take a closer look at these issues.

If an organization's computer security policy states that passwords must be eight characters in length and must include at least one number, computer systems can be configured to only allow this type of password to be used. Alternatively, if the organization's policy says that passwords are not to be written down or shared with other employees, there is no automated mechanism to determine if this policy is being followed. It may be necessary for the security department to interview each employee

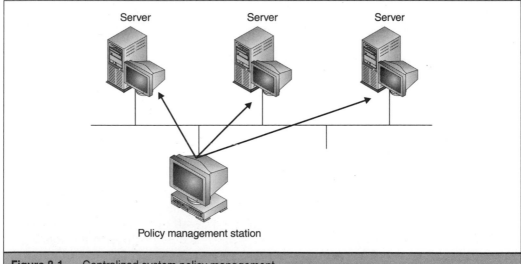

Figure 8-1. Centralized system policy management

to find out how they are choosing their passwords and remembering them. In addition, the security staff member may need to examine the work area for each employee to see if passwords have been written on Post-it® notes, left under keyboards, or even written on the ceiling above the employee's seat.

As far as policy compliance being a management issue, there is little the security department can actually do. At the same time, security is often asked to assist in identifying employees who are violating certain policies such as computer use or sexual harassment policies (we will talk more about computer use policy monitoring specifically in the next section). The reason this type of monitoring is more of a management problem is that it directly affects the employee's productivity and work habits. If, for example, an employee spends all day surfing Web sites for information on golf, the employee is unlikely to be very productive. Is this employee violating a computer use policy? Possibly. Is this a security issue? Unlikely.

Yet the security department may be in the best position to monitor the employee's actual habits on the Internet and thus may be used to help management manage the issue with the employee.

Generally speaking, the monitoring of employee policy compliance is a difficult and time-consuming task. There are no good automated methods for doing this and thus we are left with a manual approach. Unfortunately, the manual approach is rarely cost-effective for the security department. If the security department needs to monitor employee behavior, it is best to randomly select employees to interview on the policy in question.

Computer Use

Many organizations have developed policies on computer use. The policies usually state that the computer provided to the employee is for business use only. This is a very easy policy to write (and there is rarely any dissent from employees—which employee is going to argue that business computers should also be used to play games, for example?). Unfortunately, this is not an easy policy to monitor effectively.

Certain parts of computer use compliance lend themselves to monitoring. For example, it is easy to monitor where employees go on the Internet. All that is needed is a proxy server. The logs of the proxy server can be matched to specific user IDs or system addresses. This would then provide a complete list of where the employee has gone on the Internet. However, this may not be what is needed to accurately monitor computer use policies. It should also be noted that the use of DHCP on the network will make tracking who is going to what Web sites more difficult. If this is an issue, the users could just authenticate to the proxy server before being allowed to surf the Web but this does add another layer of complexity to the entire system.

Let's say that an employee visits a travel site on the Internet. Is this appropriate? If the employee is visiting the site to plan a vacation, it is not business-related. However, if the employee is using the site to plan business travel, it is business-related. The simple tracking of Web sites does not show the intent of the use. There are exceptions to this. A visit to a sex site is rarely business-related, for example.

Other issues in monitoring computer use stem from the fact that employees may use a desktop system for non-business-related tasks (such as playing games) that are hard to monitor in an automated fashion. While it certainly is possible to do, the time, expense, and privacy issues involved may outweigh any benefit to the organization.

The most effective way to monitor computer use (or specifically Internet use) is through the use of a proxy server. The proxy server should log all Web site visits. This information can then be used to monitor the use of various Web sites as well as the times of the visits. Certain individuals can be spoken with regarding their habits if they are obviously abusing the organization's time. Information can also be charted so that management can see trends in Internet use.

NETWORK MONITORING

The monitoring of network traffic is very important for a security department. The reason for this is that the security department can identify attack traffic as well as inappropriate system configurations by monitoring network traffic. Figure 8-2 shows a typical network. The locations that are marked on the figure show places where network monitoring can take place. We will refer back to this figure in the following sections.

System Configurations

Security has a great interest in making sure that the configurations of certain systems are appropriate. This is especially true of security devices like firewalls. By monitoring network traffic, the configurations of various devices can be determined.

If you look at Figure 8-2, you can see that monitoring traffic around the firewall can confirm a firewall's configuration. A monitoring device placed on the internal network (at location 3) could monitor traffic coming from the Internet to the internal network. If the firewall configuration is supposed to prevent inbound telnet traffic and the monitoring device detects an inbound telnet packet, there is clearly a problem with the firewall configuration.

The same type of monitoring can be performed for a specific system. If a server configuration is supposed to require TFTP (Trivial File Transfer Protocol) to be disabled and TFTP traffic is detected from a server, the system should be checked for a misconfiguration.

Figure 8-2 should not be considered to be a complete description of all possible monitoring locations. Monitoring an internal network can be fairly complex when servers are located on different parts of the network. The key to network monitoring for configuration information is that the monitoring device must be located where it will see the traffic that is of interest.

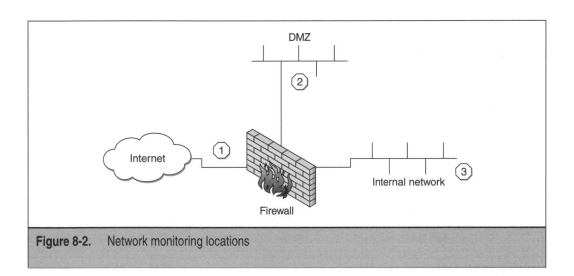

Figure 8-2. Network monitoring locations

Attacks

Attack traffic is very much an item of interest for most security departments. Attack traffic that actually makes it to potentially vulnerable systems is even more interesting. By monitoring network traffic, the security department can be alerted to such traffic.

A monitoring device located at location 1 in Figure 8-2 can detect all attack traffic targeted at any of the organization's addresses. This location cannot, however, determine if the attack actually made it to the targeted system. To determine whether the attack made it past the firewall, monitoring devices at locations 2 and 3 would be necessary.

Keep in mind that attacks do not only come from the Internet. Attacks can also originate internally (according to the latest Computer Security Institute/FBI survey, as much as 70 percent of attacks are from the inside). These attacks may be targeted against systems on the Internet or they may be targeted internally. A monitoring device at location 3 (somewhere on the internal network) may detect this traffic. As before, the exact location of the device will be dependent on the actual network topology.

Mechanisms to Monitor the Network

The only way to effectively monitor network traffic is to use a network sniffer. A sniffer is a device that captures all of the packets on the network and performs some analysis. For the security department, the most effective sniffers are those used for network intrusion detection systems such as ISS RealSecure, Network Flight Recorder, Enterasys Dragon, or Symantec NetProwler.

CHALLENGE

As a staff member in the security department, you have the job of building a system to monitor network traffic and attacks. Your network is not terribly complex—there is a single firewall, a DMZ (a separate network that is somewhat protected from the Internet but not fully integrated and thus trusted by the internal network) for the Web servers, and the internal network. The internal network is all switched and the servers are on their own network segment.

Where do you start? How many monitors will you use and where will they be placed? How will you configure each monitor? Are there any areas that you will not be able to monitor effectively?

Start by defining why you want to set up network monitoring. The answer to this question will help you to identify which traffic is of interest and thus where you can set up your detectors. Generally, setting up a detector outside the firewall will capture all of the attempted attacks. Setting up a detector on the DMZ will show all of the attacks that reach the Web servers. A detector inside the firewall will show any attack that gets to the internal network. You can then set up your monitors to alarm appropriately based on their location.

Monitoring the internal servers may be a potential problem as the network is switched. However, since the servers are on their own network segment, it may be possible to place a network tap on the link from the router to that segment. If this is not possible, it may not be cost-effective to monitor traffic to and from the internal servers.

Commercial tools are not the only ones that can be used for this purpose. Snort is a free tool that can be made to be as good as any of the commercial systems. It should also be noted that there is now a commercial version of Snort from Sourcefire. Another free tool called Shadow is also available. Either of the free tools can be used in the same way as the commercial tools.

 SECURITY ALERT!   The sniffer must be placed in an appropriate location on the network in order to be effective. Sniffers placed on switched segments may not be effective since the switch does not show every packet to each device. Make sure you understand the network architecture before deploying a sniffer.

AUDIT LOG MONITORING

Capturing audit information on systems is an appropriate and necessary security measure. Unfortunately, if these logs are not examined in some manner, the information is nearly useless in managing the risk to the organization. Many organizations capture audit information because they have to—often it is an audit requirement. The information actually does them very little good in this case.

Audit logs can be examined manually. Unfortunately, humans are not very good at examining long log files. Eventually, all of the lines begin to look alike and the really important information gets lost. The most effective way to examine the log files is through an automated process. We will talk more about this in "Mechanisms for Effective Log Monitoring," later in this chapter.

Unauthorized Access

While network monitoring is effective in identifying attack traffic and configuration errors on systems, host log monitoring is the only way to detect successful unauthorized access. Therefore, log files on systems should be monitored for such indications.

To examine a log file for indications of unauthorized access, you will first need to define what authorized access is (and thus what unauthorized access is). Keep in mind that some unauthorized access may come over legitimate channels. For example, having an administrator log into a system using SSH is appropriate but having a normal user log in via SSH is not. The same can be said for where the login comes from. Here again, a login from the administrator's workstation is appropriate but a login from another employee's desktop may not be.

There are other types of unauthorized access that must be watched for as well. What about the authorized user of a system who tries to access files that belong to another user? This is usually classified as an unauthorized access attempt. In this case the logs that indicate such an attempt are of interest to the security department.

 SECURITY ALERT!   Keep in mind that the systems must also log information that can indicate unauthorized access attempts. If the system is not logging failed file access attempts, you will not be able to see such events.

The final type of unauthorized access is the use of an attack to bypass the authentication mechanisms on a system. Often these attempts will be logged by the system but the log message may not specifically say that this is an attack or unauthorized login attempt. For example, if a buffer overflow is attempted on a system, the program that is attacked may write a log message that indicates a bad argument (if, and this is a big if, the program is still working after the buffer overflow). Such a message should cause a review of the system for a potential compromise.

Inappropriate Behavior

In addition to unauthorized access or access attempts, there may be some behavior that is also of interest to the security department and therefore should be monitored. The types of behavior covered by this category will depend upon the acceptable use of your computer systems. Some behavior that may fall into this category includes

- Adding new devices to systems
- Opening connections to other systems
- Adding new services

- Adding new software
- Changing system configurations
- Changing account parameters
- Starting or stopping services

As you can see from the list, some of these activities may be standard system administration activities. It may depend upon the time that the event occurs, who performs the action, or other factors to determine if the event is something of interest or not.

Another type of event that may be of interest to the security department is the changing of files such as data files or program files. If the changes are made as part of a software upgrade, changes to binary program files may be appropriate. However, if the changes are made outside of the standard configuration control process, they may not be appropriate and thus should be monitored.

The same is true for certain types of data files. Some files, such as databases, may change every second based on transactions that go through the system. Other data files, such as Web site home pages, may only change as part of the standard content control process for the Web site. If they change at odd times or outside of this process the event may be of interest to security and thus should be monitored.

Mechanisms for Effective Log Monitoring

As we already mentioned, the most effective way to monitor log files is to do it with an automated process. Computers perform this type of repetitious job very easily. In that vein, there are several ways to do it:

- Purchase a commercial product
- Write scripts or programs that look for information specific to your organization

The choice of which route to go will depend upon your expertise and the budgets available to you. Commercial products in this category include Symantec's Intruder Alert and ISS RealSecure Server Sensor. In both cases, you will be able to configure the system as to what events are of interest to you.

SECURITY ALERT! There is one disadvantage with log monitoring—if the logs are kept on the local system, the individual who is being monitored can modify them.

It is good practice to move log files off of the local system as soon as possible to prevent their unauthorized modification. If this is not possible, strong access control must be placed on the log files but even this will not prevent an administrator from gaining access to the log files.

Figure 8-3 shows how log files can be moved and consolidated on a logging system. The logging system is responsible for collecting log files and for running the programs or

Incident Response Procedure

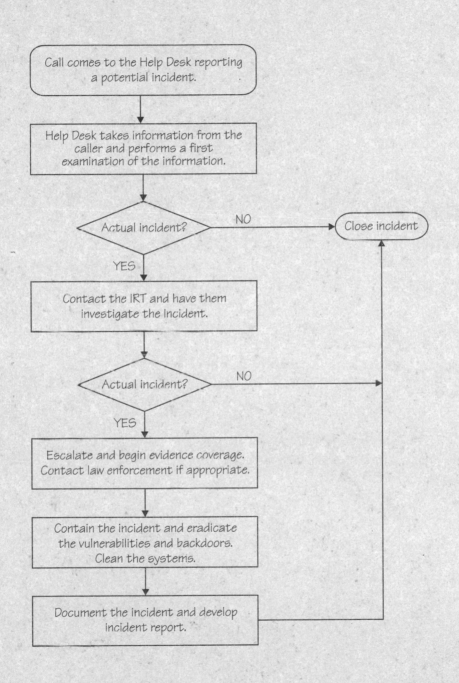

Call comes to the Help Desk reporting a potential incident.

↓

Help Desk takes information from the caller and performs a first examination of the information.

↓

Actual incident? — NO → Close incident

YES

↓

Contact the IRT and have them investigate the Incident.

↓

Actual incident? — NO →

YES

↓

Escalate and begin evidence coverage. Contact law enforcement if appropriate.

↓

Contain the incident and eradicate the vulnerabilities and backdoors. Clean the systems.

↓

Document the incident and develop incident report.

Monitoring

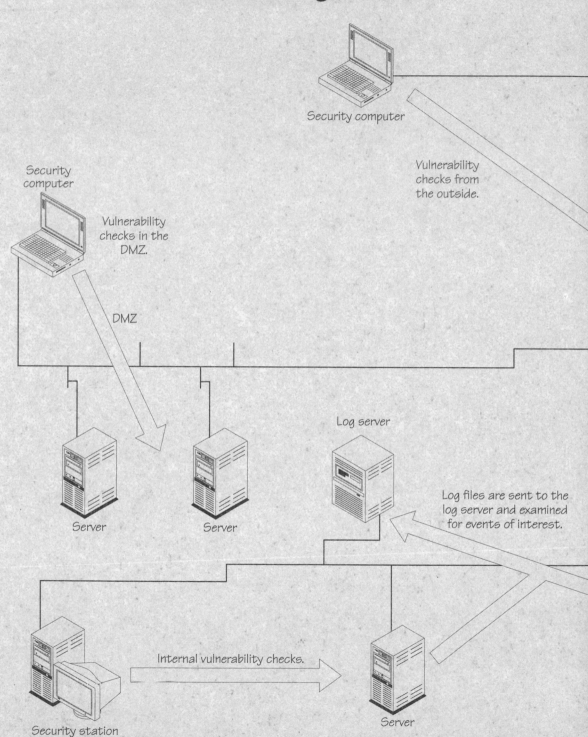

Security computer

Vulnerability checks from the outside.

Security computer

Vulnerability checks in the DMZ.

DMZ

Log server

Log files are sent to the log server and examined for events of interest.

Server

Server

Internal vulnerability checks.

Security station

Server

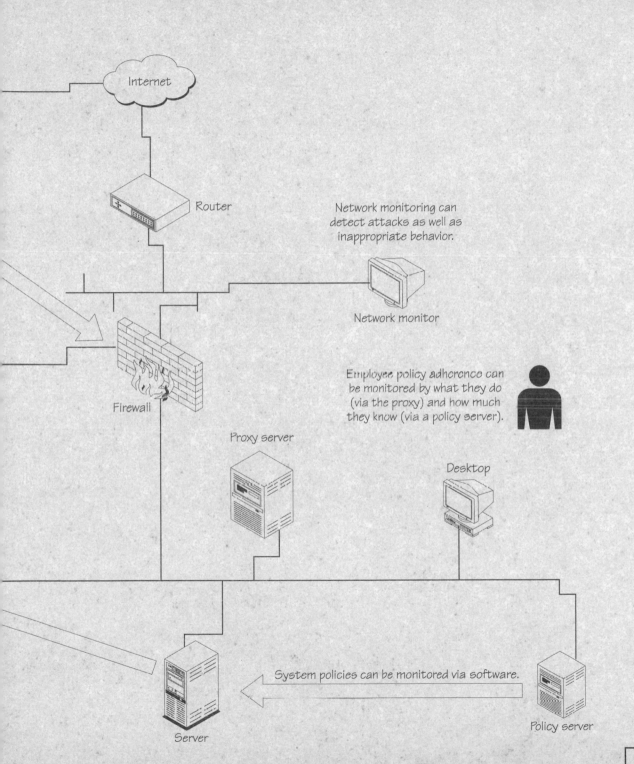

Internet

Router

Network monitoring can detect attacks as well as inappropriate behavior.

Network monitor

Firewall

Employee policy adherence can be monitored by what they do (via the proxy) and how much they know (via a policy server).

Proxy server

Desktop

System policies can be monitored via software.

Server

Policy server

5

Range of Security Assessments

Make sure you know what you want out of an assessment and choose the right one. You may not have much choice about audits, but you should know what you can expect out of the other types.

Administrative Controls

Business
processes

Policies and
procedures

Physical and Environmental Controls

Power management

HVAC

Fire
suppression

Building
security

Technical Controls

Applications	Hosts	Network infrastructure	Perimeter
	Workstations	Routers	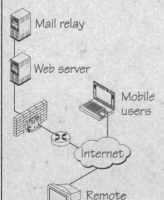 Mail relay Web server Mobile users Internet Remote users
CRM			
Financials	Servers	FDDI ring	
Office automation			
Web applications			
Intranet	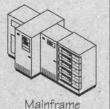 Mainframe	Switches, bridges, and hubs	

AUDIT	VULNERABILITY ASSESSMENT	PENETRATION TEST	RISK ASSESSMENT
☑			☑
☑			☑
May include a cursory look at physical and environmental controls.			
☑	☑	☑	☑
Usually focuses on a single system at a time.	Usually focuses on checking technology for vulnerabilities.	Focuses on the perimeter of the network—firewalls, border router, DMZ, IDS, Internet-facing applications, etc.	Comprehensive look at all aspects of protecting information.

Phases of a Disaster

```
        ╭─────────────────────────────╮
        │       Disaster occurs       │
        ╰─────────────────────────────╯
                      │
                      ▼
```

Response
- Limit human injury
- Limit damage to the organization
- Contain the disaster as much as possible
- Make an initial assessment as to the extent of the damage
- Determine the amount of activity required to contain and control the disaster

```
                      │
                      ▼
```

Resumption
Identify and bring back online the most important and time-sensitive capabilities of the organization

```
                      │
                      ▼
```

Recovery
Restore the less time-sensitive functions of the organization to operation

```
                      │
                      ▼
```

Restoration
- Return the organization to permanent quarters
- Return the organization to normal business operations

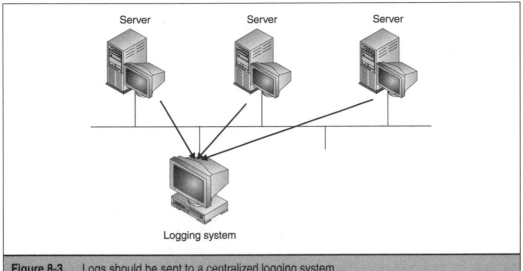

Figure 8-3.   Logs should be sent to a centralized logging system.

scripts that monitor the logs. Access to this system is extremely limited so that only members of the security department can gain access to the files. Ideally, the files will also be written to some type of protected media so that they are extremely difficult to modify.

Monitoring systems for unauthorized changes to files (either binary or data files) depends on how often the files change. If the files change very often, there are few mechanisms that will work effectively. If the files change rarely or as part of a defined process, it is relatively easy to set up a mechanism to monitor for such changes.

The mechanism usually requires the use of a cryptographic checksum. When the files are placed on the system, a checksum is taken of each file. This checksum is stored on some unchangeable media. At periodic intervals, the checksum is recomputed and compared to the original checksum. If the checksum has changed, the file has been modified in some manner.

The most common way to perform cryptographic checksums is to use a product called Tripwire (sold commercially by Tripwire Security Software). The original version of Tripwire is still freely available on the Internet. The new commercial version has some additional management features and is also available for Windows systems.

VULNERABILITY MONITORING

The identification of vulnerabilities on computer systems and network equipment is part of risk identification. It is important to monitor the number and type of system vulnerabilities so that the organization understands the security risk to these systems from an external or internal threat.

Unfortunately, identifying vulnerabilities once does not suffice when managing risk. The reasons for this are as follows:

- Changes to the number of vulnerabilities on existing systems (both increases and decreases) need to identified.

- New systems come online and the vulnerabilities on these systems must be identified.

- New vulnerabilities are discovered that may affect existing systems.

The vulnerability picture for organizations is, therefore, constantly changing. We cannot rely on a single snapshot of the vulnerabilities to completely represent the risk to the organization.

Software Patches

Just about every piece of software on the market has vulnerabilities that can be exploited to cause problems for an organization. Some of these problems are relatively benign while others may allow an intruder to gain administrative access to a system (and thus to all of the information on that system).

When we speak of vulnerabilities in software, we are talking about programming errors. These errors tend not to affect the functionality of the software (in most cases) but they may allow information to leak out or an intruder to gain additional privileges or access. The vast majority of these vulnerabilities are corrected by the vendors through the release of software patches.

By checking the software patch state on the system, we can identify which vulnerabilities the system is likely to be vulnerable to. Alternatively, we can check for each of the vulnerabilities and see if the system is in fact vulnerable. A combination of the two techniques is usually the best course of action.

Configuration Issues

Software problems are not the only way vulnerabilities can get into systems and network devices. Configuration mistakes can also cause vulnerabilities. Some configuration issues are part of configuration policies and procedures but some parts of the system configuration may not be covered by the organization's policy. For example, very few Web server configuration procedures specifically state that directory browsing should be turned off (usually this is understood by the administrators and they do it as a matter of course). However, if this particular configuration issue were forgotten by the administrator of the system, anyone could browse all of the files on the Web server.

There are many other examples of configuration errors on systems that can allow intruders to gain information or direct access to systems. If a configuration error is made on network devices it is possible that vulnerabilities on other systems will be exposed (see Figure 8-4). Take for example a configuration error on a firewall that protects an organization's DMZ. Instead of just allowing ports 80 and 443 (HTTP and

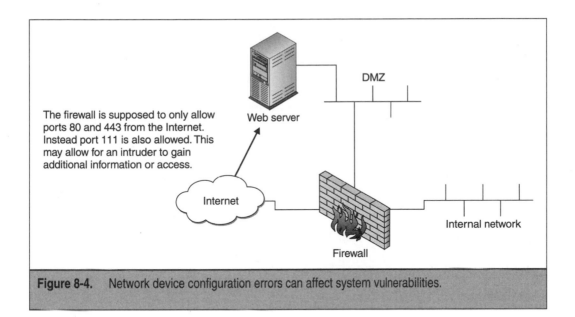

Figure 8-4. Network device configuration errors can affect system vulnerabilities.

HTTPS) to the Web server, the firewall also allows access to port 111 (SunRPC). An intruder will then be able to use this open connection to gather additional information about the system and possibly to exploit a vulnerability to gain access.

Configuration problems can be operating system-related (such as inappropriate services left running) or they can be application-related. In any case, configuration errors can leave an organization as vulnerable to attack as any software error.

TIP Don't forget to perform port scans periodically to identify what services are actually running on each system.

Mechanisms to Identify Vulnerabilities

There are many tools that allow you to identify vulnerabilities on systems (both software patches and configuration errors). The tradeoff that needs to be done is one of time versus cost versus accuracy. Let's take a look at the two primary mechanisms.

On-Host Scanning

Several commercial tools will identify missing patches on systems. These include ISS System Scanner, Symantec Enterprise Security Manager, and Pentasafe Vigilant Security Manager. These tools work by placing an agent on the systems to be checked. The agent then reports to a manager on some other system (look back at Figure 8-1 for the architecture of these systems).

The commercial tools can be expensive and if all you are interested in doing is looking at patch levels for Windows systems, Microsoft has developed a free tool to do this. The name of the tool is HFNETCHK and is available at the Microsoft Web site. In order for this tool to function, the user must have Domain Administrator access to the systems. If this is the case, the user can perform a check against all of the systems in the domain. Keep in mind that this tool only works on Windows systems.

As a general rule, this type of vulnerability check will identify the actual patch levels on all of the systems as long as the tool is run as an administrator on the system. Unfortunately, with the exception of HFNETCHK, the tools are fairly expensive (upwards of $600–1,000 per system). If cost is a major factor, it is possible to check for patch levels manually but this takes time and staff to perform the work. If this task can be automated, it is the best way to go.

Remote Scanning

A somewhat less expensive alternative is to use remote scanning tools. Examples of remote scanning tools that will look for vulnerabilities and services on systems include the ISS Internet Scanner, Network Associates Cybercop, and the free tool Nessus. There are a number of other port scanners as well (such as nmap) but they do not perform vulnerability checks. Port scanners will only identify open services.

Figure 8-5 shows how remote scanning works. The scanning system sends network traffic to each server to be scanned. Some of the traffic will be TCP SYN packets to attempt to connect to the services on the system. Each system that responds has a service open. In addition, the scanners will look for software version numbers and other indications of vulnerability. Normally, the scanners will not exploit a vulnerability but instead they will look for indications that the vulnerability exists.

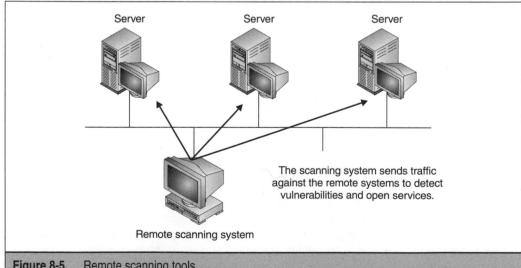

Figure 8-5.   Remote scanning tools

SECURITY ALERT!   Since the remote scanning tools look for known indications of a vulnerability, it is possible that they will miss some existing vulnerabilities. This is especially true if they have not been updated recently.

As the previous Security Alert says, it is possible for remote scanning tools to miss some vulnerabilities or give false indications that a vulnerability exists. Simply changing the banner that is reported by applications can cause false negatives in the scanner (this means that an existing vulnerability would not be reported). In some cases (especially on Windows networks), false negatives can be reduced by scanning the network as a Domain Administrator. By scanning as a Domain Administrator, the scanning system can gain additional access to the Windows systems and get better results.

Scanning Locations

A question that we hear often is "Where should I scan from?" In other words, where should the scanning system be placed to get the most valuable information about my systems? Figure 8-6 shows three locations that should be included in a proper scanning program.

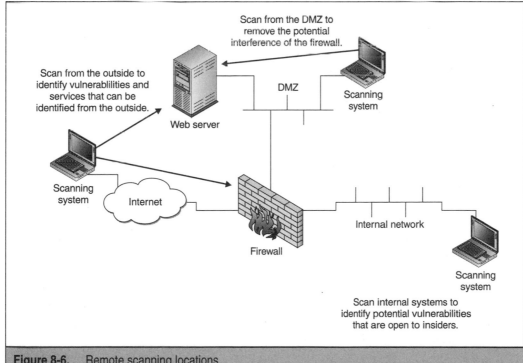

Figure 8-6.   Remote scanning locations

Scanning the firewalls and Internet-accessible systems from the Internet provides a view of your systems that any outside intruder would see. You can identify (very accurately) what services are open from the outside on your DMZ as well as on your firewall and any internal systems that may be accessible. Scanning this way will also give you a good idea of the types of vulnerabilities that an outsider can find.

The scans from the outside will not give you a complete story on the vulnerabilities and configuration issues with your systems primarily due to the interference of the firewall. Since the firewall will block traffic that is not specifically allowed, you may not see some services that are open on the systems. To get a complete picture of the DMZ and internal systems, you will need to conduct a scan that does not go through a firewall. It is therefore best to scan from the DMZ against DMZ systems and from the internal network against internal systems.

CHECKLIST: KEY POINTS IN MONITORING SECURITY

The following is a checklist of key steps in monitoring security:

- ☐ Identify any employee privacy issues and discuss them with HR and the organization's General Counsel.

- ☐ Determine what policy compliance means for awareness, system configurations, employee actions, and employee use of computer systems.

- ☐ Determine how each area can best be monitored.

- ☐ Establish systems or procedures to monitor for policy compliance in each area.

- ☐ Determine what needs to be monitored on the network.

- ☐ Establish monitoring points where the monitoring systems can see the traffic of interest.

- ☐ Determine what is appropriate behavior on computer systems.

- ☐ Set up a centralized logging system to gather log files.

- ☐ Establish a mechanism for reviewing the log files for important information.

- ☐ Determine the systems that need to be monitored for vulnerabilities.

- ☐ Establish a mechanism to test systems for software patches and proper configurations.

PART III

Plan Administration

CHAPTER 9

Budgeting for Security

Building a budget for your information security program includes more than just going to a few Web sites and trade shows to get costs for the latest security products. It is much more complex than that and yet some organizations do it that way. When it is done that way the organization ends up with a bunch of partially deployed tools, no real strategy, no way of showing return on investment and a lot of risk exposure.

To effectively budget for your information security program, you must consider many factors including the overall IT budget, new and ongoing IT projects, the actual risk level to your environment, staff size, training needs, software subscription maintenance, cost of assessments and penetration tests, and outsourced security services. Unless you are just starting a program from scratch you will likely have a previous budget from which to work. There will probably be some security technology in place and a few staff. Those, of course, carry over into the new budget and then you have to plan for the new stuff.

According to a survey conducted by the Computer Security Institute (CSI, www.gocsi.com/mangsumm.htm), the average 2003 annual information security budget is expected to increase by almost 24.5 percent over the 2002 budget. In a survey conducted by *InfoSecurity Magazine* (www.infosecuritymag.com/articles/september00/pdfs/Survey1_9.00.pdf) in 2000, 66 percent of respondents said their information security budgets were not sufficient.

In this chapter we will explore the budget building process for the information security program budget. You may begin to see why it is so important to have the security program recognized formally. A formal program clearly demonstrates the company's seriousness and commitment to the program.

ESTABLISHING THE NEED

Throughout this book we have stressed the criticality of recognizing the information security program as a "formal" program. Obtaining funds is one of the primary reasons for establishing the program on paper and in the minds of the executive board. If the organization is to succeed at lowering and managing its information security risks, then it must have an ongoing program with upper management support in terms of people and money.

Assuming you have to submit a budget proposal yearly like most organizations, you will probably have to justify every penny you ask for. Some information security departments have to kick and scratch for every thin dime and others have more money than they know what to do with. Although the second one sounds wonderful it turns out to be a nightmare. In the case of the deep pockets you usually end up with too many projects going on all at once and it becomes a less effective organization. On the other extreme you have organizations that can't lower risks effectively because they don't have enough resources. There is some happy medium that you must establish. You can do that by obtaining upper management buy-in and proper budgeting.

By "proper" budgeting we mean accurately forecasting your need and then sticking to your budget as closely as possible throughout the fiscal year. As with all budgets you win support from above when you spend money wisely and efficiently. Show a return on investment and you are a winner in the budget wars. With today's shaky financial markets and some organizations being more cautious with their spending, the information security department is likely to see budget shrinkage. Like most of the other IT departments (assuming your department is in IT), you are expected to do more with less. The good news is there are tools that can help you do just that.

Keys to good budgeting include review of previous budgets and spending patterns and looking ahead at what it will take to reduce the risks identified throughout the year. In previous chapters we talked about the importance of having a risk assessment conducted. From the assessment you will derive a list of issues and risks to mitigate. With the help of the business units, you can effectively prioritize those risks and develop a project plan. It will take time, money, and other resources to complete those projects. To a large extent that constitutes the bulk of your budget.

Let's try an example. Let's assume it is October and you recently completed a comprehensive risk assessment of your network infrastructure. The assessment vendor provided you with a report showing findings and recommendations ranked by risk. You brought this report to your information protection panel, which consists of representatives of the business units and others (see Chapter 5). With the panel you identified five major projects to be accomplished over the next year to lower the risks identified in the risk assessment report. Let's assume the sample project plan shown in Table 9-1 is the plan you developed with the panel.

Risk Level	Project	Description	Owner/Size/Resource Requirement
High	Credit card data on network	The assessment revealed that an older application for conference registration allows members to submit credit cards to pay for registration. Although the link to the browser is encrypted, the credit card number is stored on the Web/application server unencrypted and is then sent via SMTP from the Web server to the marketing department. From there the credit card numbers are stored on local hard drives, in cache, on mail servers, and in backup tapes.	**Owner:** Marketing department **Size:** Large (three months) **Resources:** One FTE as project manager; developers, security, network, desktop, and server personnel periodically.

Table 9-1.   Risk Reduction Project Plan

Risk Level	Project	Description	Owner/Size/Resource Requirement
High	Host vulnerabilities	A number of vulnerabilities were discovered on the hosts scanned during the assessment. These are a combination of operating system and application/server vulnerabilities. To eliminate these vulnerabilities, the IT department will have to download, test, and install security patches.	**Owner:** IT department **Size:** Medium (one month) **Resources:** Two FTEs
High	Remote access points not protected	The assessment pointed out that there are some remote access points in the network that bypass security controls including the firewall. These include modems on desktop computers, servers, and a RAS server for one of the applications used by the sales department. The recommendation is to locate all such points, relocate them to a DMZ, and force them to traverse a firewall or find another suitable protection.	**Owner:** Security and networking **Size:** Large (three months) **Resources:** One FTE for project manager and participants from the network team throughout the period.
Medium	User account management	The assessment pointed out that user account procedures are not sufficient or consistent. A single access request and change form needs to be developed, key data/system stewards need to be appointed, and a new process for requesting/approving requests must be instituted. This will involve awareness training after the new process is implemented.	**Owner:** Security **Size:** Medium (two months) **Resources:** One FTE and participation by at least five other personnel periodically.
Medium	Data classification	The risk assessment pointed out that although some policies refer to "confidential" information, there is no information classification and protection policy. Data owners and stewards have not been assigned and it is unclear who should decide what information is "confidential." The recommendation is to create a data classification and protection policy and procedure guide.	**Owner:** Information protection panel **Size:** Large (four months) **Resources:** One FTE as project manager and participants from the panel.

Table 9-1.   Risk Reduction Project Plan *(continued)*

BUILDING THE BUDGET

As stated in Chapter 5, it is important to get the business units to agree to the priority of these projects. As the security professional you will have to help them understand the risks in terms that they can understand. For example, the first project on the list talks about the exposure of member credit card numbers. The business unit should fully understand the criticality of such an exposure for both legal liability and customer perception reasons. Most other business units will agree that this is a high-priority exposure and should be dealt with first.

This prioritized project list is a key element in creating your planned budget. It also aligns the security issues to the business need. That is a huge issue when dealing with management. For the holders of the purse strings, it will be hard to dispute the importance of these projects, especially since the business units will be there lobbying for funding on your behalf if there is any pushback at all. If, during the fiscal year, an issue arises that may impact the completion of any of these projects, you can go back to the panel and present the issue and alternatives for dealing with it. For example, if some new vulnerability is exposed in an existing application for which a fix is necessary but unplanned, you might have to re-prioritize the projects and corresponding budget to fix this problem.

Since your budget might not accommodate fixing this issue you will have to drop something off of your plan. You should take this before your information protection panel, explain the alternative, and let them re-prioritize the projects. Let the marketing department battle it out with the department whose application has the new vulnerability. If they agree to a plan, that's fine. If they both want to get their projects completed, then more money will have to come your way. Once again, let them battle it out and give your budget more funding. You can only do so much with your budget and resources. To do more, it costs more.

OTHER CONSIDERATIONS

The project plan to mitigate risks to systems and information is only one part of the budget. You must also include the cost of software subscriptions for the products you have in place, training your staff, giving your staff increases in pay, hiring contractors and consultants (part of this cost may be tied to the projects in the plan), performing assessments and penetration tests, using managed security services, and purchasing new products. Let's look at each in more detail. In some cases the salaries of staff contractors and consultants will not be in the same budget for security products.

Staffing Requirements

Staff will likely be the most expensive part of your budget. People cost a lot of money. According to a recent CSI survey (the same one cited earlier), organizations expect a 64 percent increase in the percentage of total workers devoted to information security activities. According to this survey, nearly 37 percent of the information security budget is used for in-house staff.

Keeping good security staff, training them, and growing them is a fundamental part of your information security program and must be properly planned in your budget. In Chapter 10 we discuss the required skills for the security staff. We identify at least six major roles as follows:

- Security administration
- Policy development
- Architecture
- Research
- Assessment
- Audit

Remember that this does not necessarily reflect the size of your staff. For smaller organizations you might have one or two staff handling all these roles. In other organizations you may have entire departments handling each of these functional areas. Your staffing size and corresponding budget will depend on the number and size of the projects on the risk reduction plan.

Unless you are specifically going through staff reduction you will have to maintain your current staffing level or increase it to meet the demands of the coming projects. According to the CSI survey mentioned previously, information security staff currently make up 0.1 percent of the total company staff, on average. Staffing for information security is anticipated to increase by almost 15 percent next year. If you estimate that your current staff can handle the load of the projects in addition to the tasks they already perform, then you must consider their compensation in your budget. Make sure you plan for pay increases, bonuses, and other incentives. We'll talk about training in another section.

If you have to grow your staff to meet the demands of upcoming projects then, of course, you will have to build that additional planned compensation into your budget. There are several considerations for new staff costs in your budget. First, the new breed of security professionals are asking for a lot of money. It has been our experience that security professionals with at least five years experience are in the $85,000 to $100,000 range. A recent salary survey conducted by Foote Partners (www.footepartners.com) for *InfoSecurity Magazine* supports our experience. You can find the results of the survey at www.infosecuritymag.com/articles/august01/securitymarket.shtml.

Our recent search for security professionals has revealed that there are quite a few folks looking. There are a fair percentage that are out of work as a result of the ".gones" and recent market fluctuations that have caused organizations to tighten up their budgets. If you are looking, be patient, screen them carefully, and make sure you are getting what you pay for. With this soft market you may be able to get them to come down in their compensation requirements.

If you use recruiters remember that they charge a substantial fee—up to 25 percent. Remember to include this cost in your planned budget if you are the one to absorb it. If you are recruiting for a specific, niche position for which there are only a few candidates qualified, then you may also have to plan for a "signing bonus." In at least one case, one of our clients was paying up to a 10 percent signing bonus (cash) without so much as a hiccup.

To keep staff from leaving to take better paying jobs, you will also have to provide fair incentives to compensation. This may include pay raises, bonuses, and rewards. These are all important to plan into your budget. There are resources to help you determine fair compensation for information security professionals on your staff. Your H/R department is a good start. Additionally, some industry organizations and trade magazines conduct periodic salary surveys. These can help provide a realistic baseline for you to use in budget planning. *Computerworld* magazine (www.computerworld.com) conducted a salary survey in 2001 that shows the average salary for an information security specialist at approximately $65,000. Another survey conducted during 2001 by *InfoSecurity Magazine* (www.infosecuritymag.com) shows a marked increase in the salary levels for information security job titles. Figure 9-1 shows the results of the survey.

In terms of planning the budget for salary increases, bonuses, and rewards, use your company standard. You may have some leverage in the size of salary increases but stay within acceptable boundaries for your company and the industry. If your

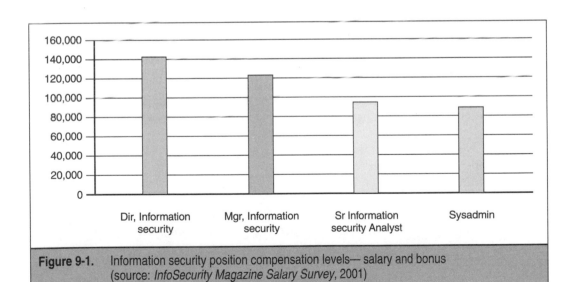

Figure 9-1.   Information security position compensation levels— salary and bonus (source: *InfoSecurity Magazine Salary Survey*, 2001)

company provides bonuses such as a profit sharing plan or year-end bonus, you may not have to incur that cost in your budget. If there is no such thing, you may want to consider a program for giving your exceptional performers some type of reward for hard work. Remember to include this in your budget plan.

Training Costs

In Chapter 7 we discussed the different types of awareness training you have to consider in your program. You must conduct awareness training for everyone to ensure they know the risks of using IT and the policies and procedures in place to manage those risks. You also have to train the security and IT professionals on specific security technologies that you have deployed in your infrastructure.

You must budget for the ongoing security awareness program. Depending on your program this might include the cost of developing material, producing materials such as newsletters and handouts, and awareness "giveaways" such as hats, pens, gadgets and other items to help users think of information security. Your program costs might also include buying videos and other purchased awareness materials from vendors. Make sure you consider the amount of time your staff will contribute to the awareness program. As your program grows, your staff may have to grow too.

Other training costs include sending your staff and other IT staff to formal, classroom training. This is generally for product-specific education for the tools you have deployed in your environment. If you are deploying new firewalls, content filtering, or other security products, you should seriously consider sending your staff to formal training for those products. The vendors might provide that training or you can go to the multitude of other training facilities. Resources for information security training include MIS Training Institute (www.MISTI.com) and the SANS Institute (www.SANS.org).

Formal classroom training is not cheap. Classes can run in the several thousands of dollars. If you have staff going for specific certifications such as Checkpoint's Certified System Administrator and Security Engineer, you can dump plenty of cash. You should have at least two people trained in every security technology in your environment. If possible, make sure it is not the same two people all the time. Spread out the knowledge a little for division of duties and to protect yourself from being too dependent on only a few folks.

If you plan for formal training then you must also plan to give your staff free time to be in that training. Don't expect them to do it all on their own time. If they get too busy then they will never have time for training and your effectiveness as a security organization will falter. Keeping staff well trained is important.

In addition to the formal, product-specific training, you should also budget for seminars and conferences. Although not specifically for training, these provide opportunities for your staff to learn what's new in the security marketplace, experience new products, and share ideas with other industry professionals. This can also be a reward for your staff since, no matter how you slice it, conferences are not hard work.

If you have security staff with specific certifications you should also consider that they have to keep those certifications current through continued professional education (CPE) credits. This basically means they have to attend some training throughout the year and send that information in to the body that governs the certification process. Just remember to include this in your training planning.

Software and Hardware Maintenance

If your department owns the security products and corresponding hardware platforms, then you must remember to budget for software license subscriptions and upgrades as well as hardware support and upgrade costs. Your costs in this area will vary depending on how you handle the cost of such systems. For example, in some organizations the information security department does not own or manage the hardware platform and operating system but they do own and administer the security applications. In this case they would be responsible for the cost of the software subscription and support.

In other organizations the information security department owns both the hardware and the applications. Obviously, in this case, the budget would have to consider the additional cost of hardware supports as well as operating system licenses. When obtaining cost quotes for security-related products, make sure you ask for the support and upgrade costs also. You will probably find that there is a cost break for longer-term support contracts.

Also consider what type of support you will need for hardware and software. Depending on your business type, firewalls may require 24/7 support with a very quick response time from the vendor. You don't want to wait 24 hours for a response while your firewall is down and the Web server is getting no hits. Suddenly, your security product is the reason for lost revenue. This makes for a bad impression with the rest of the company. Likewise, don't buy the most expensive support for products that are not time critical such as a log collection and analysis product.

If you can work with other IT departments when ordering hardware that supports your security products you should do so to take advantage of the volume discounts they likely receive from their hardware vendor. If your staff is small you may want to consider having other IT departments administer your platforms while you administer the security applications.

CAUTION   If you do have other IT departments administer your hardware platforms, be aware that as the system administrator they probably can have full access to your security application and its functions. If this is an issue or concern for you then administer the platform yourself.

Outside Services

Even the biggest organizations need help from vendors, consultants, and contractors once in a while. Outsourced help often makes sense. First, you may not have the specific expertise on your staff. Secondly, consultants can be very cost-effective, especially for limited engagements. Finally, using outside help is necessary to get an unbiased, third-party opinion.

Typically, organizations use outside help when they don't have the expertise they need on staff or their staff is too small to complete a particular security project. Installation of firewalls, deployment of an IDS, risk assessments, penetration tests, audits, and product integration are all types of projects for which external consultants and contractors can be very helpful. Additionally, it has become very popular to engage vendors for managed security services such as managing firewalls, VPNs, and intrusion detection systems. According to the CSI survey cited earlier, organizations use outsourcing for approximately 7.5 percent of their information security projects.

There are several benefits to using contractors and consultants. They bring specific expertise to the table. For example, let's assume you are planning on deploying network intrusion detection sensors throughout your network to identify possible attacks and give you better network visibility. Your information security staff consists of four people—two are technical security administrators, one is focused on application security, and the other is a junior network security engineer.

Let's further assume that none of these four staff members has more than a cursory understanding of network IDS. You have a pretty good, high-level understanding of how it works and what purpose it serves. You know enough to determine you need it in your enterprise. Unfortunately, you can't install or run it. An obvious choice is to outsource this work. You could do this two different ways.

First, you could have a vendor come in and deploy the products, teach you how to use it, then let you run it. The other option is to outsource the whole thing to a managed security service provider. Either one might fit your circumstance. Only you can decide. In either case you will use an external organization for some part of the project. It makes sense because you do not have the expertise on staff to deploy and operate the IDS. For smaller organizations it is probably more cost-effective to use a managed security service provider. This is especially true for IDS.

To budget appropriately for using consultants and contractors and outsourced managed service providers, you must have these projects in your plan. Consultants cost anywhere from $100–$250 per hour on average. One can get really good consultants for projects for as little as $100 per hour. Going with the big accounting and consulting firms will cost an organization well over $500 per hour for a senior consultant. If you are to budget well you should try to make your project plans as accurate as possible. It's pretty hard to just put place-holders in your budget for consulting without knowing precisely which projects you will use them on. Make sure you get cost quotes from multiple vendors prior to making any decisions. Vendors are happy to provide you with cost quotes during budget-building season in hopes that they might get work once the budget is approved.

It is nearly always recommended that you use an external entity for risk assessment and penetration testing. There are several reasons to use outsiders for this work. They include the unbiased nature of the contractor, their specific expertise, and their cost-effectiveness. Since assessments are only done periodically it does not make sense to have an on-staff assessment team. Chapter 3 provides a detailed discussion of using outside vendors for different types of assessments.

Budgeting for assessment and penetration tests is a bit easier, especially if you plan on periodic assessments. This is, by the way, highly recommended. Risk assessments should be conducted about every 18 months. Penetration tests should be run at least twice a year and when you deploy new applications or modify your perimeter. External vulnerability assessments should be run more frequently. Some organizations have vulnerability assessments conducted monthly to ensure that no new weaknesses are exposed at the network perimeter.

New Products

Deploying security products is another important part of the overall information security program budget. In a security survey respondents said they were spending their security product budgets on firewalls, access controls, client/server security, and LAN/WAN security. Although an older survey, it does indicate that organizations spend a fair portion of their budgets on information security products.

Product purchases can be associated with specific projects as defined by your information protection panel that are required to mitigate risks found during risk assessments or as part of infrastructure changes and growth. Most product purchases should be able to be in your planned budget. This is especially true if you have conducted a risk assessment and can use the results of the assessment to develop your planned budget for the next fiscal year.

As former system analysts we find it irksome when security professionals buy point products without considering an enterprise approach. We understand that not all product purchases happen after a thorough requirements analysis, design, product evaluation, and final selection. However, buying products to fix individual issues is like putting a small bandage on a huge cut. Let's use an example to show you.

CHALLENGE

While working for a former employer we got involved in a project to help select anti-virus software for the servers. The organization had anti-virus software deployed on all desktops but the servers had been ignored for several reasons including a fear that it would impact the server stability and performance.

As we got involved in the project we began to realize that the entire anti-virus problem had not be fully addressed. A review of the virus logs from the virus console revealed that the bulk of the virus infections were coming from e-mail attachments. Further investigation showed that not all desktops were protected at the same level. In fact, some desktops had no anti-virus protection at all while others had virus detection signature files that were almost a year old.

CHALLENGE (continued)

After much prodding it was agreed that the project had the wrong scope and direction. It was not going to be prudent or cost-effective to just purchase anti-virus software for the servers. In fact, anti-virus software might not even been necessary on the servers if the desktops were properly configured and an anti-virus product was deployed to the mail gateway.

Ultimately, the project ended up as a product evaluation for an enterprise-wide anti-virus solution for desktops, laptops, and servers. Additionally, the project also identified a need for an anti-virus solution at the e-mail gateway. Requirements for each platform were derived and documented. Vendors were brought in to demonstrate their products' ability tomeet our requirements.

When the project was completed we had deployed a new, enterprise-wide anti-virus product on all servers and desktops. Additionally, an anti-virus product was deployed on the e-mail gateway. We developed an incident response team and rehearsed our responses through drills. When all was said and done we all but eliminated the occurrences of virus infections on servers and desktops primarily because we deployed the anti-virus product on the e-mail gateway.

Had we simply budgeted for anti-virus software on the servers we would still have had a serious problem and would have not realized a good return on investment.

Unexpected Costs

All the planning in the world cannot protect your environment from the unexpected. There will always be the sudden change in plans that may result in the need to alter your information security priorities. The company may suddenly merge with or acquire a competitor. The business units may do a rapid, unplanned system deployment. A new security threat may appear and target you. There are a multitude of things that can affect your information security program budget.

For this reason it is recommended that you put a percentage of "slush" in your budget for these unplanned events. The worst that can happen is that this slush gets cut from your proposed budget. It is better to try to get this in.

STICK TO YOUR BUDGET

Once you have an approved budget it is important to hold close to it. If you come in way under or way over budget, senior management will have reservations about your ability to run a program. You may lose credibility. Stick with your spending plan. If you have to deviate make sure it is made clear why. This is especially important if the deviation is caused by some entity outside of your program. To stick to your budget you will have to utilize good project planning.

CHECKLIST: KEY POINTS IN SECURITY PROGRAM BUDGETING

This checklist summarizes some of the main points from this chapter and should prove useful when you begin your budget building.

- ☐ Start with a project plan.
- ☐ Get business units to contribute and buy in.
- ☐ Refer to previous years' budgets and spending records.
- ☐ Include funds for:
    - Staff compensation, including bonuses, raises, and rewards
    - Training
    - Products
    - Outsourced services
    - Software and hardware maintenance
    - Unexpected events
- ☐ Stick to your budget.
- ☐ Go back to the business units if priorities change.

CHAPTER 10

The Security Staff

Security departments range in size from a single person to several hundred highly skilled professionals. The abilities and skills of the department staff will be the main difference between an effective and ineffective security program. Therefore, hiring the right people with the correct skill sets and properly organizing their efforts is a key part of the security manager's job.

In this chapter we will explore the skill sets that are needed within a security department. A second topic of discussion will be the hiring of good security people. Understanding that there is a significant range in the types of security departments different sized organizations will need (and be willing to fund), we will discuss issues surrounding small organizations and large organizations.

SKILL AREAS

Every security department, no matter how small, requires the same general set of skills (see Figure 10-1):

- Security administration
- Policy development
- Architecture
- Research
- Assessment
- Audit

That is not to say that each security department requires a minimum of six people. On the contrary, the number of people required by a security department depends on many other factors (which we will discuss later in this chapter). These skills form the

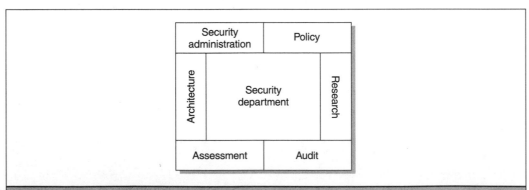

Figure 10-1. Security department skill areas

basis of the department's tasks. Whether the skills are found in various individuals on the staff or if the skills are available through some outsourcing arrangement is immaterial for the discussion of this chapter.

The following sections examine each skill area and how it will be used within an organization. It should be noted here that there are some skills that security staff will need that are not security-specific. For example, each member of the security department will need basic communication and interpersonal skills. Without the ability to communicate ideas, risks, and information to management, the security department cannot fulfill its role.

Security Administration

Another way to describe this skill area is "security operations"—in other words, the day-to-day operations of security systems within the organization. These systems may be:

- Operating systems security and access control
- Firewalls
- Intrusion detection systems
- Authentication systems
- User accounts
- Vulnerability scanners
- Policy management systems
- Public key infrastructure
- Encryption systems

The potential list of security systems is very large and each organization may have their own configurations. Some organizations place the operations of any and all of these systems under the security department. In these cases, the staff required to manage these systems may be large. For example, organizations that use mainframes with RACF, ACF2, or Top Secret may have the security department administer all user accounts. This may require a staff of six or more people depending on the number of users with accounts on the mainframe.

In other organizations, the operation of security-related devices and systems (such as firewalls) is handled by system or network administration staffs. This type of situation requires that the security department have someone who understands operations and can work with the administration staffs to troubleshoot security issues and deploy new systems. However, the staff can be smaller as day-to-day operations are not part of the security department's duties.

The operations staff will also have the responsibility for responding to security incidents. This means that these skills may be used infrequently yet still need to be very sharp when needed.

In any case, staff members responsible for security administration must understand the products that they are responsible for. Training must be up to date. This means that each staff member must be trained on the products they will be working on.

 SECURITY ALERT! As the products change and as new individuals enter the department, training must continue. It is illogical to expect staff who are not trained to properly administer the systems.

Policy Development

It is sometimes argued that policy development is not a special skill as it only entails writing a set of standards to be followed. At times it seems that all that the policy developer really needs is copies of policies that have already been written. While it is true that there are a number of books on policy development (*Information Security Policies Made Easy* by Charles Cresson Wood [Baseline Software, 2001] comes to mind), policies should not just be copied and dropped into an organization.

 SECURITY ALERT! If a policy does not fit the requirements of an organization, it will invariably fail.

The reason for this is that security policy development affects the entire organization. Each and every employee will be affected by the requirements of the policies. Thus the writing of security policy entails two other skills: the ability to build consensus with other departments and an understanding of proper security practices.

The security staff member who works to develop policy must be able to work with other departments. In so doing, he or she must be able to explain why the policy must be a certain way. The staff member must be able to explain the potential threats to the organization and the vulnerabilities that incorrect policy may allow. In this way, the policy developer hopefully can achieve an understanding with the business departments of the organization that will allow the policy to be employed appropriately. A policy developer who lacks these skills will be writing polices for naught, as policies that do not represent the business goals of the organization will habitually fail to be heeded.

In order to provide the detailed explanations of vulnerability and threat, the policy developer must also understand what types of countermeasures can be employed to reduce the risk to the organization. This means that the security staff person must understand the current recommended best security practices.

The policy developer cannot be completely rigid, however. Business units may have valid objections to certain types of security safeguards. The policy developer must be willing to listen to concerns and to work with the business units to come up with alternatives so that business can continue when the policy is implemented.

Finally, the policy developer must be able to provide security awareness training or must at least work with the training department to develop awareness training. This training should be for all employees, new hires, and administrators.

Architecture

The security architect is the visionary of the department. It is his or her job to set the long-term course for how security will be handled (and thus risk managed). The security architect is looking at the interaction of security systems and business systems and working to develop ways in which this interaction can be smoother.

The architect is the staff member who will be involved in the development of new business projects. When a new business project is being developed, it is the architect who will work with the business unit to develop appropriate security requirements and to see that the requirements are implemented in the final system.

The architect will also assist the development staff by providing training on the proper way to prevent security vulnerabilities in software. This means that the architect must either do the training or work with the training department to develop the material.

Research

Research in the security department consists of two primary tasks: identification of new vulnerabilities and threats, and the identification of new security technologies. The staff member charged with this responsibility must be able to perform basic investigations and testing.

The researcher works closely with the architect on the development of new systems. Some new system designs will require an examination to determine if a vulnerability exists. Information on new security technologies is passed to the architect so that they may be incorporated into the future vision of the department.

Assessment

The security department will need to conduct periodic examinations of the security of the organization. Generally, these examinations are called *assessments*. Depending upon the information that is needed, an assessment may cover the entire organization or a single site or department. The security department will need someone with assessment experience to properly identify risks to the organization.

As discussed in Chapter 3, the assessment of an organization can be a fairly complex process. The members of the security staff who conduct assessments must be well versed in security technologies, vulnerabilities, threats, and business practice. It is especially important for the staff members to be able to communicate their understanding of the security environment to executive management.

A subset of the assessment skill is the ability to conduct penetration tests. Members of the staff who conduct penetration tests need to have a good understanding of testing methodologies as well as security vulnerabilities and risk.

Audit

The final skill that is needed in the security department is the ability to audit. Auditing is a very structured approach to the examination of a system or procedure. It is generally a separate skill from that of assessment although it is possible to find individuals who can both sense risk and audit systems to determine compliance.

The security department will sometimes need to conduct audits for policy and standards compliance. The staff member who possesses the audit skill will need to identify areas of noncompliance and communicate this information to business units and other members of the security department.

HIRING GOOD PEOPLE

Every organization wants to hire the best people. Security departments are no different. The question, of course, is how do we go about identifying the right people to hire when we only have a limited amount of opportunities to identify important qualities and traits. The following sections discuss key aspects that should be examined when evaluating candidates. If you look closely you'll notice that very few of the items that we'll discuss are specific to security (the notable exception being the certifications section).

Work Ethic

Obviously, the individuals hired into the security department need to have a good work ethic. This means, among other things, that they will do the job that they are paid to do. While this may seem like an obvious statement, it is amazing to see how many individuals do not live up to it.

Some important things to find out about potential candidates include their view of their job. For example, most security departments will want professional people. They are people who will act like professionals while they are part of the organization. What does acting like a professional mean? Generally, it means the following:

- The employee arrives for appointments on time.
- The employee completes work when promised.
- The employee shows up for work every day.
- The employee does not look for ways to get out of work.

There are, of course, caveats to some of these items. For example, if a job is not going as planned and there are unexpected roadblocks on a project, it should be expected that the employee would inform the project manager or the department head as soon as the schedule slip is noticed. In this manner, the employee can give the project manager or department head the maximum amount of notice that a job will not be completed on schedule.

Skills and Experience

When new employees are hired, organizations often focus on their skills and experience. Most job descriptions define very clearly the skills that are expected in a candidate for a position and the amount of experience that is necessary in order to apply. The level of experience that is needed for a given position will, of course, depend on the duties of the position. It will also depend on the amount of salary the organization is willing to pay for someone in that position. Generally, the more experience (and skills) a person has, the higher the salary that will be commanded.

As far as experience goes, larger security departments should always have a mixture of experience levels. This means that there will be a few staff members with many years of experience and a larger number of staff members with only a few years of experience. This mixture allows the more experienced staff to tutor and mentor the less experienced staff.

As far as skills are concerned, it is obvious that the security staff will require technical security skills (of the type described earlier). However, the security staff will also require business skills.

Technical Skills

It is unreasonable to assume that every security staff member will have every skill necessary. That being said, it is not unreasonable to require experienced security staff to understand basic risk management and security concepts. Basic risk management concepts would include:

- Definition of vulnerability
- Definition of threat
- Definition of risk and risk equations
- Identification of attack categories
- Identification of security services

All security staff should also have an understanding of TCP/IP networking and basic system administration. This does not mean that every member of the security staff should be able to configure and manage a Unix system, but they should understand enough about the operating system to be able to speak intelligently about potential vulnerabilities.

It is not necessary that a candidate for a junior staff position have much experience performing security tasks. It is necessary however, that such a candidate understand networking and system administration. It is much easier to teach someone security concepts (while working in a security department) than it is to teach networking and system administration.

Business Skills

Business skills are perhaps more important than technical skills for some staff positions. When we talk about business skills we are specifically talking about listening skills, presentation skills, writing skills, and the ability to communicate ideas clearly. One common mistake that many security people make is thinking they will get by on their security skills alone. This is not the case. Management often couldn't care less about a specific encryption algorithm—they want confidence that the staff is supporting the needs of the business.

 SECURITY ALERT! Given the activities of the security department, it is extremely important that every member of the security staff be able to communicate technical and business concepts clearly and succinctly. Whether the staff member is developing a policy or writing a report, the issue of risk management must be relayed to the audience. Failure to do this will greatly hamper the ability of the entire department to perform its mission.

Listening can be just as important as talking for the security staff member. The staff member must understand the business issues associated with the job at hand. If the business issues are not properly understood, inappropriate recommendations may be made. Therefore, it is extremely important that the security staff be willing to listen to the concerns and issues raised by business units.

Personality

In most cases, the personality of the individual is more important than the skills that are possessed. If an individual is the most brilliant security expert in the country but cannot communicate his ideas to the organization, he is of little use to the security staff. The security staff member must also work with the team. That means that an individual who is too arrogant or who is unwilling to live up to schedules may hurt the team more than help.

Integrity

Integrity is important for the security staff member. Since important business decisions will be made based on the advice of security, it is important that the organization (and the senior management of the organization) have trust in what the staff member is saying. If the members of the security department are considered to inflate their risk presentations or to ignore or hide their own failures, the organization will loose confidence in the department. This will be detrimental to the department's ability to complete its mission.

Reliability

The reliability of each member of the security department affects how the department is viewed by the organization. Remember, security is generally viewed as a cost item that can be done without by many business units. The security department must prove to be reliable in its dealings with business units on new projects and on other security issues. If the organization views security as unreliable, it may not use the department in new projects or (in some cases) even hide new projects from security so that the new project can be done on schedule.

Reliability means doing what you say you will do when you say you will do it. If a staff member says they will have a report done on Monday, it should be done on Monday. The same is true for meeting attendance. On time or early should be the requirement of all staff members. It does not take long for others to build an impression of unreliability if staff members are consistently late for meetings.

Events that are out of our control do happen. And such events will eventually cause someone to miss a date. These occurrences must be expected. If such an event occurs, the staff member must inform the project lead or the person to whom the report was promised as early as possible that it will be late and reschedule. The security manager should also be informed so that other plans can be made.

Outgoing

A security staff member must be outgoing. This is not to say that all security staff members should be "the life of the party" but they should be willing to speak with people and gather information. There will be cases where security staff members will have to make a point very strongly. It is also likely that many of the points that security staff members will have to make will be unpopular. When such an event occurs, the staff member must present information strongly and clearly.

There will also be cases where security staff will have to seek out other employees and managers of the organization. This will be done to either gather information or to seek assistance for a security project. The security staff member cannot be afraid or unable to do this.

Pride

Security staff members must take pride in their work. However, they should not be arrogant about the place of security within the organization. Security is a support department of the organization. In the vast majority of cases, security does not provide income to the organization. Therefore, the security staff member cannot attempt to force his or her view on a business unit just because he or she is "right."

In affect, all we're saying is that security staff should generally be humble rather than arrogant. As mentioned before, this does not mean the staff member cannot express strong opinions. But it does mean that the staff member must to be willing to listen and understand other points of view.

Paranoia

It seems obvious that security staff must be somewhat paranoid. Of course, we are not speaking of a psychological disorder. However, security staff are charged with looking for threats, vulnerabilities, and risk. To do so, the security staff member must look for avenues of attack that may not be obvious to other employees. In effect, the security staff member must be looking for the worst-case scenario almost all the time.

The ability to look for worst-case scenarios must be tempered with realism. In order to identify appropriate risk levels, the security staff member must be able to examine the worst-case scenarios and identify the likelihood that they will or could occur. So perhaps it is better to say "realistic paranoia" when speaking of the trait for a security staff member.

Certifications

There are many certifications available for security people. These include security-specific certifications such as the Certified Information System Security Professional (CISSP), the Certified Information System Auditor (CISA), and the Certified Protection Professional (CPP), to name just a few. Many security vendors also have certifications for their products and there are also other technical certifications for operating systems and networking equipment. The question that comes up is which of these certifications should be required for a position.

Certifications will not help you identify individuals that will fit well into your organization. Certifications can help you identify candidates in areas where you do not have strong technical knowledge. For example, the security department would like to hire a staff member to work with the network administrators. Therefore, it would be good to have a candidate who understands networks. If the security manager does not have sufficient knowledge to judge the technical qualifications of the candidate, a certification from Cisco might be helpful. The alternative would be to seek assistance from the network department in determining the skills of the individual.

TIP Certifications should not be relied upon to tell the whole story about an individual. During the interview, ask questions and see if the individual's skills are really there. Also, try to determine if the individual has the necessary experience to apply the certifications to real-world situations.

CHALLENGE

As the head of the security department, keeping and hiring good staff members is a constant problem. After placing an ad in the various papers and posting on Web sites used by job seekers, you are deluged with resumes. Many of the resumes show certifications on products and in various security areas. Some of the resumes have no certifications at all but they do have (what seems to be) significant experience.

How to you approach the resumes? Do you sort by certification or do you look at experience first?

Certifications can be used as a first-level gate, but do not ignore the resumes with significant experience. Often the individuals who have worked with products in the trenches have a better feel for how the products really work than the candidates with the vendor certifications. Also keep in mind the position that you are trying to fill. Does the position require specific product knowledge? Do you have someone on staff who can interview the candidate and find out what he or she really knows?

SMALL ORGANIZATIONS

Because of their size, small organizations usually cannot afford to have large security departments. In fact, if a small organization has any security department, it is usually a single person. Clearly, there are many more tasks (even in a small organization) than one person can handle. These tasks will require a number of skills that may not be found in one individual. Therefore, the small organization must make some compromises.

In this section, we will examine the skills that a small organization needs to have on staff and how other skills can be found and utilized to manage the organization's risk and still keep costs down.

Skills on the Staff

The small organization is likely to have a security department of one. Therefore, this person must be able to manage the security of the organization. At the very least, the security manager must be able to deal with the day-to-day security needs of the organization. Where the one person will run into resource problems will be handling day-to-day activities while implementing new projects (such as new policies, new security systems, and so on).

Given this, the security manager must be able to handle the project management of these new projects. At the same time, he or she must be able to work with the rest of the organization on new projects and handle the administration of existing security systems. It should be noted that in most small organizations, the day-to-day administration of authentication systems, firewalls, and so on is usually handled by the system and network administration staffs.

The security manager then needs to be able to work with business units in meeting policy requirements and designing new systems. So at the very least, the security manager should also be the security architect. Additionally, most organizations choose to keep policy work in house. The reason for this is that policy work tends to require a good understanding of the overall business and thus can usually be handled well by internal staff.

Finding Skills Outside of the Staff

Small organizations will not have all the necessary security skills in house. Therefore, some amount of the other skills must be found. Appendix B provides more details on outsourcing security functions, but here we will go into the types of functions and skills that a small organization will outsource.

Policy

While it is likely that the security manager of the organization can develop and implement policy, it may be necessary to outsource some policy development. The reason for this is that a single security person may get overwhelmed if the number of policies that are needed is too large. For example, a small organization that has no policies hires its first security manager. This manager is now faced with handling day-to-day operations and working with the business on new projects. At the same time, the organization needs policies. Depending on how the organization organizes the policies, five or even ten new policies may need to be created. While the security manager is capable of creating them, it may take him a significant amount of time.

In this case, it may be more cost-effective and time-effective to hire an outside organization to help develop the policies. The maintenance of these policies can then be turned over to the security manager.

Research

Part or all of the research function will be performed by the security manager as he examines new architectures and new technologies for use within the organization. Researching new vulnerabilities and the appropriate patches for systems can be performed through a number of services, e-mail mailing lists, and Web sites. While the examination of this information takes some amount of time, it takes significantly less time than attempting to perform the research in the first place.

In a small organization, the research function is still extremely important but it can be more efficiently performed by using the information available on the Internet. Certainly no one person will know all of the security answers but a security professional must know where to look when he has a question.

Assessment

In Chapter 3 we discussed the various types of assessments that should be performed for an organization. With a small staff, it is very difficult to conduct meaningful assessments while still maintaining operations. The security manager can and should perform informal assessments of the organization. These may take the form of walking down the hall and noting the physical security of building. The results of these informal assessments are then fed into the plans for future technologies and security systems.

More complete assessments can be outsourced. An assessment is generally a project of fixed scope and defined time period. Therefore, it is usually more cost-effective for a small organization to outsource this type of work.

Audit

The audit function is normally outsourced in most organizations. Even when there is an internal audit staff, organizations conduct financial audits by hiring outside auditing firms. Very often these financial audits are accompanied by an information technology audit. There is no reason why these external audits cannot be used to audit policy compliance within the organization. Keep in mind, however, that the external audits may have a very limited scope in the information technology arena and thus a change in scope may be required for policy compliance to be properly audited.

LARGE ORGANIZATIONS

Large organizations may have a sufficient need to justify a large security staff. It should be noted, however, that even large organizations might have very small, limited security staffs. In this case, the previous section on small organizations may be applied.

For organizations with large security staffs, proper organization is important. Large security staffs will also allow the organization to maintain most security skills on staff. The organization will likely only outsource security for particular projects (where an unavailable skill is needed) or as a means of staff augmentation.

Basic Organization of the Security Department

As Figure 10-2 shows, the security department can be organized according to function. Keep in mind that security administration may have a need to maintain operations twenty-four hours a day while the other functions do not generally need this capability.

For large organizations, especially those with mainframe systems, the security administration function may have the largest number of staff in the security department. Other functions that require fewer staff members may be grouped together. For example, the architecture and research functions work together very often and thus would fit together nicely under a single supervisor.

The audit function may or may not fall under the security department. Some security departments will maintain a capability to review system configurations. In other organizations, the internal audit department takes care of the auditing of system configurations.

Finding Skills Outside of the Staff

As can be seen from Figure 10-2, the security department maintains all of the various security skills on staff. This is a fairly expensive proposition and thus the skills should all be used regularly. If this is not the case, that particular skill or function should be outsourced when needed.

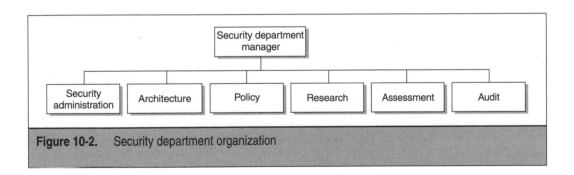

Figure 10-2.   Security department organization

Even with a large organization, it is still likely to be more efficient to use the various research services to track new vulnerabilities and patches for operating systems. This means that the research function is focused more on new technologies than it is on the finding of vulnerabilities.

It is also appropriate for the organization to periodically outsource assessment functions. The reason for this is that even very good departments can become "ingrown." By this we mean that the department has been designing and managing the security of the organization for some period of time. During this period, the members of the security staff believe they have identified all vulnerabilities and have managed that associated risk. In reality, they may have become blind to some of the risks associated with their organization. An outside view of the risk to the organization can assist the staff in seeing areas of risk that they may have missed.

CHECKLIST: KEY POINTS IN HIRING STAFF

The following is a checklist for the key points in hiring security staff:

- ☐ If staff already exists, identify the skills of that staff.
- ☐ If no staff exists, identify the skills that are of the greatest importance to the organization.
- ☐ Create a technical skills job description for the positions that need to be filled.
- ☐ Identify candidates who meet these skills.
- ☐ Interview candidates to determine their work ethic.
- ☐ Verify the candidate's skills and experience by giving them technical questions and problems to solve.
- ☐ Determine the candidate's business skills. Ask for examples of writing or presentations that they have given.
- ☐ Verify the candidate's personality traits by checking references and by asking appropriate questions during the interviews.
- ☐ For a small organization, determine the skills that are vital to the success of the department.
- ☐ For a small organization, determine the skills that can be outsourced.
- ☐ For a large organization, determine the most appropriate organization of the department.
- ☐ Identify good supervisors to lead each function.
- ☐ Identify the skills that should be outsourced.

CHAPTER 11

Reporting

Reporting is a necessary and important part of a security program. The senior management of the organization needs to understand what is happening with security and how the information security risk of the organization is being managed. Remember that it is the job of senior management to manage all of the business risks to the organization. Therefore, they need to understand how information security will affect the overall risk of the organization.

There are various types of reports that should be provided by the security department. In this chapter we will examine each of the primary reports. For each type, we will identify the content of the report and the importance of the report to senior management.

PROGRESS ON PROJECT PLANS

The organization is providing the resources for a project. Therefore, it is only reasonable that periodic reports be made on the status of that project. Various organizations require reporting on different schedules. Some require weekly reports while others are willing to receive only monthly reports. In any case, the senior management of the organization should receive a report on the progress, risks, delays, and corrective actions of any major project.

As was mentioned in Chapter 6, every project should have a project plan. Since the project plan as well as the projected costs of the project were approved by senior management before the project started, it is appropriate to report on the progress against the plan on a regular basis. In most cases, the easiest way to show progress against the plan is via a Gant chart (see Figure 11-1). Products like Microsoft Project and Primavera can be used to generate such charts. For large projects, tools such as these become extremely important.

ID	Task Name	Start	End	Duration	Jan 27 2002	Feb 3 2002	Feb 10 2002	Feb 17 2002
1	Requirements definition	02/01/2002	02/07/2002	1w				
2	System design	02/08/2002	02/11/2002	2d				
3	Development	02/12/2002	02/15/2002	4d				
4	Test	02/18/2002	02/20/2002	3d				
5	Production turnover	02/21/2002	02/21/2002	1d				
6								
7								
8								
9								
10								
11								
12								
13								

Figure 11-1. Project progress can be shown on a Gant chart.

Each line on the chart defines the parameters of a separate task. The chart provides a visual representation of the schedules begun and any dates of each task as well as progress against each task. Any delays in the beginning or ending of a task can also easily be shown. Every project has what is known as a *critical path*. By adding dependency information to the Gant chart this critical path can also be shown.

A Gant chart does not provide the whole story, however. It is appropriate to provide a written narrative that identifies issues in the project. These issues may relate to resource constraints, unexpected risks or difficulties, or delays. For each issue, the project manager should identify potential solutions, expected additional costs, and the corrective action that will be taken. If appropriate, senior management may be called upon to decide if the additional costs are acceptable.

Different organizations use different mechanisms for project reporting. Some organizations have a scheduled time where senior management meets with all project managers. All projects are reported on during this meeting, with each project manager being given a few minutes to identify issues and provide scheduling updates. In other organizations reports are provided to managers in a written format to be examined at their convenience. In this case, the project manager must take special care to call to the attention of senior management any decisions that need to be made.

Regardless of how the report is presented to senior management, the following information should be provided:

- **Current Progress Against Schedule**   This is simply the examination of the Gant chart showing the progress of the overall project. There is no need to provide gory details on each task unless there is or has been an issue that has caused project delays or cost overruns. Remember, the report is being provided to senior management and they are not likely to be interested in the details of the solution to a coding problem.

- **Major Issues Resolved**   If there were issues that affected the project in the past that have been resolved, the solution should be presented to senior management. When the solution is presented, it should be presented as the most appropriate solution to the problem. Since the issue has been resolved, the project manager is not asking for assistance but telling of the solution. New risks should be identified and the impact to the overall project should be mentioned.

- **Major New Issues**   If a new issue that will affect the schedule, costs, or risks to the project has surfaced since the last report, it should be mentioned. If potential solutions are available, they should also be mentioned. A date for a resolution of the issue should be identified or assistance should be requested.

- **Expected Progress over the Next Reporting Period**   At the end of the report the project manager should project progress over the next reporting period. These should be realistic expectations. The project manager should not be overly optimistic nor should he project less progress than expected. Senior management will be able to identify these types of trends and adjust their expectations accordingly.

TIP   Do not be afraid to report problems or delays in a project. It is better to be honest with senior management than to cover up problems.

STATE OF SECURITY

It is up to the manager of the security department to provide reports on the state of security within the organization. To do this, there must be some way to measure the state of security. Without a method of measuring security, any type of report becomes pure opinion that is not necessarily based in fact.

In the following sections, we will discuss two methods of reporting on the state of security: metrics and risk. As you will see, neither is a perfect science and each security manager must tailor his reporting to the organization in which he resides.

Metrics

Reporting on metrics is simply the reporting of something measurable. Thus the most important part of a reporting system based on metrics is defining the metrics. In order to use the metric reporting method, the security manager must identify metrics, determine how they relate to the overall security of the organization, and find a way to measure them.

Identifying Metrics

Many things can be measured. The question for the security manager becomes "what things can be measured that will provide reasonable information about the security program?"

The last part of the question is the most interesting part. The metrics need to show something about the security program. Obviously, the number of breaches that have been found can be measured. However, this number will (hopefully) be very small and thus may not really give an accurate picture of the security posture of the organization. Therefore, there needs to be something else that provides meaningful measurements of security and yet can be monitored and measured periodically.

Table 11-1 provides a list of some potential metrics and their advantages and disadvantages. As you can see from the table, each of the potential metrics provides indications of the security posture. None of them, however, provide direct information about the strength of the program.

The exact metrics that should be used will depend on the responsibilities and tools of the specific security department. If the department is responsible for user account administration, for example, it may be appropriate to report on the number of accounts and the time between request and actual set up of an account.

Metric	Advantages	Disadvantages
System vulnerabilities	Identifies real system vulnerabilities that may be exploited	Does not take into account the accessibility of the system and thus the risk the vulnerability truly poses to the organization
Policy configuration violations	Identifies how the administrators are configuring systems	Does not identify the potential for successful penetration
Blocked attacks (firewall or IDS)	Identifies what is being attempted against the organization and thus some information about threat	Does not indicate real vulnerabilities and cannot differentiate between a true attack and a test
Number of employees through the Security Awareness Program	Identifies how well employees are following the directive to attend training	Does not show whether the employees are following what they have been taught
Internal failed access attempts (system or files)	Identifies potential threat	Does not take into account accidents or mistakes
Number of security incidents	Identifies actual security issues	Only identifies known incidents

Table 11-1. Advantages and Disadvantages of Various Security Metrics

An important question that should not be overlooked when using metrics to paint a picture of security within an organization is the meaning of the metrics. For example, if the number of vulnerabilities is increasing, does this mean that the security of the organization is getting worse? Perhaps. It may also mean that a number of new systems have been added to the network or that a new tool was being used that found newer vulnerabilities. In this case, it is necessary to correlate the number of vulnerabilities with other activities (in this case new systems coming online).

As another example, consider the number of security incidents being reported. If the number increases over time, does this mean that security is getting worse? Again, the answer is perhaps. Other explanations for this increase might be an increase in the visibility of the organization (major news stories or press releases, for instance) or it might be an indication of better detection or reporting. The latter might be an indication that the security program is getting better rather than worse. Also, not all incidents are equal. The severity of the incident should figure into the metric somehow.

 SECURITY ALERT! Identifying metrics must be done carefully. The meaning of these metrics must be fully understood by those reporting on them so that they may be properly explained to management (see "Reporting on Metrics," later in this chapter).

Measuring Metrics

To provide proper information about the security program, the metrics must be measurable. How often should they be measured and how should they be measured? The answers to these questions will be driven by the capabilities of the security department. The department cannot report on information that it does not have. Therefore, the only metrics that should be reported must be measurable by the security department.

If we take a look back at Table 11-1 we see that each of the potential metrics listed requires some mechanism for measuring. Some of the mechanisms can be manual (the number of security incidents for example) while others may require automation (the number of attacks blocked by a firewall or IDS). These are the easy ones to measure. The only real question that should be answered is how often should the measurement be taken? Should it be daily, weekly, monthly? This will depend on how the metric will change over time. Daily reports from the firewall logs may be appropriate while monthly incident numbers may be necessary to register anything other than a zero.

Some metrics can be measured manually or through the use of tools. For example, a vulnerability scanner can be used to measure the number of vulnerabilities on various systems. This job could also be done manually by checking to see which systems are patched and which are not. However, if the job is performed manually it will take much longer than a vulnerability scanner. In this case, it may be more appropriate to measure a sampling of systems over each measurement period rather than every system.

Reporting on Metrics

The reporting of metrics should be focused on trends, not on individual numbers (see Figure 11-2). The reason for this is that the security department is attempting to paint a picture of the organization's security program and its progress over time. In short, what matters most is that the program is improving the security posture of the organization, not how many vulnerabilities were found in January. Please note that this is not to say that the individual numbers are unimportant, but that they must be read and used in context.

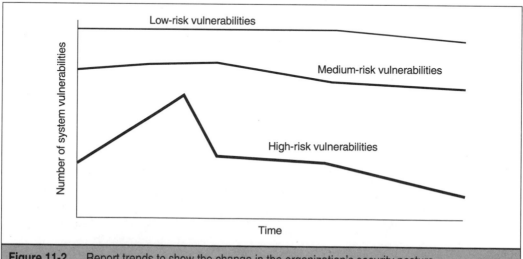

Figure 11-2.   Report trends to show the change in the organization's security posture.

Just reporting the raw trends is not completely helpful either. Take a look at Figure 11-2. You can see that the high-risk vulnerabilities go up and then trend downwards. At the same time, the medium- and low-risk vulnerabilities show significantly less reduction. What does all of this information tell us about the security posture of the organization? Since the trend in high-risk vulnerabilities (those that may allow an immediate system compromise) is trending down, it can be surmised that the overall security posture is improving as there are fewer ways to compromise the organization's systems. But should management be concerned with the relative lack of reduction in medium- and low-risk vulnerabilities? This question should be answered in the report. If the answer is yes, then there must also be a report of the actions that will be taken to reduce these other vulnerabilities.

Risk Measurement

Measuring an organization's security posture using metrics really only paints half a picture. Metrics provide indicators but they do not tell the true danger to an organization. The measurement and reporting of information security risk provides the other half of the picture.

What Risk Means

Risk is the potential for something bad to happen to the organization. Every organization and every person in the world lives with risk every day. Most risks have such a small likelihood of actually occurring that we don't worry about them. Others require some type of management so that the potential of occurrence is reduced. For example, most homes have locks on their doors to reduce the likelihood that someone will walk in and steal items of value. By placing the lock on the door, the owners of the house are managing their risk.

In terms of information security, we must examine the risks to

- Information confidentiality
- Information integrity
- Information, system, and capability availability
- Accountability mechanisms

Each of these categories of risks may have many specific systems or points where an attack can be made and damage suffered by the organization. The senior management of the organization should be made to understand these risks so that they may be managed. Remember that risk can never truly be eliminated. Risk must be managed and this is the core of information security.

Identifying Risk

Risks are identified through risk assessments (see Chapter 3). All types of risk assessments identify risks by looking for threats (the perpetrator of an attack) and vulnerabilities (the method of entry of the attack). Each type of attack is then compared against existing countermeasures (such as firewalls, access control systems, and so on) to determine if the risk is likely to occur. Therefore, to completely determine the real risks to the organization, we must first identify vulnerabilities, threats, and countermeasures.

Identifying Vulnerabilities   When identifying specific vulnerabilities, start by determining all of the entry points to the organization's networks. In other words, find all the access points to information (in both electronic and physical form) and systems within the organization. We do this by identifying the following:

- Internet connections
- Remote access points
- Connections to other organizations
- Physical access to facilities
- User access points

Once the entry points are identified, we need to see which information and systems are accessible by each entry point. Be sure to include in this list any known vulnerabilities in operating systems and applications. This exercise will identify the major vulnerabilities of the organization.

Identifying Threat   Threat assessment is a complex and sometimes abstract task. There are some specific threats that are very obvious, such as competitors. Unfortunately, true threats often remain hidden from view. True targeted threats may not show themselves until an event has occurred.

A true threat is the combination of a known individual or individuals having known access with a known motivation performing a known event against a known target. Thus we may have a disgruntled employee (the agent) who desires knowledge of the latest designs an organization is working on (the motivation). This employee has access to the organization's information systems (access) and knows where the information is located (knowledge). The employee is targeting the confidentiality of the new designs and may attempt to brute-force his way into the files he wants (the event).

As you can see from this example, finding true threats can be very difficult due to the fact that the individuals involved will try to hide the fact that they are a threat. How could an organization identify the disgruntled employee as a true threat? Without the employee providing an indication of his intentions, it would be very difficult or almost impossible.

An alternative to identifying targeted threats is to assume a generic level of threat. If it is assumed that there exists a generic level of threat in the world, and if we can generally define the level of this generic threat, then we can use this information in our risk assessments. This generic threat exists because some individuals may choose to do bad things. If we assume a generic threat (somebody probably has the access, knowledge, and motivation to do something bad), we can examine the vulnerabilities within an organization that may allow the access to occur. Any such vulnerability then translates into a risk since we assume there is a threat that may exploit the vulnerability.

When using generic threat models, keep in mind that most threats are internal. All of the security surveys (CSI/FBI, SANS, and so on) continue to show that the vast majority of security threats (and incidents) occur internally and can be traced to an internal threat.

Identifying Countermeasures   Each potential avenue of attack must be examined in the context of the organization's security program. Any countermeasures that are already in place must be taken into account. Countermeasures may include

- Firewalls
- Anti-virus software
- Access controls
- Two-factor authentication systems
- Badges
- Biometrics
- Card readers for access to facilities
- Guards
- File access controls

As the risk assessment progresses, countermeasures around each access point should be identified. These countermeasures will help determine how severe the risk is around each entry point.

Determining Real Risks   To determine the real risk to the organization, we take the likely threats (or generic threat) and examine the vulnerability through each access point. Based on the damage that can be done to the organization, we can determine the real risk areas.

The risks can be rated based upon the probability that such an attack will happen and the potential damage that may be caused. Generally, risk can be qualified based on Table 11-2.

	Damage: Low	Medium	High
Probability:			
Low	Low	Medium	High
Medium	Low	Medium	High
High	Medium	High	High

Table 11-2.   Typical Risk Levels Based on Probability and Damage

Measuring Risk

In order to be reportable, the identification of risk must be measurable. While identifying each risk as high, medium, or low can provide some information, it may not convey the seriousness of the risk to senior management. Thus we must find a way to quantify risk so that it can be understood in an objective manner.

When measuring risk, it is important to keep in mind that each risk can be measured in a number of ways such as

- Money
- Time
- Resources
- Reputation
- Lost business

While it is certainly possible to gel all of this information into some manufactured risk value, it may be more appropriate to provide senior management with the information for each category.

Money   The cost of an information security incident is perhaps the most obvious way to measure risk. When something bad happens, money will have to be expended to correct the situation. This cost may be measured by calculating

- Lost productivity
- Stolen equipment or money
- Cost of an investigation
- Cost to repair or replace systems
- Cost of experts to assist
- Employee overtime

Many of these costs may need to be estimated for the risk measurement since (hopefully) the incident has not yet occurred. There is also a difficulty in the measurement of costs. How does an organization quantify the cost when an intruder copies sensitive information?

Time   The measurement of time is difficult. Before the time component of risk can be measured, you must determine how time can adversely affect the organization. For example, a delay in a project or the deployment of a new system can cause scheduling problems. In this case, a scheduling delay may be the best way to express the risk. In another situation, the time component of risk measurement may mean the amount of time a key resource must be devoted to restoring operation. A third way to look at time may be the time a system is unavailable.

Time and money are closely related in the sense that delays or downtime can be directly related to costs. However, the time component of risk measurement may mean additional risk. For example, a new system is to be online on a particular day. The organization has geared its marketing activities to make sure business is available on that day. If the system is delayed the entire marketing program may be for nothing or may require a major investment to publicize the new date.

Resources   When an incident occurs, resources (people, systems, communication lines, applications, access, and so on) must be used to correct the situation. These resources may not be available for normal business purposes if that happens. While the monetary cost of using a resource to correct a situation can be computed, there may also be a non-monetary cost of not having a particular staff person available to perform other duties.

The same may be true for non-people resources. How can a dollar value be assigned to a slow network connection or slow system response time? This is also very difficult to measure in pure dollar terms. Thus we should measure risk by the resources that may be potentially unavailable if an incident occurs.

Reputation   If certain types of incidents occur, the monetary loss may be small, however, the incident may be highly visible to those outside the organization. Consider, for example, a Web site defacement. In many cases, the dollar cost is small (possibly just two hours of staff time to replace the correct Web page). The defaced Web site is seen by hundreds or thousands of customers and potential customers. The company's reputation suffers due to the defaced Web site. How can this be measured in monetary terms?

The answer is that it cannot. In many industries (banking, for example), reputation can be considered equivalent to trust. This is the trust that the general public puts in the organization. Just think what would happen if a bank got a reputation for lax security. Surely, some customers will leave and that would affect the health of the bank.

A strong public image and reputation requires time to build. The loss of this image is not easy to equate to monetary terms but the potential of this happening must still be part of the measurement of the risk.

Lost Business   Some incidents pose the risk of the organization not doing some amount of business. This missed or lost business is unrealized potential. The monetary cost of lost business is almost impossible to measure. Certainly, if an organization does $1,000 worth of business every hour and the system is down for two hours, we could say that $2,000 worth of business was lost. But this calculation does not take into account the number of customers who may try again later and still do business with the organization. On the other hand, if the system is down for three days there may be some customers who do not return and this would surely be considered lost business.

As with some of the other measurements we have discussed, assigning a monetary value becomes very difficult. Thus the category will require its own terms of measurement to define the risk.

Reporting on Risks

When the security department reports on information security risk, what it is actually doing is showing progress in managing this risk for the organization. The report should show specific projects that are meant to reduce specific risks to a manageable level.

The organization should conduct risk assessments regularly. These assessments will indicate issues that need to be managed. Ideally, the assessment report will provide measurements of risk that match the way the security department measures risk. For each issue that is identified, the security department should identify a method for managing or reducing the risk.

The methods may, in turn, develop into projects that will be tracked and reported on, or may possibly turn into metrics. For example, if the assessment report indicates a high risk to the organization due to the lack of patches on systems, the security department may institute a program to patch systems for the latest vulnerabilities. The progress of this work may be reported via a metric on the number of vulnerabilities on systems or the number of patched systems.

Once the project or program is completed (in this example, a first pass over all systems to patch them appropriately), the risk can be reported as reduced. In some cases, risk levels may be reduced gradually as extensive projects are implemented. This type of report shows senior management how expenses related to security directly affect the overall risk to the organization.

CHALLENGE

As the manager of the organization's security department, you are called into a meeting with the CEO and the executive vice presidents. They have one question for you—what is the state of information security within the organization?

It is clear from their question that they either have not seen or not read the reports that you have created. How do you answer the question?

If you have created a good reporting process, you will have much information at your fingertips. You could answer with regard to existing security projects or you could answer with regard to the various metrics that you have established. Lastly, you could answer with your current risk calculations. Based on your audience, discussing the current risk calculations is likely the best place to start. If the group asks more detailed questions, you can follow up with your metrics (and their trends) as well as the status of various security projects (since they were instituted to manage some risks).

RETURN ON INVESTMENT

Return on investment (ROI) has long been a problem for security departments. Most security is looked at as a bottom-line expense and a cost of doing business and thus, there is little tangible benefit to the organization for money spent on security. This means that it is possible to debate the usefulness of security (even more reason to show via reporting that security is helping the organization to manage risk).

What many security departments miss is that security is also an enabler of business. To see this, think of a bank. If a bank did not have security (bank vault, guard, access controls, and so on) would it be a good bet to put money into it for safekeeping? Of course not. Thus in the case of banking, security actually allows the bank to exist and to do business.

In other cases, security has encouraged and allowed businesses to take orders over the Internet. The use of Secure Socket Layer (SSL) over Web connections secures the credit card number and other personal information as it traverses the Internet. If these technologies did not exist, Internet commerce would be more difficult.

These examples prove that an ROI does exist for some security expenditures. The question becomes how to report this to senior management.

Business Projects

Anytime there is a business project that requires some type of security mechanism to function, this should be reported to senior management. We are not speaking of the need to comply with organizational policy but rather projects (such as Internet commerce) where security technology becomes an enabler of the project. This means that if security did not provide something to the design, the project or system could not work.

Ideally, this type of reporting would be done by the business units and project managers. However, their focus will not be the ROI for security but for the business project as a whole. Therefore, the security manager should identify how security has allowed the business projects to open up new business opportunities or cost savings.

Direct Savings

There are some cases where security expenses can be tied directly to cost savings for the organization. A good example of this is insurance. Every business carries various types of insurance. Some insurance companies may charge lower rates on some policies for better security. Take a policy that insures an organization against losses from hackers. The premium on the policy will likely be reduced if the organization has certain levels of security. The security department can show how the expenditures to achieve the required level of security will reduce the premium and thus provide a direct ROI to senior management.

INCIDENTS

Incidents happen. There are no two ways about it no matter how good a job of risk management the organization does. When an incident occurs, the information about the incident should be reported to senior management. Please note that we are not suggesting that every time a user types his or her password incorrectly three times and gets locked out that senior management should be told. Senior management should, however, be informed of any serious security incident (any incident that may cause loss to the organization, for example).

When these reports are presented, they should contain the following information:

- A factual account of events
- The method of attack or the vulnerability exploited
- The actions taken by the organization to correct the problem
- Recommendations to prevent further occurrences

Factual Account of Events

Senior management should be provided with a complete factual account of the events of the incident. Keep in mind when this account is written that the executives of the organization may not be interested in the gory details. Therefore, make sure to include an executive summary along with the complete report.

The complete report should include the following:

- A time-line of events
- An estimate of the damage to the organization, if possible
- Information regarding any publicity the incident received
- Outside organizations that were contacted, along with the reason for the contact and who authorized the contact

The report should not attempt to place blame for the incident but it should provide all of the available information as to what happened and who took what actions. The more information that is gathered here, the easier it will be to conduct a lessons learned exercise.

Vulnerabilities Exploited

During the investigation and response to the incident, the response team will be looking for information as to how the attack occurred. In the best of all worlds, the team will be able to identify exactly how the system (or systems) was penetrated and which vulnerability was used to compromise the system.

If this is the case, the incident report should document what was found. In the final description of the attack, the report should document the entire path that was used by the attacker through the organization's network. Keep in mind, as this section of the report is written, that there may have been more than one vulnerability exploited to gain access to the compromised system. This is why the identification of the entire path is so important.

Actions Taken

The incident report should describe actions that were taken during or following the incident to correct the vulnerabilities that allowed the attack to occur. These actions may include changes to network architectures, firewall rule sets, or system configurations. The key point for this section is to show that the risk to the organization from this type of attack is being appropriately managed.

There may be some cases where corrective actions are not immediately possible. This may be because the vulnerability that allowed the successful compromise exists in an important system for which a patch is not immediately available. In such cases, the report should highlight the fact that the risk of further compromise still exists. Ideally, the recommendations section of the report (see the next section) will include recommendations to at least monitor the vulnerability, if not manage the risk, through some other means.

Recommendations

The final section of the report describes additional actions that are recommended to manage the risk of further intrusions. These recommendations are normally focused on technical security issues (firewalls, system and network configurations, and so on); however, policy and procedural changes or physical security issues should not be overlooked.

Each recommendation that is made should be tied into an identified risk. The fact that an incident occurred does not mean that the risk of such an intrusion was not known. It may be that the organization had determined that the risk was low enough as to not warrant an expenditure to manage it. In this case, further recommendations may not be accepted. Regardless of this, recommendations should be made to manage risk appropriately and this means that the cost of the recommendations must be taken into account.

AUDITS

In most cases, audits will not be performed by the security department. Rather, formal audits will be performed by the organization's internal audit function or by an external audit firm. The reports of these audits are usually not provided directly to the security department. The reports are presented to the organization's board of directors or to senior management. Therefore, the security department may not even find out what is in the reports until after the organization's senior management has already read and digested the report.

Audit reports generally require a response from business and support departments. The report is sent to the various departments with instructions as to which departments must respond to which issues. It is at this time that the security department will need to provide information.

Security Department Response

The security department must address each issue that is raised by the auditor. For each finding, the security department should indicate whether it agrees with the finding and what action will be taken to correct the issue.

As with any external examination of an organization's security, an auditor does not have a complete understanding of all of the issues an organization faces. Thus some of the recommendations may not be completely correct. If the security department disagrees with the finding, a complete description of the issue should be provided. This should include known vulnerabilities and countermeasures as well as the security department's understanding of the risk posed by the issue. If corrective actions have already been taken, these must also be provided.

CHECKLIST: KEY POINTS IN SECURITY REPORTING

The following is a checklist for the key points in reporting:

- [ ] Report on major security projects by providing narratives as well as Gant charts to senior management.
- [ ] Security issues in business projects should be reported on by the business project manager.
- [ ] Use a combination of metrics and risk to report on the state of security for the organization.
- [ ] Identify metrics that are measurable and meaningful to the state of security within the organization.
- [ ] Make sure that the security department and senior management understand what the metrics mean.
- [ ] Define appropriate measurement standards for each metric.
- [ ] When reporting metrics to senior management focus on trends, not raw data.
- [ ] Use consistent methodologies when identifying risks to the organization.
- [ ] Make risk measurements meaningful to the organization. Don't just use High, Medium, and Low.

- [ ] Tie reporting on risks to projects and metrics to provide a mechanism to reduce the identified risks.
- [ ] Identify security enablers that can provide an ROI on security investment.
- [ ] Identify direct cost savings that occur in response to security expenditures.
- [ ] Provide complete reports on any security incidents.
- [ ] Follow up incident reports with lessons-learned sessions.
- [ ] Provide appropriate responses to findings in audit reports.

PART IV

How to Respond to Incidents

CHAPTER 12

Incident Response

Bad things happen. Bad things even happen to well-prepared organizations with good security programs and strong security departments. The security department tries to manage the information security risk to the organization but even so, bad things happen. When they do (and it is a matter of when rather than if), the security department must be ready to take the lead in the response.

Ideally, a security incident will never happen—or at least not until the organization's *incident response plan (IRP)* is completed. The IRP should define the team and the steps to take during an incident. As with most contingency plans, an IRP can only go so far. It is not reasonable for the IRP to cover every possible scenario but a well-designed IRP should cover every reasonable scenario. The response of the organization to an incident is still dependent upon the technical capabilities of the security department and the other members of the team.

This chapter will discuss the make-up of the incident response team as well as the various stages of an incident. For each stage, we will provide guidance on how to respond. However, each incident is different and will require creative solutions to problems, many of which will not be thought of before the incident.

THE TEAM

The *Incident Response Team (IRT)* is the core of the organization's response to a security incident. The team provides the leadership and authority to do what is necessary to correct the problem and accomplish the goals of the organization during the incident. That being said, it is important that the team be made up of appropriate individuals, have strong leadership, and have the proper authority to carry out its work. It is also critical that the team be prepared for an incident. Testing the IRP and drilling the procedures is absolutely essential to make the team function properly.

Team Members

Who should make up the Incident Response Team? Each organization needs to define the individuals who will be part of the IRT. In this discussion, we can recommend functions and skill sets that the team needs to have. Figure 12-1 shows the basic layout of the IRT.

As you can see from the figure, the IRT composes a number of functions that are not technical. In the following sections, we will examine the purpose of each function during an incident.

 SECURITY ALERT!   The members of the team should be chosen carefully. The members not only should have the necessary skills but also should be completely trustworthy.

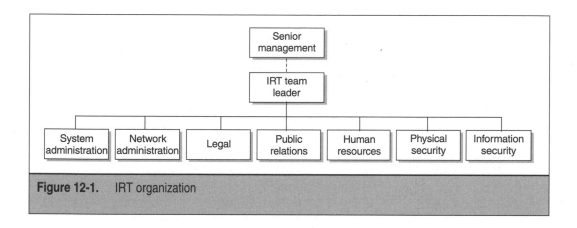

Figure 12-1.   IRT organization

System Administration

System administration is part of the team to provide expert knowledge of the various systems that may be part of the incident. System administrators should be able to work their way through a system to identify problems or suspicious files (see the upcoming section "What to Look For" for how to do this properly). Each organization should assign one system administrator who has expertise in each major operating system in use at the organization. This may require that the team have two, three, four, or even more system administrators as team members. However, for a given incident, it is likely that not all will be needed.

Network Administration

In the same way that system administrators provide the technical expertise on the systems, the network administrator provides the technical expertise on the network and the devices associated with making the network function. The network administrator provides the expertise to install network monitoring equipment in the correct place or to isolate portions of the network for containment. The network administrator will also help to identify whether network devices have been compromised.

While the network and system administrators have similar roles (and may in fact be the same person), the roles played on the team are slightly different. The system administrator is concerned with the systems and how the intruder gained access to them. The network administrator examines the network traffic and devices to see if the devices have been penetrated, but also examines the network traffic to determine how the intruder's traffic is being routed over the network.

Legal

The member of the team from the legal department will be the primary interface between the organization and law enforcement. The legal function is critical to managing the risk that an incident poses to an organization. It is this team member's job to identify the legal liability issues and to advise on what information should be allowed outside of the organization.

Public Relations

Not every incident will become public. In the event that the incident does come to the attention of an outsider (for example, the press), the public relations function should be the primary interface between the public or press and the organization. Based on the direction of legal, the public relations staff member will provide information to customers, the public, investors, and the press. It is important that the individual providing this information work with the technical resources in the team to make sure that inappropriate promises are not made.

To illustrate the importance of the relationship between public relations, legal, and the technical resources, let us take a look at a real-world example. The Web site of a bank is defaced. The report of the defacement is made by a customer who also reports the defacement to the local press. A local TV station sends a reporter and camera team over to the bank's headquarters for a statement. An employee of the bank makes two statements to the reporter. First, that no customer information was compromised and second, that the system would be up in three hours. On the face of this, it sounds fine. In the background, we find out that the technical team was not consulted on the information that was provided. In order to make the deadline, the system administrators had to fix the system and bring it up without several security patches. At the same time, the investigation to find out if customer information had been compromised was not conducted. The legal department was not consulted and thus the public statement may have opened the bank up to severe liability.

Human Resources

A member of the HR staff is on the team to handle any internal employee issues that may arise from the incident. If an employee is found to have violated corporate policy (either in creating the incident or allowing the incident to occur), it is up to HR to handle the disciplinary actions. It should be noted that HR must work with the legal department to make sure that the organization is protected during this action.

Physical Security

Not every incident takes place purely in the electronic realm. Some incidents also include a physical component. In this case, the physical security staff of the organization may be needed to assist. This assistance may be as simple as providing the access logs to an office or it may include actually escorting an employee out of the building.

Information Security

The information security department provides the primary investigative and security expertise for the incident. It is the job of the security department to lead the team. The security department should have procedures in place that cover the identification of the incident, containment of the damage, investigation of the incident, and reporting.

Leadership

Every team must have leadership. In the case of an IRT, the security department should provide that leadership. The leadership of the IRT consists mainly of the lead investigator and the coordinator of information. Keep in mind that leadership does not mean that the team lead has the knowledge or skills to perform all of the functions that the team will require. The team leader must rely upon the skills and knowledge of the team members.

The team lead will gather the information about the incident and work with legal and system administration to determine the damage and risk to the organization. The team lead will present this information along with recommended actions to senior management. The team lead will provide the final report on the incident as well. Finally (or more correctly, firstly), the team lead is responsible for preparing the team to work on an incident (see "Team Preparation," later in this chapter). It is important that during a live incident, the team leader be the single point of contact between security and management. Having too many cooks can make an incident more difficult to ameliorate.

Authority

One issue that often comes up when we talk about incident response is authority. How much authority does the IRT have? The answer to this question depends on the organization and the incident. In some organizations, the IRT has the authority of senior management to do what is necessary without consultation. This means that the IRT could cause a system to be removed from production and rebuilt if a compromise is even suspected.

This type of model does not fit every organization. It is important that the IRT also have an understanding of the business so that the impact of any decision can be weighed against the impact to the organization of taking down a system.

It is usually best to make a member of senior management a loose member of the team. While this person may not be involved in all of the team preparation and work on an incident, he becomes the final authority to gauge the business impact. In this case, if the team determines that a business system is compromised, the team would formulate a recommended course of action (for example, take the system offline and rebuild it). The member of senior management would listen to the recommendation and decide to follow it (and take the system down) or not.

A second piece of the authority question deals with law enforcement. Not every organization will want to contact law enforcement in the event of a security incident. This decision may have an impact on the organization's business or its reputation. Such decisions should not be made by the IRT but rather they should be made by senior management in conjunction with the legal department. Time is of the essence in making the decision to contact law enforcement as an extended delay in doing so can have a negative effect on the ability to prosecute.

SECURITY ALERT!   Make sure that the issue of authority is handled during the preparation phase of incident response. If it is left until a real incident happens, there will be misunderstandings that can adversely affect the organization.

Team Preparation

No team should be expected to perform properly without some training and preparation. It is expected that the various team members will have certain skills (system administration, and so on) but to properly work as a team on an incident requires that the team understand its role as well as organization procedures and good investigative steps. Once the IRT is identified, the team should work through several simulated incidents.

The first training sessions should be open discussions while sitting around a conference table. The team leader describes a training scenario and each team member talks through his or her individual actions. As the team increases in knowledge and skill, these simulated incidents become more realistic. This will include unannounced simulations as well as real-world training where a real attack is simulated on a system. The importance of these tests and drills cannot be overstated. The events of September 11th showed that companies that had real drills in their DR/BCP/CIRT teams fared much better than those that never drilled.

 SECURITY ALERT!   This item cannot be stressed too much. *Training must occur for the team to be effective.*

IDENTIFYING THE INCIDENT

The identification of an incident is not an exact science. Certainly, there are methodologies that can be used to identify incidents (see the next section for exactly such a checklist), but when something happens only once it is often difficult to identify the issue as a security incident or a system problem.

What Is an Incident?

Before we go any further, let's define what a security incident really is. We will define a security incident as "an event that causes some level of disruption to normal business activity and that is precipitated by an individual through malicious or accidental actions."

Please note the various parts of this definition. First, the event must cause some disruption to normal business activity. This is all well and good but many non-security incidents can cause such disruption. That is where the second part of the definition comes in. The event is caused by a human performing some malicious or accidental act. The reason that we include accidental acts is that the motivation behind the act may not be apparent until the incident has been completely investigated.

Given this definition, what can be categorized as a security incident? Here are some examples:

- Computer intrusions or attempted intrusions
- Denial-of-service attacks
- Unauthorized access to information

Clearly, this is not a complete list but it gives you some examples of events that fit the definition.

What to Look For

Some incidents are really obvious. For example, an organization's Web site is defaced. The IRT checks the Web site to see if it has been defaced. If it has, we have an incident. Unfortunately, not every incident is as easy to identify. Take, for example, a Web site that goes down. There is no obvious explanation for it and nothing obvious in the log files. Is this a security incident or is it just a bug in the operating system or application software?

What can be done to identify security incidents quicker and more exactly? There is usually some indication that a true security incident has occurred. Such indications can be found in:

- Log files (from firewalls, IDS, routers, systems, and so on)
- Network traffic
- System configurations

Log Files

Log files are a great place to look for indications of a security incident. Of course, you have to know what to look for. Often there will be indications of failed intrusion attempts. For example, attempted buffer overflows may appear in log files as error messages. You may also see failed login attempts. Unfortunately, many system log files will tell you what attacks failed rather than what attacks succeeded.

A successful intruder will likely attempt to remove evidence of the successful intrusion. When looking at log files, we need to not only look for obvious error messages but also for missing entries. In some cases this is very obvious. Some attackers will remove an entire day's worth of logs to erase their activity. Since most systems generate logs everyday, the absence of the day's worth of log files obviously means that someone erased the file. More sophisticated attackers may only remove certain entries in a log file. In this case, it becomes much more difficult to find evidence of the intrusion.

System log files are not the only log files where information about an incident can be found. Firewall logs, network logs, and intrusion detection systems may all provide some information. These logs, while they may provide information about the actual attack, may also provide indications of a system compromise. For example, a Web site begins to attempts outbound connections. These connections are blocked by the firewall and the firewall log records the attempts. Since it is known that this Web site should not be making outbound connections, we now have evidence that the system may have been compromised.

Network Activity

Network activity can also provide indications of an incident. The easiest type of incident to verify by examining network activity is a denial-of-service attack. By examining the type of network traffic inbound to the organization it is fairly easy to identify most denial-of-service attacks.

However, network activity can also be used to identify other types of intrusions. For example, if a system attempts to open connections (such as the example in the previous section) or if a connection exists between an internal system and an external system that is not expected for normal operations. The network traffic can be monitored through a number of mechanisms that include the firewall logs, an intrusion detection system, or a network sniffer.

System Information

The systems themselves are often the best source of definitive information about a potential security incident. It is difficult to completely hide the evidence of an intrusion on the compromised system. The attacker will usually make changes to the system in some manner and these can be detected.

Processes   One way to identify if a system has been compromised is to examine the list of processes running on the system. If some of the processes cannot be identified as normal, they may belong to the attacker. Carefully examine the names and the other attributes of the processes. Names can be set to look like a legitimate process, so also examine the amount of processor time and memory each process is taking up. It is important to note that the number of processes on a system can impact the administrator's ability to identify rogue processes. Large servers with hundreds of processes can be extremely difficult to analyze in this manner.

Accounts   Attackers like to have other ways of getting into systems (in other words, backdoors), therefore, if the attacker can gain access to an existing account or create one of their own, they will. Look at the accounts on the system and make sure that they are all legitimate. Closely examine any account that belongs to the administrator group on the system. In the best of all possible worlds, the organization will have a good user administration procedure. Assuming that this procedure requires records to be kept of all system accounts, these records could be used to identify unauthorized accounts.

Files   Examine the files on the system. There are two things that an attacker may do to files. First, the attacker may move his own files onto the system. These may be placed in hidden directories. If a hidden directory is found where one should not be, it may contain files belonging to the attacker.

The second thing that an attacker may do to files is to modify existing files to hide his presence. Ideally, the organization has made cryptographic checksums of all binary files on the system. This will allow a system administrator to identify quickly which files have been changed. If not, it may be necessary to compare known good files to the files on the system. This can be a very tedious process. Don't forget that it is possible to change the file access times so that the files do not appear to have been changed. The only truly reliable method of determining if a binary file has been changed is to use a cryptographic checksum. To be truly effective, the checksum must be created before an incident occurs (so that checksums from files after the incident can be compared to the originals). Doing the checksums after an incident has occurred will require the IRT to compute the checksums of files from known good media.

The Help Desk Can Help

It is very likely that the majority of potential security incidents will be identified by the user community. In such a case, the first call will be to the organization's help desk. If the help desk staff is educated about security incidents, they will be able to assist the organization in the identification of incidents.

To perform this function, the help desk should be educated as to the indications of a security incident. For example, in a real incident a Unix system generated messages indicating that inetd could not bind to the telnet and FTP ports. Further investigation revealed that this was because a second copy of inetd had been started (which is not a usual occurrence). The second copy was started by an attacker's script during the compromise of the system.

To further assist in the investigation of an incident, the help desk should capture the following information from the caller:

- Name of the caller
- Time and date of the call
- Time and date when the indications began
- Type of indications
- Type of systems (including OS and hardware)
- Location of the system (IP address if possible)
- Is the activity ongoing or was it a one-time event
- User actions on the system (what did the user do)
- Help desk actions (what did the help desk do or advise)

If a security incident is suspected, the help desk should advise the user to leave the system as it is and wait for assistance. The information is then passed to the security department for follow-up.

TIP   When dealing with the help desk, the security department should not rebuke help desk technicians for identifying a security incident (even if it is not) as this will make the help desk reluctant to identify further events as security incidents. Instead, if a large number of non-security events are being handed off to the security department, the security department should respond with additional training for the help desk staff.

ESCALATION

If a potential incident is identified, the IRT is contacted and the organization's IRP is invoked. Keep in mind that the first job of the IRT is to determine if an actual incident has occurred. This means that the IRT must identify the systems involved and look for indications of a serious security incident.

CHALLENGE

Your phone rings. It is the supervisor from the help desk informing you that she believes an employee has identified a security incident. Based on the procedure that security provided to the help desk, the help desk staff member walked the caller through the steps to gather more information. The supervisor is forwarding the information to you via e-mail. As you hang up, you see the e-mail in your inbox. You look it over and it sure looks like a security problem.

What is your next step? Should you activate the incident response team? Should you escalate the issue? If so, how?

Ideally, your organization has developed an incident response plan. You have worked out a procedure with the help desk to gather initial information. Based on what you see in the e-mail, the event meets the criteria for a security incident and therefore, you should activate the incident response team and begin working the event as a security incident. The plan should specify how to contact the team members and the steps that need to be taken to resolve the incident.

Investigation

It may be that the IRT will perform the initial steps of investigation, including the examination of log files. In performing this examination, the team will be looking for indications of a security incident and at the same time taking care not to modify the system. In the best of all possible worlds, the team will be able to collect system images before it even begins investigation. However, since the team may not know that an incident has occurred, it may be necessary to begin the system examination before system images are performed.

During the investigation of the incident the IRT will attempt to determine the scope of the problem. Just because the incident was noticed on only one system does not mean that the incident is confined to only one system.

Another key point to determine during the investigation is the seriousness of the incident. Different systems in the organization have different value to daily operations. The criticality of the system, the sensitivity of the information on that system, and the type of intrusion will all have a bearing on the response that the organization is likely to pursue. Ideally, these criticality levels are known in advance via the risk analysis and assessment for each system and application.

Collecting Evidence

During the investigation of the incident, the IRT should take appropriate precautions to safeguard information that may be valuable as evidence if law enforcement is contacted. Until law enforcement is called into an incident, the information that is collected is not evidence per se. While it may not be evidence from a legal perspective, it is crucial in the legal process that it be treated as evidence. If at any point it is tainted, then that is all a defense attorney needs to have it thrown out. When law enforcement collects evidence, they will take the appropriate measures to safeguard the evidence so that it can be used in court.

Before law enforcement is called (and they should be called only by appropriately authorized members of the IRT), there are two different situations that may cover what is going on as the organization conducts its own investigation. First, information that is collected as a normal part of business activities (such as regular backups, and so on) can be used as evidence without additional precautions. If, however, the organization takes special steps during the incident (such as calling in an outside consultant or activating an internal IRT), other precautions must be taken to make sure that the information is protected.

Ideally, the IRT will have contacted law enforcement prior to any type of incident (usually during training or the development of the IRP). One of the questions to ask should be "What do we need to do to protect evidence?" The law enforcement officer should be able to provide detailed procedures to allow the best chance for information captured by the IRT to be used in court. Keep in mind that anything can be challenged if the case actually gets to court and the final decision on what is evidence and what is not will be left to the judge.

At the minimum, the IRT should be prepared to take image copies of the systems in question. Along with the images of the system's hard drives, the team should also be able to record the following:

- System date and time
- A list of who is logged on to the system
- A record of open sockets
- A list of processes that opened the sockets
- A list of processes that are running on the system
- A list of remote systems that recently connected to the system

The exact procedure for gathering this information on the various systems of the organization should be part of the organization's IRP.

Once the information has been gathered, nothing should be done to the original copies of the disk. If the disk copies are to be used for part of the investigation, a second copy should be made using appropriate forensic tools. The original copies should be placed in a plastic bag, sealed, labeled, and locked away where they will be protected from unauthorized access. Obtaining evidence bags and not Ziploc bags will make the operation look much more professional and impressive to a judge, who will decide whether to accept the evidence or not.

The label that is placed on the bag should include who made the backup, when it was made, and what it should contain. Be sure to work with the organization's legal department when the procedure for protecting potential evidence is developed. Two good references for exactly how to protect evidence are: *Handbook of Computer Crime Investigation: Forensic Tools & Technology*, by Eoghan Casey (Academic Press, 2001) and *Computer Forensics*, by Warren Kruse and Jay Heiser (Addison-Wesley, 2001).

Determining Response

Once the initial investigation is conducted, the IRT develops a recommended response to the incident. This recommendation is then made to senior management by the IRT leader. The recommendation should take into account the impact of the incident on the business as well as the stated goals of incident response outlined in the organization's IRP. Some potential recommendations to senior management may be:

- Contact law enforcement
- Take the system down, clean it, and rebuild it
- Leave the system up for some period of time and then perform the cleaning operation

There are many other recommendations that may be made depending upon the actual incident. For example, if an internal employee is found to be attacking systems, it may be appropriate to have HR speak with the employee in private and ask for his resignation. This may be more appropriate if the organization does not wish the greater publicity of a public termination.

Other parts of the response to consider have to do with how publicity will be handled. If information about the incident has not been leaked outside of the organization, senior management must decide if the information should be publicized or not. Likewise, the legal department must provide some information on the potential liability to the organization. It may be necessary to report the incident due to industry regulations.

One other aspect to consider when determining the organization's response is the type of incident. Computer intrusions are fairly common types of incidents but they have different response options than a denial-of-service attack. Most denial-of-service attacks will be successful even if the target organization has taken all appropriate precautions. In the case of a denial-of-service attack, it is usually necessary to get assistance from the organization's ISP to contain and stop the attack.

CONTAINMENT

During the investigation of the incident, it is hoped that the method of attack was determined. In other words, one of the important pieces of information to determine is how the attacker gained access to a system. A second very important point to determine is how many systems were affected. This information provides some of the pieces to determine the extent and the cost of the incident (this information is needed if the organization will be pursuing prosecution). In addition, this information tells the IRT where to collect evidence.

Once the extent of the compromise has been determined and the potential evidence is collected, the IRT switches to a containment mode. This means that the IRT is now attempting to prevent the compromise from extending to other systems in the organization. Keep in mind that the compromise may extend based on system similarities (meaning similar vulnerabilities on various systems) or it may extend because that intruder was able to identify other vulnerabilities because of the first compromise (see Figure 12-2).

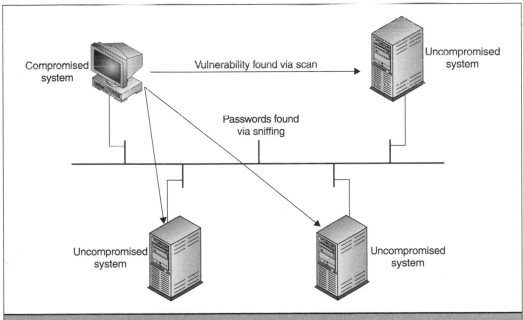

Figure 12-2.   An intruder can extend a compromise based on new vulnerabilities.

The IRT prevents access to any of the compromised systems. This may require that the systems be taken offline. If this is the case, senior management must be informed and approve that decision based on the business requirements. In other cases, it may be possible to prevent access from the outside by blocking such access at a firewall or router. The exact method of preventing the attacker from accessing the compromised system will depend upon the location of the system and the method of compromise.

ERADICATION

Once the attack is contained in such a way that the ability of the intruder to continue the unauthorized access of systems is prevented, it is time to clean up the mess. In a few rare cases, it may be possible to clean a system without rebuilding the operating system from scratch. However, these are very rare. It is generally a better practice to clean a system by formatting the hard drives and reloading the operating system from known good media. This does not mean copying the operating system from another system but actually going back to the original CDs or tapes. The reason for this type of procedure is that it is very difficult to determine all of the changes that were made to a system by an intruder.

Let's take a look at a real-world example of what an intruder may do to a system. In one incident that we investigated, the intruder compromised several Sun systems. During that attack, the intruder performed the following actions (we know this because we were able to find the attack script on some systems):

- Deleted several binaries (including the programs used to gain initial access)
- Replaced the ps command
- Replaced the inetd binary with one that contained a backdoor into the system
- Copied a sniffer into a hidden directory and started sniffing the network

During the investigation of the incident, we found the sniffer. If we had not found the script that was used by the intruder to perform the other actions on the system, we may also have found the deleted binaries, but identifying the compromised ps command and inetd binary may have been more difficult as they both performed normally under most conditions.

We should note that it is possible to check system binaries using a cryptographic checksum (such as MD5). Checksums are computed for all system binaries and they are compared against the checksums of known good media. If any of the checksums do not match, the file has been changed and needs to be replaced with a good copy. Products like Tripwire perform this type of check and can be invaluable during an incident investigation, assuming that they have been installed prior to the incident.

Once you have located all of the changed binaries (or have reloaded the operating system) do not assume that the data on the system is obviously good and reload it. It is possible that the intruder left a backdoor in the passwd file or in a user's home directory. A modified .rhost file is a wonderful way to reenter the system when you need to. The files must also be checked. Ideally, documentation on all authorized accounts exists so that the accounts can be checked quickly. Since .rhost files (files that allow users to log into a system without a password) are generally poor security practice, it may be wise to remove them anyway. The data files should also be checked for inappropriate cron jobs and SUID and SGID (programs that can run as another user, usually root) files. As you can see, the files to check can be extensive.

DOCUMENTATION

Documentation is the key to all incident response. This means that how you document procedures and policies before an incident, how you document what is done during the incident, and how you document the incident after it is over are all key to properly dealing with a computer security incident.

Before Documentation

So how do you document before an incident occurs? Clearly, you cannot document the details of the incident but you can document the groundwork for how you will handle the incident and the policies and procedures that will help you when you must begin to deal with a system compromise. In some cases, the policies that the organization creates before an incident occurs may decide whether an intruder can be prosecuted or not.

Monitoring Policy

The policies of an organization define what is allowed on the part of the employees and set the expectations for things like privacy. Generally, organizations are allowed to monitor their own networks (see more on this in the "Legal Issues" section later in this chapter), however, it is a good practice (and may in fact be necessary) to tell employees that the traffic on the network and things that they may consider private (such as e-mails) may be read as part of normal administrative operations.

This policy applies to incident response since it is likely that the IRT will be monitoring network traffic and reading files on affected systems. This policy must be done before any such monitoring or snooping is performed.

Account Management

Why is it important to have account management procedures in place before an incident? Because it makes life easier on the IRT. Think about the case of a system compromise where the intruder has left backdoors but they are not obvious. The system has a large number of accounts on it. Are all of the accounts legitimate? Do they all belong to current employees or contractors? How can the IRT determine the answers to these questions quickly and efficiently? If good account management procedures exist, it is a significantly easier task. If account management procedures (and the records of those procedures) do not exist, it may become an impossible task.

System Configurations

Having procedures for building new systems has many benefits outside of security. With regard to incident response, system configurations and good configuration control will provide information to the IRT as to what the system should look like. In the best case, the standard system configuration procedure will require the administrator setting up the system to make cryptographic checksums of all of the binaries on the system. If this is the case, the IRT need only compare the checksums of files on the system with the originals to find files that may have been modified by the intruder.

Strong system configuration procedures and good system administration will also help with potential backdoors in user data files. If the procedure states that no .rhost files should exist and some are found, it is easy for the IRT to simply remove the files. Good system administrators will also run periodic checks on systems to locate files that should not be there (such as .rhost, SGID, and SUID files).

Incident Response Plan

The IRP is probably the most important document to have before an incident occurs. The IRP should set out the organization's goals when dealing with an incident. This means that the organization has thought out how it will respond to the potential publicity, information compromise, and system unavailability.

In addition, if the IRP has been written correctly, it will cover most of the issues that we have discussed in this chapter. In order to write the document appropriately, the security staff must work with IT, legal, public relations, and HR as well as with senior management. The primary issues will have been discussed, drilled, and tested before an incident occurs when the pressure of the incident is not hurting the thought process of the individuals involved.

During Documentation

When an incident is actually occurring, the IRT will have many things to do. In addition, it is likely (especially in the case of a serious incident) that the organization's senior management will be looking for answers and action. In this type of environment, the stress level will be high and the last thing on the minds of the IRT members will be documentation. However, this is an important time to maintain proper documentation about the incident and the steps that are taken to resolve the issue.

After the incident is over, it will be necessary to write reports (see the next section). In order for these reports to be accurate, the IRT members will need to remember the actions that were taken and the order in which they were taken while the incident was occurring. If the intruder is eventually identified, it may be necessary for this information to be available to prosecutors and for testimony in court. In all cases, the information must be accurate.

The IRT members must maintain good notes regarding their actions while the incident is occurring. This means that each action should be recorded. Each member should record the following:

- The date and time
- The action that was performed
- The system in question
- Anything that was noticed (files, suspicious processes, and so on)
- Others that witnessed the action or suspicious thing

The information should be written into a bound notebook. Ideally, the IRT will be issued a notebook at the beginning of the incident. If the notebook is bound, it automatically provides a history in order (as it becomes difficult to add pages to the notebook and deletions can be noticed).

TIP   Keep a stack of bound notebooks around in case an incident occurs. If one does, hand out a notebook to each team member and explain its use. When the incident is over, collect the notebooks and keep them with the other information from the incident.

After Documentation

Once an incident has ended, a report and lessons-learned document should be written. The IRT leader should write the report with input from each team member. Once written, the report should be sent to each team member for additions, corrections, and agreement.

The purpose of the report is to document what happened and how it could be prevented in the future. The report should be a factual account of the incident. It should not attempt to assign blame. The report may reach some conclusions (for example, how the intruder gained access to a system) but it should not identify the employee who was responsible for leaving a patch off the system.

The report should make recommendations to prevent the same type of incident from reoccurring. This may mean changes to existing procedures or the addition of new ones. All recommendations should be made to assist the organization in managing the information security risk of the same incident happening again. However, the recommendations cannot be blind to the business needs of the organization or the costs involved. A recommendation that calls for the removal of the organization's e-commerce Web site is not likely to be followed and does not truly help the organization manage its risk. It would be more appropriate for a recommendation to discuss architecture or procedural changes rather than complete removal.

LEGAL ISSUES

With all legal issues associated with incident response, it is appropriate and usually mandatory that the organization get competent legal advice. In most cases, the organization's general counsel is the appropriate person to consult. If the general counsel does not have the expertise in this area, he or she will be able to find someone who does.

The general counsel should review and provide comments on organization policies. The general counsel should be involved in the discussions with law enforcement on the best way to preserve evidence and should also be involved in the discussions about calling in law enforcement if an incident should occur.

With that said, let's take a look at two key areas relating to handling an incident.

Monitoring

The provider of a communication network is allowed to perform monitoring of that network for administration purposes. This is an exception to the wiretap laws (18 U.S.C. 2511). That being said, there are still potential privacy issues that may come up with employees. Employees should be informed that they have no expectation of privacy for any files or communication that is stored on organization computer systems or that traverses the organization's network.

This statement should be made in a formal organization policy as well as in banners on all computer systems. A banner such as the following may be appropriate:

This system is owned by <organization name> and provided for the use of authorized individuals. All actions on this computer or network may be monitored. Anyone using this system consents to this monitoring. There is no expectation of privacy on this system. All information on this or any system or network belonging to the organization is the property of <organization name>. Evidence of illegal activities may be turned over to the proper law enforcement authorities.

However the policy statement and banner are written, they should be reviewed by the general counsel before being placed on any systems.

Evidence Collection

Technically, information that is gathered during an incident is not evidence until it is in the hands of law enforcement. That said, there are things that can be done during the incident to assist law enforcement in gathering and using such information.

Keep in mind that law enforcement can use backup tapes and other system information that is kept as part of normal business procedures. These can be used as evidence even if the tapes are not specially protected after they are made. If the organization takes special and extraordinary steps during an incident, the information gathered may not be usable as evidence unless it is specially protected after is it made or gathered. In any case, contact local law enforcement and your organization's general counsel to determine the most appropriate way to protect potential evidence.

Another point to make about evidence: Law enforcement does not require a subpoena if the organization is willing to give information willingly. However, before any information is given to law enforcement, the general counsel should be consulted. Some of the information may have privacy or regulatory protections and the organization may become liable if the information leaks out. In many cases it is better to let law enforcement get a subpoena or warrant for the information. This provides some protection from such liability to the organization. Again, consult with the organization's general counsel on this matter.

CHECKLIST: KEY POINTS IN INCIDENT RESPONSE

The following is a checklist for the key points in incident response:

- [ ] Identify the incident response team.
- [ ] Include representatives from the following departments on the IRT: system administration, network administration, legal, public relations, human resources, physical security, and information security.
- [ ] The security department should provide the leader of the IRT.
- [ ] Define the authority of the IRT.
- [ ] Identify the organization executive to contact for actions outside of the authority of the IRT.
- [ ] Provide proper training for the IRT to include announced and unannounced tests of the IRP.
- [ ] Define what an incident is for the organization.
- [ ] Define a standard set of procedures to use when determining if an event is or is not an incident.
- [ ] Train the organization's help desk in identifying an incident.
- [ ] Define a standard procedure for the IRT when investigating a potential incident.
- [ ] Define a standard procedure for the IRT when collecting evidence.
- [ ] Define a standard procedure for cleaning compromised systems.
- [ ] Develop appropriate "before" documentation, including procedures and policies on monitoring and system configuration.
- [ ] Develop an Incident Response Plan.
- [ ] Maintain a set of notebooks to allow documentation during an incident.
- [ ] After an incident has occurred, prepare a proper report and lessons-learned document.
- [ ] Consult with the organization's general counsel on the legal issues surrounding incident response.

CHAPTER 13

Developing Contingency Plans

isasters of all shapes and sizes occur to businesses. Because organizations have become so dependent on their IT infrastructures it is essential that they develop and keep up to date an IT disaster recovery plan. This plan will derive from existing policies and procedures with roles and responsibilities for preparing for, responding to, and recovering from a variety of disasters. This chapter explains the key steps in developing an IT disaster recovery plan. It is important that we first distinguish between disaster recovery planning (DRP) and business continuity planning (BCP). Disaster recovery planning is planning aimed at the definition of business processes, their infrastructure supports and tolerances to interruptions, and the formulation of strategies for reducing the likelihood of interruption or its consequences. An example of this is shown in Figure 13-1. Backup tapes (and their rotation scheme) are used to reduce the consequences of a disk failure and the associated loss of information.

Business continuity is the overall process consisting of disaster recovery, business recovery, business resumption, and contingency planning. DRP's place can best be seen in Figure 13-2.

DEFINING DISASTERS

A *disaster* can best be defined as the occurrence of any event that causes a significant disruption in IT capabilities. It is typically an event that disrupts the normal course of business to the extent that monetary losses can be quantified.

Disasters come in many forms, but generally are either "natural" or "man-made":

- **Natural:**
  Earthquake
  Tornado
  Fire
  Flood
  Hurricane

- **Man-made:**
  Bombings
  Power blackouts
  Application failures
  Hardware failures
  Hacking, distributed denial-of-service (DDoS), and virus attacks
  Internal sabotage

While we can't discuss every possible scenario in this chapter, the ones that we will cover can be readily applied to similar scenarios. Some disasters have a higher probability based upon your geographical area, or maybe even your line of business. For instance, the southeast United States region has a higher probability of hurricane occurrence than other areas of the country. Drier areas, or areas subject to drought conditions, have a higher probability for fire than wetter areas, such as the northwest or south central United States. Quite recently, California was subject to rolling blackouts during which businesses lost power without a moment's notice.

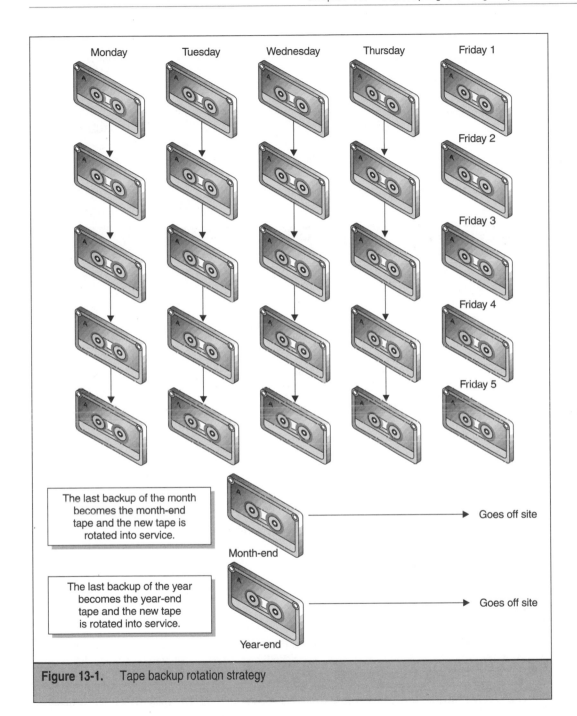

The last backup of the month becomes the month-end tape and the new tape is rotated into service.

Month-end

→ Goes off site

The last backup of the year becomes the year-end tape and the new tape is rotated into service.

Year-end

→ Goes off site

Figure 13-1. Tape backup rotation strategy

BCP	Disaster recovery	Business recovery	Business resumption	Contingency planning
Objective	Critical computer applications	Critical business processes	Process restoration	Process workaround
Focus	Data recovery	Process recovery	Return to normal	Make do
Example event	Mainframe or server failure	Laboratory flood	Building fire	Loss of application
Solution	Hot site recovery	Dry out and restart	New equipment New building	Use manual process

Figure 13-2. DRP's place in the BCP process

TIP Look for the most obvious natural disasters for your particular area and plan accordingly.

If the nature of your business involves a heavy Internet or online presence, you might find yourself subject to hacking, virus, or distributed denial-of-service (DDoS) attacks. A DDoS attack is one of the more difficult hack attacks to combat, and has resulted in millions of dollars damage to many a company doing business on the Internet. In January 2002, a DDoS attack lasting several days forced Cloud Nine Communications, Ltd., an Internet service provider, to close its doors for good. Some good remediation methods and additional information on DDoS attacks are available at:

- ciac.llnl.gov/ciac/bulletins/k-032.shtml
- staff.washington.edu/dittrich/misc/ddos/

In this particular type of attack, an attacker (Client) compromises several systems (Handlers) on someone's network. These systems are used in turn to compromise other systems (Agents) until the total numbers of compromised systems are well into the thousands. Each Agent system generates a stream of packets, which are directed toward a potential victim. The Client system can change the potential victim just by issuing commands to the Agent's Handler.

This type of attack can cause the actual infrastructure (network connections and devices) of the organization to become unavailable. While this is certainly not the only type of disaster that can cause this type of damage, it is something that should be planned for.

TIP Coordinate the DRP for this type of event with the incident response plan for the organization.

IDENTIFYING CRITICAL SYSTEMS AND DATA

Identification of critical assets and data is the first crucial step in creating a functional and effective disaster recovery plan. If you don't know what systems and data are critical to the running of your business, putting together a contingency plan to deal with recovery and restoration is a moot point. It's also important to understand that there are no "canned" solutions on the market today that can "automagically" lay out every single aspect of a DRP solution for every business and scenario. If you plan on using DRP templates that are freely available on the Internet, plan on modifying them extensively for use in your particular environment.

 SECURITY ALERT!   The use of canned DRP plans is a recipe for disaster in and of itself. DRP solutions require significant customization to take into account the way your business functions and its needs. Do not expect to be successful if you use only a canned plan.

Business Impact Analysis

Part of determining what items are critical and essential to the survival of your business, is in doing a business impact analysis. How will certain disasters affect key elements of your business? What would be the impact, for instance, of your central database going offline for an extended period of time? How would you quantify loss in this situation, and how would it affect the company as a whole monetarily? In this analysis, you should draw on the interview process for particular areas of focus that are considered business critical. Circulate a questionnaire among key personnel, asking essential questions such as:

- Who are your key internal/external customers? What impact do you have on them if your group cannot execute required functions?

- Who are your key internal/external suppliers (people you depend on for support)? What would happen if they failed to deliver the required support to you?

- What key processes are required to take place daily, weekly, and/or monthly to support the business requests and overall deliverables? Please try to list all events in the order in which they must occur, especially if there are interdependencies among processes and provide a ranking in terms of importance (1–low and 5–high). Also identify the person in your group responsible for performing each task.

- What primary and secondary information systems are vital to the success of your area's business objectives?

- What particular manual processes exist to support data entry to the information system and also provide support to the overall business objective(s)? Can these processes be extended or new ones created to support your group's daily/weekly/monthly objectives if no system support is available?

- Has your department already completed a formal procedure that stipulates what is to be done in the event of a disaster to resume normal or near-normal operations? Is there a maintained and updated emergency call list for your group? If so, has this plan ever been executed or tested? Who is the lead facilitator of your group?

- What would you do to ensure a rapid recovery takes place in regard to establishing temporary processes needed to support customer requests and maintain critical support from suppliers? Do you feel you have all that is needed in the event of a disaster, such as equipment, people, and other vital resources?

- Where are your vital records stored, and who are the people that are authorized to retrieve them? How often are the records backed up? Please include in your response which persons you depend on for storage and retrieval of these records.

Identify critical systems, data, and current processes from the questionnaire's results. Chart and tabulate them so that you can refer to key points later. You can then prioritize all areas for further insight and information gathering in the next step, the interview process.

CHALLENGE

You have been named the organization's disaster coordinator and now it is your job to begin building the organization's DRP. Knowing that you needed information before any real steps could be taken, you sent a questionnaire to each department asking questions about their critical systems.

As you analyze the results, you are seeing a disturbing trend—each and every department is using critical systems that cannot be down for longer than four hours without adversely affecting the organization! You had no idea that every system in the data center was so important. How can you even begin to construct a DRP based on this information? It would cost a fortune to be able to recover the entire organization in four hours!

The initial information provided by each department may or may not be completely accurate. In most cases, there are some systems that are absolutely critical and others that fall into the "nice to have" category. You may also find that some systems that you think are absolutely necessary for the operations of the organization do not need immediate recovery due to the way they are currently used.

After the questionnaires are analyzed, you, as the DRP coordinator, must visit with each business unit and determine exactly what the business requirements are for the systems. Use the interviews to validate the information on the questionnaires and do not hesitate to ask pointed questions.

The Interview Process

The interview process is the next step that should be taken in order to identify critical systems and data. Knowing what is important and why it is so to a particular business unit or organization will help you justify priorities when the inevitable politics come into play. Interview department heads, programmers, information technology and support people, telecom folks, and the average end user to get their perspectives.

You should start at the top and work your way down, soliciting everyone from the "big cheese" down to the mailroom. Generally, the higher up you go on the "company food chain" the more of a generalized perspective on critical systems and data you are likely to get. The further down this chain you go, the deeper the understandings of the day-to-day workings of the business typically become. A CEO, for instance, may have quite a different perspective on critical systems and data than would a payroll processor or human resources representative. Your findings from the questionnaire process will assist you in identifying key people and processes worth delving into in greater detail.

Key questions to ask during the interview process include

- What applications are critical or essential to the functioning of your company role, and why?

- Would you be able to accomplish your job by manual means if the information systems were not available for any length of time? If yes, for how long? If no, why?

- What company organizations do you depend on to do your job? Who in turn is reliant upon you?

Ensure that all questions for each of the interviewees are the same (for a given business unit), and that the interviewees have had a chance to review their answers. This will assure that no answers were taken out of context, and that the answers given can be readily tabulated along the same scale of relevance.

PREPAREDNESS

Preparing for a disaster is a function of thinking of the worst thing that could possibly happen to your organization and planning accordingly. Obviously, we hope that this event will never come to pass, but we want you to be ready if it does. In preparing for a disaster there are several areas that must be examined:

- Risks of various event types
- Equipment inventories
- Funding
- Justification for spending
- Organizational culture

Risk Analysis Items

Risk analysis is the first step of formulating your DRP. During this phase you should determine which threats are the most likely to happen within your environment and prioritize them. Rank each threat into two main categories of "probability" and "impact." Then rate each of the risks as low, medium, or high. You can assign a numerical weight of your choice to these items; we'll use 1, 3, and 5. A matrix, such as the one shown in Table 13-1, is a great way to accomplish this.

Inventory

Having a current inventory in your arsenal of information is an absolute must. Try to account for every tangible asset the company has, what the asset's current value is, and what it would cost to replace or make redundant in another location. Inventory your assets based upon two distinct areas: hardware and software.

Hardware

This will include computer systems, telecom equipment, routers, switches, hubs, cooling systems, racks and anything else that is not considered to be "software." List everything you can think of; the more complete your inventory is, the better off you'll be. Finding out that you need a particular piece of information later and not having it will be much more time consuming than writing it down in the first place. List purchase dates, amount of

Risk	Probability	Impact
Fire		
Flood		
Tornado		
Hurricane		
Earthquake		
Power loss or blackout		
Bombing or terrorist action		
Hacking and DDoS attacks		
Tsunamis or tidal waves		
Volcanoes		
Blizzards and ice storms		
Landslides		
Nuclear disasters		
Avalanche		

Table 13-1. Risk Analysis Matrix

original purchase, serial number, revision, manufacture date (if available), physical location, responsible area or area owner, operating systems, service packs/hotfixes/ patches, and revision numbers.

You should also note any associated software packages that came preloaded or installed (break this down further when you do the software inventory) and contact information of the vendor/reseller where you purchased the equipment. Many vendors can assist you greatly in this process by supplying their warranty information. Dell Computer Corporation, for instance, keeps a database on each system associated with the system's service tag number (on the back of the machine) listing nearly everything about the system in question. All the crucial information, such as original factory configuration, all service calls and parts replaced, purchase date and purchase order numbers, are readily available.

Software

The software inventory becomes a bit more challenging than the hardware inventory. Start out with the enterprise applications first, and then work down into each functional area of your company. You can then get system-specific. The recent "Y2K non-event" did more to help companies in this regard than any other event. Much of the information gathered during this initiative can be leveraged here and updated accordingly. Much like the hardware inventory, a few critical items should be established:

- Original software vendor or preinstallation source
- Original cost (include upgrades)
- Number of licenses
- License number/key(s) and version number(s)
- Location (which system or device, by serial number or device common name)

It is especially helpful to have a network blueprint, or "map," of your environment. A simple Visio document listing systems and interconnectivity will go a long way when trying to restore things to the condition they were before.

In general, when doing your analysis, there are seven factors that can help determine a particular application or data's criticality:

- The time that can elapse before the application recovers after a disaster
- The unique resources required if the application is to be restored
- The application's ability to withstand relocation during restoration
- The IT operations staff's experience in testing the restoration process
- The limits on loss that can be tolerated if application restoration is delayed or not possible
- Structural or operational defects that may be present in the application
- Security considerations regarding structure or performance

Funding

The first step in obtaining executive sponsorship is the determination of needed funds. You'll never get executive sponsorship/buy-in without knowing what it will cost the company. Start off with comparative pricing on disaster recovery service providers. As these will generally cost a great deal more than a solution developed in-house, you'll have a somewhat more accurate baseline to go against.

Once the cost of potential solutions has been determined, it is time to apply a risk management approach to the situation. During the data gathering process, the criticality of each system and application was identified. Ideally, each business unit was able to identify the cost to the organization of the loss of the system (or at least the loss of use of the system) for some period of time. These cost estimates can now be used to determine the most appropriate alternative for disaster recovery.

As you put together the alternatives and recommendations for senior management, examine the potential disasters very closely. You have identified the probability or likelihood of an event occurring and the impact that the event will have on the organization. Now factor this information into your funding needs.

The complete set of alternatives, along with your well-reasoned recommendations, can now be provided to senior management. The work that you have done and the analysis you present will assist in getting the buy-in from the executives. You can show that you worked with the business departments and conducted a reasoned and thorough analysis.

Which Mode?

Partial recovery or full recovery?

With *partial recovery* only the critical systems are restored to full or nearly full functional capacity so that the business can accomplish the tasks that are most crucial to its survival.

With *full recovery* the entire business information infrastructure is restored to its pre-disaster condition.

It is important that both modes are accounted for so that any given situation or scenario can be readily applied to devise the appropriate plan.

Hot or Cold Sites?

Hot sites are a complete mirror of your current operating environment. This includes connectivity, space, systems, power requirements, applications, and data. Most times a mere DNS change is all that is needed to switch over to the hot site environment. It goes without saying that this is the more expensive of the available options.

A *cold site* is an environment with everything except the equipment. Businesses typically relocate all of their equipment to this separate facility and assume operations there. These are typically used when certain disasters strike that do not harm the equipment in the first place. One such disaster might be a flood that cripples your particular power grid for an extended period of time, but does not extend to your facility housing the equipment.

It is important to understand that a third option, known as a *warm site*, does exist and is a combination of the two scenarios just presented. If this is your option, you'll have more work to do restoring a warm site than you would a hot site, but less work than with a cold site.

Justification

In order to obtain funding for establishing a DRP within your company or organization, you will probably have to cost-justify it. As with any crucial new business initiative, justification is the first aspect. Why do you need a disaster recovery plan? While this may seem obvious to you, the executive staff, board of directors, or other higher-ups will no doubt need to see concretely what it will cost the company if a disaster should occur and a plan of this nature is *not* in place. Spell out in monetary damages what areas would be affected, and by how much. While it is normally not necessary to be exact to the penny, a realistic approach will buy you much more credibility than just making something up. There are numerous studies available on the Internet that you can reference, and research companies such as Gartner, IDG, and META also have a wealth of information available that will aid you in this regard. Be thorough in your "homework" and try to anticipate the questions before they come at you from what will seem like all sides. Some of the more obvious questions will include

- What do our competitors do in the way of disaster recovery?
- How much is this going to cost?
- Who will participate, and how much time do they need to devote to this?
- What will the company gain by doing this?

You'll face other questions, but most will have the same flavor to it. As long as you are able to show your company they can't afford *not* to have a DRP in place, you'll do fine. Make sure you have hard, concrete facts and examples of actual scenarios where business or revenue was lost, what was the overall detrimental outcome, and so on. While you are not trying to scare anyone, you certainly want to raise the red flag of concern in the proper light.

Allocation of Funds

Now that you've got the justification out of the way, and the powers-that-be have given their blessing, you'll have to give an estimate of how much it will cost. Be prepared to break the cost down by each specific area of the company, for if the company wants to initiate the charge-back approach, you'll certainly need it. The main reasoning behind this level of detail in fund allocation is that not every area will have the same needs for returning to business as usual, so some areas will more likely incur more of the total financial brunt than others.

Some key points to consider when determining allocation of funds for your DRP are

- Criticality of the particular business unit—how much does that business unit contribute to the "bottom line" of the company. Some of this can in part be dictated by existing service-level agreements.

- Number of systems and personnel.

- Amount of data and total restoration time.

- Number of remote users.

- Dependency upon other functional areas such as other companies, departments, vendors, and so on.

Interorganizational Cooperation and Corporate Politics

This is not normally an "official" or recognized part of a disaster recovery plan, but it is certainly important enough to mention here. Every company has certain political overtones to it, and understanding a bit of how that can affect you in your DRP endeavor will assist you in making the overall process a smoother one. First, try to get as many area heads or executives involved as possible. The more important or influential the person in the organization, the more cooperation you are liable to get. While they don't need to be involved in every aspect of the process, or even hold a substantive role, being included is everything. It's human nature and the more people you have on your side, the easier your job will become. Find a role for these people based upon their experience and importance in the organization, and more importantly, where the least competent can do the least "damage."

 SECURITY ALERT!   Failure to include the various business departments in the DRP process will cause problems later. Build on your relationships with your peers and the other departments. Show them how this planning can help the organization as a whole and get their buy-in.

PUTTING THE RECOVERY TEAM AND STEERING COMMITTEE TOGETHER

Before you go into picking names out of a hat for the DRP team, bear in mind that overall direction will be needed from start to finish. A DRP steering committee should first be established to watch over the DRP creation process. Ideas and draft plans should be presented at frequent meetings of this committee so that all areas of the business are adequately represented. A typical DRP steering committee will have at least one representative from all affected business areas, as well as executive management. It should not just be technical people.

There are several roles for a DRP team that you should be familiar with, including their responsibilities and selection criteria. Bear in mind that some of these roles and responsibilities can be outsourced to a competent vendor who specializes in this area. This is especially helpful when your organization is very small or when you are working with a tight budget. The first role is someone to pull all of this together. That person will be the DRP coordinator. This is the "top dog" in the DRP strategy with the most responsibility and antacids available. If you're the one developing this plan, chances are it will be you. The coordinator has the overall responsibility for designing, implementing, overseeing, and periodically revising the entire DRP process plan, or parts thereof.

In most organizations, there will be a corporate DRP team as well as departmental teams. The membership of various teams is shown in the following table:

Corporate-Wide Recovery Team	Business Systems Recovery Team	Administrative Systems/Operations Recovery Team	Network Communications Recovery Team
Disaster Recovery Coordinator	Director, Business Systems Computing (Team Leader)	Manager, Systems & Operations (Team Leader)	Manager, Computer & Network Services
Manager, Computer & Network Services	Training Coordinator, Business Systems	Manager, Computer & Network Services	Network Administrator
Manager, Systems & Operations	System Administrator, Business System Computing	Manager, Systems & Operations	Telecom Analysts
Manager, Technology Support	Business System Computing staff	System Administrator, Systems & Operations staff	Manager, Technology Support
Network Administrator	Manager, Systems & Operations	Programmer/Analysts	Director, Business Systems Computing
Director, Business Systems Computing	System Administrator, Systems & Operations staff	Computer Operators	Manager, Systems & Operations
Training Coordinator, Business Systems		Director, Business Systems Computing Business Systems Computing staff	

While each team leader has overall ownership of their given areas, they still report to the Disaster Recovery Coordinator for enterprise/corporate-wide accountability. You'll also notice a certain degree of "cross-pollinating" between functional business areas. This is done for additional communicative purposes. One of the last things you desire in a situation such as this is for one hand to not know what the other is doing.

For each position on the team, a description of responsibilities and duties should be created. The description should cover the following details:

- Position title
- Responsibilities with regard to DRP (use a bulleted list of items)

- Reports to (identify the position that this person reports to for DRP)
- Alternate (identify the alternate for this position)

The list of responsibilities should be as detailed as possible so that the individual and the rest of the team understand what each position does. This will enable the team to understand how to work together more effectively.

TIP Make sure that every member of the team understands the responsibilities of each position. This will enable each team member to go directly to another team member for help during the recovery, rather than requiring each team member to work through the coordinator.

Although most team leaders will have similar responsibilities that relate directly to their given business areas, one commonality is that they will *all* report to the Disaster Recovery Coordinator when it is time to implement the DRP plan.

Another format for responsibility is to break groups down by existing job functions that are still applicable to a disaster recovery plan, such as:

- DRP Management Team
- DRP Administration Team
- DRP Systems Recovery Team
- DRP Site Recovery Team
- DRP Insurance and Risk Management Team
- DRP User Liaison Team
- DRP Media and Public Relations Team

This is an excellent method of integrating all of those key "political" people we mentioned previously. But just as in the other responsibility scenario, cross-pollinate the groups with at least one member of a different functional area for communication purposes.

GENERAL PROCEDURES

Procedures and policies are a key part of any DRP. As the event occurs, the more information that is written down (and trained into the DRP team), the better everyone will function. Some generalized procedures that need to be designed and conveyed to all parties include

- Maintaining and updating the DRP.
- Ensuring that all affected personnel are aware of their responsibilities in case of a disaster.
- Ensuring that periodic scheduled rotation of backup media is being followed for the off-site storage facilities.

- Maintaining a current status of all equipment affected by the DRP.

- Informing all technology personnel of the appropriate emergency and evacuation procedures.

- Ensuring that all security warning systems and emergency lighting systems are functioning properly and are periodically checked by qualified personnel.

- Ensuring that fire protection systems are functioning properly and that they are checked periodically.

- Ensuring that UPS systems are functioning properly and that they are being checked periodically.

- Ensuring that client companies, partners, or customers are aware of appropriate disaster recovery procedures and any potential problems and consequences that could affect their operations.

- Ensuring that the operations procedure manual is kept current.

- Ensuring that proper temperatures are maintained in equipment areas.

Backups and Tape Storage

Backups and tape storage are fundamental aspects that most companies, large and small, already have some kind of a plan for. Unfortunately, poorly documented or implemented backup plans will only increase the frustration level when putting together your DRP. Try to be as concise as possible with your backup plan, and more importantly, make it easy to implement and follow. A plan we've used for many years follows here.

To conserve tapes, maintain simplicity, and insure sufficient retention of history, a five-day tape rotation schedule should be implemented using a different tape for each day of the week and retaining each Friday's (week-ending) tapes for one month.

The tape used on the last day of the month is rotated out of service and retained for 12 months. At the end of each year, the tape that is used on the last backup of the year is rotated out and retained indefinitely. Using this schedule, any file that is stored longer than one day, but not past the Friday backup, will be recoverable if restore is requested within five business days of the creation date.

If the file is recorded in a Friday backup, but not month-end, the file is recoverable if requested within 20 business days. If the file is recorded on a month-end backup, but not year-end backup, the file is available for recovery for approximately up to one year from creation date. Files that are recovered on year-end backups will be recoverable indefinitely based upon the retention duration of year-end tapes.

NOTE   The backup tape name (that is, Monday, Tuesday, and so on) *does not* reflect the day that the backup occurs. The tape name indicates for what day the tape should be inserted. Typically, the tape name indicates the day before the backup is actually performed, as most backups take place in the early hours of the morning during the least amount of local activity. The following table illustrates this concept.

Tape name	Monday	Tuesday	Wednesday	Thursday	Friday
Day tape inserted into server	Monday	Tuesday	Wednesday	Thursday	Friday
Actual backup day and time	Tuesday (1am)	Wednesday (1am)	Thursday (1am)	Friday (1am)	Sunday (10am)

Now that we've covered a recommended tape rotation schedule, some additional factors regarding backups should be considered.

Tape Storage Location

Once you've defined what it is you need to back up, the tape rotational basis, and the applications/data that are crucial and essential to business restoration, you'll need to figure out *where* these tapes will be stored. Some immediate factors come into play when making this determination:

- How accessible should the data be? This will be determined in part by what type of disaster is more likely to happen to your company. For instance, storing the tapes in a vault down the street might not help you very much if that location is also leveled by the same tornado. It will, however, provide more convenient access in the case of a hacking incident.

- Who has physical access to the data? If you are relying on an archival storage and retrieval company, for instance, what constraints are put in place by that company to safeguard your data and ensure that it is safe from prying eyes and competitors? Should encryption be used on the data? If so, what is the method for recovery should the encryption key also be lost?

- What will the storage location cost, and is this cost justifiable given the company's current needs?

One common mistake that people make is not using data safes. If a safe is not data rated, they can get very hot inside in the event of a fire. While papers will not be affected by the heat (around 175 degrees), magnetic tapes will melt at such temperatures.

DRP "Fire Drills" and Post-Implementation Test Plans

All of the best-laid plans will go for naught if they are not practiced and improved upon. Don't wait until a disaster actually happens in order to find out that there is a wrench in the works. Much like a fire drill, coordinate mock disasters and follow out your plan in a given situation. Make these drills both scheduled and unscheduled. See where the areas for improvement lie and update your plan accordingly.

Figure 13-3 depicts a typical DRP testing cycle. You can clearly see that two of the areas, checklist and walk through, are under continual revision. The whole process itself is circular and cyclic.

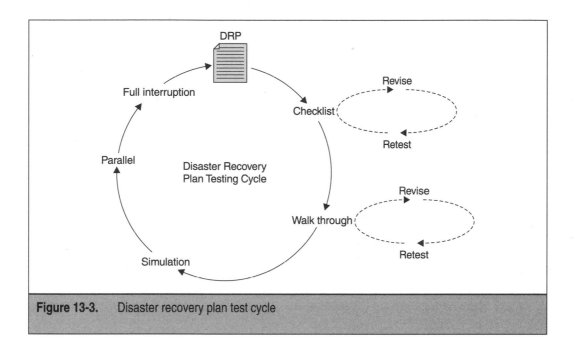

Figure 13-3. Disaster recovery plan test cycle

In closing, there is a lot more to a complete disaster recovery plan than what we've just presented, but these procedures and tips should suffice to get something workable off the ground. Getting a full disaster recovery plan working and implemented properly can be an enormous and daunting task. Depending upon your particular needs, capabilities, and business model, your mileage may vary. Try to make the plan easy to implement and easy to understand. It is a waste of effort to develop something that will never be implemented due to complexity or other shortcomings. There you have it. If you know what you're up against, then putting it all together becomes all that much easier.

RESOURCES

Some excellent resources on disaster recovery and business continuity planning are

- **The Disaster Recovery Journal**   www.drj.com
- **Globalcontinuity.com**   www.globalcontinuity.com/
- **The Disaster Resource Guide**   www.disaster-resource.com
- **Davis Logic, Inc.**   www.davislogic.com

CHECKLIST: KEY POINTS FOR CONTINGENCY PLANS

The following is a checklist for the key points in creating a disaster recovery plan:

- ☐ Create a good inventory of hardware and software.
- ☐ Create good and up-to-date diagrams of network connectivity.
- ☐ Use questionnaires to determine information about business systems.
- ☐ Follow up the questionnaires with in person interviews.
- ☐ Construct a table with all of the critical business systems and the amount of time that each can be unavailable.
- ☐ Construct a table of potential disasters, their impact, and their likelihood.
- ☐ Determine the costs of various recovery alternatives.
- ☐ Create a set of recommendations to be presented to management as to the best way to perform disaster recovery.
- ☐ Identify members of the DRP team.
- ☐ Create a DRP steering committee.
- ☐ Create a set of responsibilities for each DRP team member.
- ☐ Create and keep updated a set of procedures for backups and disaster response.
- ☐ Identify appropriate storage locations for backups.
- ☐ Drill the plan with the DRP team.

CHAPTER 14

Responding to Disasters

I n Chapter 13 we talked about developing contingency plans such as disaster recovery plans and business continuity plans. Once such a plan is developed it should be easy to respond to any type of disaster, right? Well, unfortunately, unless the plan is drilled constantly so that the entire team understands what to do when disaster strikes, the response will not be automatic. *The only way to make a specific response automatic is to constantly drill it with the entire team.* In most cases, the best that we can hope for is that the team will be familiar with the plan.

In this chapter we will discuss how the security department can improve the organization's response to a disaster and thus help to manage the risk to the organization. Disasters are significant events for an organization. Some organizations do not survive a disaster. Others suffer grave losses. How the organization organizes its response is a key part of reducing the potential loss.

REALITY CHECK

Something bad has happened to your organization. This may be the result of a natural disaster like a hurricane, flood, tornado, or earthquake or it may be a local disaster such as a fire. In any case, damage has been done to the building or buildings used by the organization. Before the organization even thinks about how it will respond to this disaster, the initial emergency must be brought under control. Clearly, fighting fires is outside of the job descriptions of most employees and such initial emergency responses as are necessary must be left to emergency personnel. For the purposes of this discussion, we will assume that the initial emergency has been called in and the emergency services of the area are being utilized to handle the situation.

 SECURITY ALERT!   We have had several clients that have written disaster plans that call for employees to fight small fires with fire extinguishers. In most cases this is unrealistic. There may be some employees who will try to do this, however, your employees are unlikely to be trained in firefighting. Thus, a plan that calls for employees to fight fires may just be exposing employees to extra danger.

First Things First

As part of the initial emergency response, the organization must provide information to the emergency responders. Such information should cover the location and condition of any victims and any hazardous material in the buildings.

Until the emergency situation is brought under control, the organization is limited in what it can do to respond or recover. If the organization has a disaster recovery hot site or the ability to shift operations to another facility, these activities should commence.

Many organizations do not maintain multiple sites (and thus the ability to shift operations) or a hot site (often due to the high cost). For these organizations, other than some initial planning, there is little to be done until the emergency is over, other than to determine the location (and the health) of the organization's employees. The organization's employees will be needed following the emergency situation to assess damage and to begin the recovery process.

TIP Alternate locations need not be expensive hot sites. It may be possible to save valuable time by identifying alternative locations within the organization that could be used as data centers in an emergency.

Damage Assessment

Once the emergency situation has been contained, the organization needs to assess the damage that was done. In some cases, the damage may be very obvious. For example, if the entire building has been destroyed, any systems that were in the building will no longer function. However, complete destruction is not the only possibility. There are many types of disasters that cause damage to parts of a building but not all of it.

Take, for example, a three-story building that is damaged by a flood. The flood waters reached a height of three feet at street level. The water entered the first floor of the building and saturated all the spaces on the first floor. Any equipment that was located from the floor up to about three feet has been submerged. Obviously, the first floor is not usable for any type of work (if for no other reason than the mud that is all over the floor). However, if the building is still structurally sound, the second and third floors may not have suffered much damage. Does this mean that the parts of the organization that used the top two floors of the building are not affected? Not quite. It may still be hard for employees to get to the upper floors due to the damage on the first floor. Elevators may be inoperable and stairways may be clogged with mud. Power and telephone service may also have been affected by the flood and thus the building may not be usable for other reasons.

A damage assessment in this type of situation may indicate that the first floor of the building will be unusable for several months as it is cleaned and rebuilt. On the other hand, the two upper floors may only be unusable for a week or two as power and telephone services are restored to the building.

The type of response that an organization will attempt is directly affected by the amount of damage that the organization and its facilities have sustained. Thus it is very important for the organization to conduct a thorough damage assessment. The following is a list of items that should be assessed:

- **Status of employees** Some employees may have been injured or killed during the disaster. Depending on the situation, some employees may not be available because they cannot get to the work location. No matter why the employees are unavailable, the organization must identify which employees are available to conduct operations and work on response and recovery.

- **Status of the building** Attempt to determine if the building is structurally sound. If so, identify the damage to various sections or floors of the building. Try to group parts of the building together by the amount of damage sustained.

- **Status of key areas**   Some areas of the building may provide key capabilities. For example, the data center will affect the ability of the organization to recover in a different way than damage to a file room. Identify the key areas and attempt to determine if each area can still carry out its intended function.

- **Status of key systems**   When a building is damaged, it is very possible that key computer systems in the building will also be damaged or destroyed. The usability of the systems in the building should be determined.

- **Status of power**   Electric power is often shut off to prevent injury to rescue workers and to prevent fire. If the power has been shut off to the building attempt to determine how long it will be until the power is restored. If a loss of power has been the primary result of the disaster, determine how long the organization can function without electricity. In some cases this may be determined by the amount of diesel fuel available.

- **Status of water**   It is very unpleasant to work in a building that does not have running water. As with electricity, attempt to determine how long until service is restored and what other options may be available.

- **Status of communications**   Communications may be lost when a disaster occurs. Most organizations use telephone or data connections to conduct business. Attempt to identify the time to repair communications and identify alternatives. Cell phones may be an alternative if phone service is cut off. Internet connectivity may be harder to restore.

DEFINING AUTHORITY AND THE TEAM

If the organization has a disaster recovery plan (DRP), it should also have a predefined disaster response team. The members of the team need to be located and assembled. Keep in mind that some of the team members may not be available either because they are out of the area, cannot get to the work site, or because they are injured or dead.

Assembling the Team

Depending on how the disaster occurred, the team may already be at the organization's location or they may be scattered. The DRP should specify how the team will be assembled and where they will assemble. Keep in mind that if the organization's building has been lost to fire, a plan that calls for a meeting in the organization's large conference room is unlikely to work.

The team may assemble in person or it may be assembled via a conference call. In any case, the team must be contacted. Again, the DRP should identify the contact method for all team members and alternates. The DRP should also have a contingency for phone lines being out of order. Such a contingency may include the use of cell phones or radios.

TIP   If the disaster is widespread (such as an earthquake), cell phones may be as useless as land lines. If the organization is worried about these types of disasters, radios are a necessity.

Organization Disaster Response Team

The organization's response team should be familiar with the DRP and the plans that were made prior to the disaster. Unfortunately, most disasters do not follow any type of plan and thus they often cause unexpected problems. One such problem may be the unavailability of team members. In this case, the DRP should have specified an alternate for each team member. If the primary team member cannot be located, find the alternate.

The DRP should also define the authority to make decisions for the organization. In reality, if the disaster is severe, the CEO or President of the organization will be the decision maker. In many cases, the senior executives of the organization may act as a decision-making team and work out the primary focus of the recovery efforts together. As with the members of the disaster response team, members of executive management may be unavailable. Each executive should have a designated deputy who can step in if the executive is not available.

What happens if the organization does not have a DRP? Many organizations do not have disaster plans. If a disaster strikes the organization, the response and the team that performs the work will have to be created on the spot. In this case, you have no choice but to start with what you have. Find individuals with expertise in the various parts of the business and make them part of the response team. Since no plan exists, it will be up to this team to work out a plan first.

Department Disaster Response Teams

The organization as a whole will have a response team. Each department will eventually be assigned the job of getting back into operation. This means that the details of putting the business back together will fall to the various business units. Each department should have a defined action plan and team based on the detailed DRP of the organization.

The job of the department teams is to focus on the business of the department. The questions that the department teams focus on are

- What capabilities are available to the department?

- What functions can be performed immediately?

- What tools (space, systems, files, supplies) are necessary to bring back some functions?

- What capabilities were lost in the disaster?

- Which employees are available to the department?

- Can the functions of the department be handled by another site? If so, where and which employees are needed to perform the function?

In essence, the department team is performing a damage assessment for the department, and is formulating the plan to respond to the disaster. Once the plan is formulated, the department will implement it.

Assessing Available Skills

One thing to keep in mind about the teams that are being assembled is that all of the necessary skills may not be available within the organization. As part of the DRP process, response and recovery skills that are not present within the organization should have been identified. In any case where the skills are not present, outside assistance should have been identified. For example, if the organization identified system administration as a skill that was not available in sufficient numbers within the organization, the DRP should have identified other sources of this skill (vendors, consultants, contractors, and so on).

The need for some skills may not have been anticipated. For example, if electrical damage was done to a building, it may be necessary to call in electricians to test the electrical system before it can be used. The DRP may have anticipated a building fire but not a severe electrical power surge and therefore it did not identify electricians to call for this purpose. Likewise, the DRP may not have anticipated the fact that the organization's network staff would be unavailable following a disaster. As with the electricians, the needed skills must be identified and a source found as quickly as possible.

Setting Initial Priorities

We will talk more about setting priorities for returning the organization to full capability in the following sections. However, as part of the initial damage assessment and team assembly it is important for the senior management of the organization to set proper priorities.

Clearly, human life is the first priority and nothing that is written in this chapter should lead one to believe otherwise. If there is danger to human life or if there is still human life at risk during a disaster, that must take precedence over the recovery of the organization.

That being said, the organization needs to have a good understanding of its own business and how it functions in order to understand what must be rebuilt first. Rebuilding computer systems may be important (and in some cases fairly easy) but other functions may be more important. Keep in mind as well that the rebuilding of some capabilities will just take time. Replacing machine tools may take months as the tools are ordered from manufacturers. Likewise, replacing a building is not a short-term project but may take many months.

All of these concerns must factor into the priorities of the organization. The response team should look for easy tasks that generate the most return. In some cases, just the reestablishment of phone service may generate significant returns regardless of where the employees are who are using the service.

TIP   Do not try to bite off too much right away. Keep in mind that some tasks may not be able to be completed promptly with a limited staff.

Setting Goals

The goals of final recovery and restoration of the business need to be laid out and they also need to be realistic. As the organization's response to the disaster begins, the executives of the organization should map out the goals for final recovery. It should be realized that final restoration will take time. No one should expect a quick fix to a major disaster.

The goals that should be established for the organization include

- Return of basic operational capability
- Return of secondary organization services
- Return of full operational capability
- Restoration of the organization

For each goal, realistic timelines should be established. These timelines should be based upon the finances of the organization and the amount of time that each type of work will require. In order to get realistic timelines, it will be necessary to conduct a detailed damage assessment while the initial recovery operations are going on.

While it is important to develop the goals and timelines, it should be realized that a lot of information will be required to fully understand what must be done in order to return the organization to full capability. This process should not be rushed but it should proceed with all due speed.

FOLLOWING OR NOT FOLLOWING THE PLAN

Before we get into a discussion about the different phases of disaster recovery, we should take a moment and talk about the DRP. Organizations today are seeing more and more reason to develop their own DRP. That is a good idea and we would encourage every organization to go through the process of developing one. At the very least, the process of developing a DRP allows the organization to identify key assets and to begin planning how it might respond and recover from a disaster.

That being said, now that a disaster has occurred, should the organization follow its plan? It should be a simple answer (yes) but it is often not that simple. For various reasons, the DRP may not have taken into account the disaster at hand. In other cases the DRP may be out of date (DRPs require a fair amount of upkeep and if they are not kept up to date, they may be of little use when a real disaster occurs). A third problem with the DRP may be that it has not been tested and practiced. Once a DRP is written it must be practiced and drilled so that the team understands what is happening and what must be done to get the organization back in operation.

Let me give you an example of a problem with a DRP. Several years ago, a severe ice storm hit the northeastern United States and eastern Canada. Power distribution systems were badly damaged (remember the pictures of big electrical towers bent over by the ice?). Montreal was without power for a significant period of time due to the storm. At the time, an insurance company in Montreal implemented its DRP. They had their primary computer facility in their building in Montreal. While the building had a backup diesel generator, the company was concerned about their ability to supply fuel to keep the generator in operation. The company's DRP called for computer operations to switch to a hot site in the event of a disaster. So the company called the hot site vendor and declared a disaster. Given the situation, they had time to verify that they could move to the hot site as the backup generator was still in operation. During the verification process, they determined that at least one large router had not been accounted for at the hot site. In other words, the DRP and the hot site equipment list had not been kept up to date. The lack of that router would adversely impact their ability to operate from the hot site. They were left with the decision to follow the plan (and thus lack some capabilities) or to not follow the plan (but deal with the issue of getting sufficient fuel for the backup generator). In the end, fuel was not an issue and the company could continue operations.

This example serves to illustrate why an organization may choose not to follow a DRP. This does not mean that your organization should or should not. It only shows that there are reasons, good reasons, why a DRP may not be followed.

PHASES OF A DISASTER

A disaster begins when capabilities of the organization deteriorate. This may happen instantaneously (such as when a tornado strikes a building) or it may happen gradually (such as in the ice storm example in the previous section). Once the disaster begins, the organization moves into four phases of action:

- Response
- Resumption
- Recovery
- Restoration

The following sections of this chapter discuss each phase of the organization's actions. Keep in mind that the timetable for each phase is indeterminate and is completely dependent on the actual events. In some cases, phases may overlap.

Response

The response phase of a disaster is the immediate reaction by the organization to an emergency situation. During this phase, the employees of the organization are taking steps to limit damage and contain the disaster. In most cases, the ability of the organization to control the disaster is limited and outside assistance is required.

Response Objectives

The primary objectives of the response phase of a disaster are to

- Limit human injury
- Limit damage to the organization
- Contain the disaster as much as possible
- Make an initial assessment as to the extent of the damage
- Determine the amount of activity required to contain and control the disaster

As was stated before, it is clear that the safety of employees and the prevention of injury or death is the most important activity. Once that has been achieved, the organization must attempt to control and contain the damage. This is done by quickly identifying the type of disaster and calling for appropriate emergency assistance.

The key to the objectives of this phase is to identify the emergency and contain or control the event to minimize damage. At this point, the organization does not have sufficient information to begin recovery efforts. It should be noted that most IT DRPs do not cover the issues of human life and injury. This is appropriate but it should also be understood that these will be key issues during the initial response phase of a disaster.

Response Tasks

In the response phase, several tasks are required of employees of the organization:

- Identifying the disaster
- Providing notification to other employees of potential danger
- Beginning the predefined emergency plans (evacuation, movement to shelters, and so on)
- Identifying the extent of the disaster (amount of the building involved, for example)
- Calling for proper emergency response assistance to contain and control the disaster
- Conducting a damage assessment as the situation is contained
- Assembling the response team

Realism needs to play a big role in the response phase of a disaster. The initial reaction of employees may be to panic or run. The organization (as a whole) needs to provide an initial assessment of the extent of the disaster (is a single room on fire or is the whole building involved). In the vast majority of cases, emergency assistance should be called. It is unrealistic to assume that employees will fight a fire without the assistance of the fire department.

Once the emergency situation is contained (the fire is under control, tornado has passed, and so on) the organization needs to conduct a damage assessment. This means identifying all of the capabilities of the organization that were lost or damaged during the emergency. At the same time, the response team needs to be identified and assembled so that initial planning and prioritization can begin.

Scenario

To illustrate the various phases of a disaster, let's take a look at a fictional but potentially real scenario. ABC Company has offices on the third floor of a ten-story building. ABC Company designs systems for waste water treatment but manufactures nothing. The company offices contain administrative functions and offices for the engineering staff. Many of the engineers work at various client locations but they rely on the computer systems housed in the data center at the ABC Company headquarters.

One day, an employee notices smoke on the third floor. The smoke seems to be coming from the offices of another tenant in the building. The employee attempts to enter the other office space but cannot since the door is locked. She pulls the fire alarm and heads to the ABC Company offices to get everyone out of the building.

If we apply the objectives of the response phase to this example, we see that the first objective is to protect human life. Getting everyone out of the building is the most appropriate way to do this. Emergency assistance is also sought and the fire alarm is pulled to summon the fire department.

The fire department arrives to find the third floor of the building highly involved in a fire. While the fire department works, ABC Company can only guess as to the damage to their own offices by the location of the smoke. They can see that some of their office space is involved but they don't know how much.

After several hours, the fire is out but the fire marshal will not allow anyone on to the third floor of the building. The entire building must be checked for structural integrity. Therefore, ABC Company must assume the worst and determine that the entire office space has been damaged and is now unusable.

Resumption

During the resumption phase of a disaster, the organization begins the process of resuming operations. Only the most important capabilities are returned to operation during this phase. The organization must prioritize its actions as not everything can be done at once. It is possible that the resumption phase may begin while the initial response to the disaster is continuing. For example, if an organization has a hot site capability, this may be invoked while a fire is still being fought in the original building.

Resumption Objectives

The objective of the resumption phase is to identify and bring back online the most important and time-sensitive capabilities of the organization.

In the resumption phase, we are moving from the initial emergency reaction to the disaster to the beginning of restoring services and capabilities. Ideally, the identification of the primary capabilities will have been done in a DRP prior to the occurrence of a disaster. If not, identification must be performed on the fly.

Resumption Key Tasks

The key tasks during the resumption phase of a disaster include

- Identifying the key capabilities and functions of the organization
- Prioritizing the capabilities and functions of the organization
- Identifying strategies for bringing back the most time-sensitive functions
- Implementing the strategies

As noted above, the development of the DRP should have identified the key functions and capabilities of the organization and prioritized the resumption of these services. If not, the organization must set about identifying the most time-sensitive capabilities.

Once identified, strategies must be developed to resume operation. Again, if the DRP has been developed properly, options for the resumption of these operations should be defined. These may include alternative locations, additional computer and communication systems, as well as locations for employees.

Scenario

Now to continue the scenario with ABC Company. The president of the company could see from the smoke billowing out of the building that the office space would be unusable for some period of time. So even before the fire was extinguished, he implemented the organization's DRP.

During the development of the DRP, ABC Company had identified the most critical functions as being:

- Remote access to files by on-site engineers
- Telephone service to allow engineers to contact clients
- E-mail service to allow engineers to send files, reports, and designs to clients and to allow clients to send feedback and requirements to the engineers

ABC Company was small and could not afford a hot site but they were able to contract for some additional services with their Internet Service Provider (ISP) in case of an emergency. In the event that the building suffered some sort of disaster, ABC Company had worked out a deal with the ISP to provide a secondary mail server as well as a Web server with additional disk space to provide access to some files for remote engineers.

The president of ABC Company told his IT staff to call the ISP and tell them of the fire and invoke the additional service. The IT staff headed off to retrieve a recent backup tape from an off-site location (bank safety deposit box) and get to the ISP. The president had other employees contact all of the off-site engineers and tell them of the fire and to wait for word from the IT staff as to how to access the files. Any of the engineers who were at the headquarters site were sent home to continue work as if they were at remote locations.

The other objective was restoration of phone service to clients. Each engineer had a cellular phone so they could use that for access. ABC Company also made sure that an up–to-date phone list was provided to all employees and that electronic copies of the phone list were available with the backup tapes. Within four hours, the critical functions of the organization were available.

Recovery

During the recovery phase of a disaster, the organization implements expanded operations by bringing online less time-sensitive functions and capabilities. It should be noted that these functions and capabilities are necessary for the survival of the organization. They are not included in the initial set of functions to be reconstituted only because they can suffer some amount of downtime without a severe detrimental effect on the organization as a whole.

Recovery Objectives

The objective of the recovery phase is to restore the less time-sensitive functions of the organization to operation.

The organization will not return to normal business operation during this phase but the vast majority of functions and capabilities will be available. This may mean that the organization identifies and uses alternative space or that the organization is split between multiple locations. In any case, by the end of this phase, the operations of the organization are available and the organization is doing business.

Recovery Key Tasks

The key tasks of the recovery phase include

- Identifying alternative locations for employees
- Restoring voice and data communication services
- Restoring non-critical business functions
- Replacing (either temporarily or permanently) lost assets and employees

During the recovery phase of a disaster, the tasks are focused on returning some semblance of normalcy to the organization's operations. Some location is provided for the organization. This may mean temporary space such as office trailers or even unfinished office space with desks. The intent is to return the organization as a whole to normal functionality. Accounting, human resources, and other support departments begin to function again.

Communication systems are reconstituted at the new location. Usually, the organization's phone numbers can be connected in the new location or can be forwarded to new numbers. The same is true for data communications. Assets that were damaged or destroyed in the disaster are beginning to be replaced (part of this may be from insurance). The same is true for employees that left the organization during the disaster.

CHALLENGE

The data center had been in the basement of the building. It had been, at least until the water pipe on the main floor burst. The organization's disaster team had responded and moved critical functions to other locations (two systems were in an office on the third floor and a third system was now working out of another office). It has been 24 hours since the pipe burst and water is still being pumped out of the basement.

As part of the work of the disaster team, the equipment in the data center has been evaluated (when the water was pumped low enough, the team waded into the data center). All of the equipment in the center has at least some water damage. Several systems were completely underwater for several hours.

How do you begin the work of recovery? What is your first step? Who needs to be involved?

In this particular case, no employees were lost or displaced (all employee offices were above the flood). Some office functions were disrupted (the elevators are not working, for example) but the building is not badly damaged. Several non-critical systems must be recovered, including a file and print server as well as an e-mail system. The backup tapes had been moved offsite so they will need to be brought back on site. The most difficult part of this particular recovery operation will be the network. The organization had been using a Cisco Catalyst switch and it was located at the bottom of one of the racks in the data center. It is still somewhat submerged. Therefore, some amount of network equipment will be needed in addition to the servers.

Scenario

ABC Company was able to restore critical capabilities within four hours of the disaster. Further information from the owner of the building indicated that the third floor would be unusable for at least six and possibly as long as twelve months due to fire, water, and smoke damage. This meant that some temporary office space would be required.

ABC Company found temporary space in a building a few blocks away. Insurance provided funds for new computer equipment, and office furniture was acquired. While the space was a little small for the company, it was available and that was the important part. The IT department rebuilt the network and computer systems and the employees moved into the temporary office space within two weeks of the fire. Due to space constraints, most of the engineers continued to work remotely.

The new location was not what ABC Company would have liked but it did allow the company to function again and continue in business. Other than the lack of space, about the only thing the temporary space was not good for was showing to clients. That would have to wait for restoration.

Restoration

The final restoration of all business functions and capabilities does not come until the final phase of a disaster. During the restoration phase, the organization finally puts itself and its operations back together again. This may not be exactly how the organization was prior to the disaster. Some organizations end up with new buildings or in different space after a disaster. Some organizations may end up losing some functions or business.

Restoration Objectives

The objectives of the restoration phase of a disaster include

- Returning the organization to permanent quarters
- Returning the organization to normal business operations

In the resumption and recovery phases of the disaster, the organization first identified the most critical functions of its business and then returned the remaining necessary functions. In some cases, this may have been the return of the entire business but in most cases, the organization has left something out, whether that be amount of space, location of various departments, or the type of space. Now in the restoration phase, the remaining issues or nice-to-haves are returned to the organization.

Restoration Key Tasks

In the final restoration phase of a disaster, key tasks may include

- Moving to permanent space
- Reestablishing work-flow throughout the organization
- Acquiring permanent replacement furniture and fixtures
- Reestablishing permanent voice and data communications

As the objectives for this phase are to move the organization back to normalcy, the tasks are to complete the final moves and acquisitions to allow the business to function normally. The movement to permanent space or back to the original space if it is available is a key part of restoration. The permanent space for the organization will provide the ability to reestablish business processes that were interrupted by the disaster.

Equipment, furniture, and fixtures are replaced and installed in the permanent space. For some organizations (like manufacturers) this may signal the first time that business can even be conducted since the disaster occurred. If the proper voice and data communication systems have not been restored to this point, they are implemented in a manner appropriate for the organization.

Scenario

Eight months after the fire, ABC Company was finally able to move back to their third floor office space. The office was remodeled and all of the employees could fit into the space once again. The president was very happy to be able to entertain and meet with clients in his company's office space once again.

With the final restoration, the company could function properly again. While in temporary space, many of the engineers were working remotely and thus had little face time with employees in other departments. This did not allow for work to proceed efficiently. With the final restoration of the company, the business processes normally in place were returned to operation.

In this example, the entire disaster took eight months to play out. While some may think that a disaster is a short-term event, disasters usually have long-term implications for organizations.

CHECKLIST: KEY POINTS IN DISASTER RESPONSE

The following is a checklist for the key points in disaster response:

- ☐ Provide information to emergency responders
- ☐ Assess the damage to the organization
- ☐ Determine the status of employees
- ☐ Determine the status of the building
- ☐ Determine the status of key areas in the building
- ☐ Determine the status of key systems
- ☐ Determine the status of power
- ☐ Determine the status of water
- ☐ Determine the status of communications
- ☐ Assemble (identify members if necessary) the disaster response team
- ☐ Define departmental teams
- ☐ Assess available skills

- ☐ Set initial priorities
- ☐ Set long-term goals for the organization
- ☐ Determine if the organization's DRP can be used
- ☐ Implement strategies to restore the organization's critical capabilities
- ☐ Restore the organization's less critical capabilities
- ☐ Identify temporary space
- ☐ Return the organization to permanent space
- ☐ Return operations to normal
- ☐ Replace furniture, fixtures, and equipment

PART V

Appendixes

APPENDIX A

Handling Audits

Audits are a fact of life in organizations. Often, the members of the organization fear audits. This is often caused by the unknown aspects of the audit: What will it cover? What will they look for? Will it affect my job? In our experience with organizations of all sizes, audits should not be feared but used as another tool to help the organization manage risk.

Why do organizations have audits? Most often, an audit is performed in response to some outside stimulus. For public corporations, audits are required so that shareholders can see that the financial statements are correct. Other organizations conduct audits in response to customer requests or other types of regulation.

Many of these audits will have a technology or security portion in addition to the primary financial focus. Other audits (such as the SAS70 or an ISO 17799 audit) have a focus outside of the financial arena. In either case, the IT and security departments will be part of the audit. This is done to make sure that the controls around the financial systems or around the organization are appropriate.

In this appendix, we will examine how the security department should deal with audits. We hope that this information will be useful in reducing the tension of an audit and that it will show security managers how to work with auditors to help manage the risk of the organization.

BEING PART OF THE TEAM

Before we begin to talk in detail about the various types of audits, we should talk about the attitude surrounding the audit process. Often, when an audit is announced, the IT and security staffs look at the announcement as a challenge to their work and skills. Another frequent reaction is fear: "The auditors are out to get me or they are going to report me to management and make me look bad."

Neither of these reactions is appropriate. They may be human nature but that does not make them right. The auditors have a job to do and every auditor that we have been in contact with has been professional. Auditors are not out to get anyone. They are out to do the best job they can and to help manage the risk to the organization.

With this in mind, let's take a closer look at the audit process and how the security department can work with the auditors to provide appropriate information. Figure A-1 shows a flow diagram of the audit process. We will take a look at each of the steps in the process in a little more detail.

Information Gathering

The auditor assigned to the project will need information. Thus, during the audit one of the tasks that the auditor will perform is to talk to individuals who have the information he or she needs. During the information gathering process, the auditor is likely to ask a lot of pointed questions. In doing this, the auditor is performing his duties. He is not trying to get you to slip up or get yourself in trouble. Very often the auditor is working from a checklist of items.

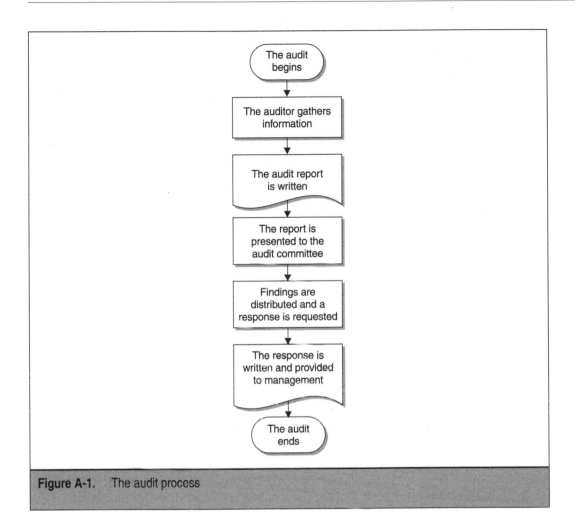

Figure A-1. The audit process

The security manager or staff member who is answering these questions should be honest and up-front with the auditor. Do not try to be evasive.

Audit Report

Once enough information has been gathered by the auditors, the information will be analyzed and a report will be written. This report will be in the form of findings. A *finding* is a discussion of what the auditors found during the information-gathering phase of the project. Each finding should discuss the issue that was uncovered as well as a recommendation as to how to correct the situation.

This audit report will be presented to the audit committee of the organization's board of directors. By its very nature, a presentation at this level of the organization will have an effect on how the organization will do business.

Audit Response

In most cases, the audit committee will require a response from the various departments in the organization. Many audit reports cover more than just IT or security issues and therefore many of the responses will be expected to come from departments other than IT and security. Let's focus on the security response at this point.

The audit report will likely identify several issues for security to deal with. The security department must examine the issues and develop an appropriate response to management. Some of the issues may not be areas of significant risk to the organization but it is important for the security department to provide details as to why certain actions will or will not be taken to correct the issue. If the security department does not agree that an issue is a risk, this should be stated clearly along with the reasons why the security department feels this way.

INTERNAL AUDITS

Many organizations have internal audit staffs. The purpose of this staff is to provide the organization with an independent internal view of potential issues within the organization. In other words, this staff is part of the risk management plan of the organization. It is a tool that can be used to protect the organization from internal problems.

Given that internal audit is part of the organization's risk management plan, there is no reason to believe that internal auditors have anything but the organization's best interests in mind as they perform their jobs. This means that the internal auditors are not out to get you. They are working to help manage the risk to the organization.

To you as the security manager or security staff person, this means that internal auditors are your friends. Internal audit has visibility to the board of the organization. Any problem that an internal auditor finds will be provided in their audit report to the board. When the internal auditor comes to you to ask questions and gather information, comply as completely as possible.

 SECURITY ALERT!   Never try to hide problems or information from an internal auditor. It is likely that they will find the information without your help and the fact that you tried to hide the information may cast you in a poor light.

Internal auditors have differing skills. Some are primarily financial auditors while others specialize in technology and technology audits. Security is usually seen as part of the technology realm of the organization and thus you are likely to have more interaction with technology or IT auditors. If your organization does not have sufficient resources to have both, you will have audits performed by the financial auditor. In such situations take the time to work with the auditor and educate him on security issues and controls. This will make the auditor more familiar with the issues that you face and will help you in the long run.

There are two primary reasons that an internal auditor will conduct an audit: it is a regularly scheduled audit or it is an audit in response to a problem. Let's take a closer look at each of these occasions.

Regularly Scheduled Audits

Most internal audit departments develop a schedule of audits to perform over the course of a year. This plan is usually approved by the board's audit committee and therefore the auditors have little freedom to change the schedule. The schedule is also usually confidential so that departments are unaware of when they will be audited.

The scheduled audits can be very specific or very general in focus. For example, a financial audit may examine all accounts receivable or a technology audit may examine back-up procedures in the data center. In either case, the auditors are looking to see if the organization is in compliance with its own policies and procedures and also to determine if the existing policies and procedures are appropriate for the organization (in other words if the policies and procedures are in accordance with acceptable practice).

When an internal audit is complete, the resulting report is sent to the audit committee. You may not see the report. If the audit committee wants a response, they will provide the relevant sections of the report to you via your manager and ask for a response or direct changes that must be made.

Audits in Response to a Problem

A second reason for an internal audit is a problem. This may be a financial problem or a problem on some internal systems. If the organization's senior management or board learns of a problem that may compromise financial information or regulatory compliance, it may direct internal audit to conduct a special audit of the problem.

As part of the security department, you may not learn the reason for a special audit. However, if a computer security incident were to occur, the investigation of the event may be given to internal audit. This is not to say that internal audit will run the incident response but rather once the immediate incident is over, internal audit may be asked to examine why the event occurred or to determine if the event may cause a financial or regulatory problem.

If this type of audit occurs, the information that you gathered during the incident will be needed by the auditor. This means that any of the documentation that your team created during the response could be valuable to the auditor. This information should be given to the auditor.

TIP Make copies of the notebooks that the team used during the incident as well as the final incident report. Keep the original notebooks locked up in case you need them in the future.

The report of this type of audit will also be given to the board. They may decide to ask for a response, depending on what the report says.

No matter the reason for the audit, the auditors of the organization are there to assist in the management of risk. This function is the same as yours and it is important for you to work with internal audit not against them.

EXTERNAL AUDITS

In our experience, external audits always seem to cause greater apprehension than internal audits. Perhaps this is because the external audits get more attention from senior management or perhaps it is the idea of some outsiders looking for problems. Whatever the cause, it helps to understand what the auditors are looking for so that you can work with them effectively.

TIP   Before an outside auditing firm comes in to perform an audit, conduct a mock audit yourself to see what areas the auditors are likely to focus on.

There are two primary types of external audits that a security department is likely to see. First, there will be computer security audits that occur as part of a financial audit of the organization. Secondly, there are specific SAS70 audits that may be performed primarily against the IT and security departments of the organization. Both of these audits will be performed by Certified Public Accounting (CPA) firms. The following sections examine each type of audit and will cover what to expect.

Financial Audits

The audit committee of the organization's board of directors will hire a CPA firm (with the approval of the shareholders) to audit the books of the organization. This will happen for any publicly traded organization and may happen at private firms. In any case, the primary focus of this audit is the books of the organization.

If this is the case, why will the auditors talk to the IT and security departments? The answer to this question is pretty obvious when you think about it a bit. Most, if not all, of the organization's financial records can be found on computer systems. If the financial records are to reflect the true financial state of the organization, they must be correct. This means that the computer systems must have some security controls to protect the financial information from unauthorized modification. At the same time, the systems must be available and the information must be safeguarded from destruction or loss. This means that backups and disaster recovery are important aspects as well.

What to Expect in the Audit

As was mentioned, the focus of the audit is the financial records of the organization. The examination of the computer systems and the controls around the financial records, while part of the audit, is actually a secondary examination in support of the examination of financial records. Therefore, it is unlikely that a team of auditors will descend upon the IT and security departments. Generally, only one or two auditors will come by to ask questions.

The auditors will talk to the security department about policy and security controls. This will cover everything from the existence of a policy to who has the authority and responsibility to see that the policy is actually followed. Expect to be asked about the mechanisms that you use to ensure policy compliance.

The auditors will also speak with the system administration staff who control the financial systems. Here they will be asking similar questions as they asked of the security department. This does not mean that they are checking your answers but they want to see the operational perspective of the security controls as well as the policy perspective.

TIP Before the auditors arrive, sit down with the system administrators and make sure you understand how policies are implemented on the various systems. This way you will be less likely to say something that is not actually how security is implemented on the systems.

Some auditors may run tools against the financial systems to look for inappropriate configurations and vulnerabilities. Some of the tools that may be used include

- ISS Internet Scanner
- Bindview
- Intrusion.com SecurityAnalyst
- Symantec Enterprise Security Manager
- Nessus
- Pentasafe Audit Express

Depending on the tool, the results may show system vulnerabilities (Nessus, ISS, Pentasafe) or policy configuration issues (Bindview, Kane, Symantec, Pentasafe). Keep in mind that the policy configuration issues may not be directly related to the organization's security policy. The auditors may use a configuration that reflects their understanding of proper security configurations. Many of these tools will also discover user accounts, group memberships, and dormant accounts. Expect the auditors to identify what they feel are inappropriate group memberships.

As the auditor is gathering information, do not be afraid to volunteer information about controls that may mitigate a security risk. For example, if a system has a weak authentication mechanism, the auditor may find this to be a problem. If this system is in the data center and only accessible by a limited number of individuals due to the physical controls around the data center, you should bring this information to the attention of the auditor.

Results of the Audit

The results of the audit will be provided in report format to the audit committee of the board. It is very unlikely that you will see the full report. If the board feels it appropriate to show anyone the results, they will likely come as excerpts so that you will only see issues or findings associated with your area of responsibility.

If the board shows any part of the report to you, they will likely ask for a response to the findings. We will discuss more about writing an appropriate response in "Security's Response to the Audit," later in this chapter.

SAS-70

A SAS-70 is an audit that must be conducted by a public accounting firm, and the team that performs the audit must be made up of and supervised by CPAs. That being said, many firms require SAS-70s to be performed because they process financial transactions on behalf of other institutions.

The SAS-70 is a specialized report format that was developed by the American Institute of Certified Public Accountants (AICPA). The format was specifically targeted at determining the adequacy of an organization's internal controls as part of its service offering. The report covers the following areas:

- Physical security
- Personnel management
- Logical access controls
- Environmental controls
- Change management process
- Policy and procedure
- Continuity planning and disaster recovery
- Problem reporting and management process
- Event monitoring

Organizations that need to have SAS-70s performed will generally have them done once a year. The final report will need to be made available to some customers and regulators.

Physical Security

The examination of physical security is focused on the physical security controls that surround the facility and the computer systems used to provide the service. The auditors will look for the following items:

- Identification badges on all personnel
- Restriction of sensitive areas to authorized individuals
- Escorting of visitors
- Logging of visitors

Personnel Management

The auditors will examine the ways in which the organization checks up on its own personnel and employees. This is not to say that the organization should not trust its own employees but that it should take pains to determine the trustworthiness of its employees and to not put them into positions where a mistake can cause inappropriate damage to the organization or a customer.

When examining personnel management issues, the auditors will look for:

- Background checks performed during the hiring process
- Non-disclosure agreements with employees and contractors
- Separation of duties among employees and contractors

Notice that some of these items apply to contractors as well as employees. The auditors will be looking at the management of any individuals who may adversely affect the information of the organization or information held in trust by the organization.

Logical Access Controls

Logical access controls determine which individuals have access to what information. Some of the items examined here are mechanisms in place on computer and network systems and some pertain to the overall architecture of the offerings provided by the organization. Some of the items that will be investigated include

- Individuals who have access to client information
- Individuals with privileged access to network devices such as firewalls and routers and computer systems
- Appropriateness of individual access to job function
- Appropriateness of user management procedures to identify dormant and unused accounts and to determine individual access
- Restriction of customer access to prevent the sharing of information
- Mechanisms in place to prevent unauthorized access to client information (both with regard to other clients and employees)

The information that is necessary to evaluate these issues is not solely related to the controls on the computer systems. The auditors will need to understand the underlying architecture that separates sensitive information and the procedures used by the organization to manage user access effectively.

Environmental Controls

The environment of the data center will come under scrutiny as well. Not only will the auditors examine the physical access controls to the data center but they will also examine the suitability of the data center to house sensitive information and systems. As such the following items are examined

- The structure of the walls, ceiling, and floor
- The security of the wiring
- Fire suppression
- Environmental controls
- Power

The auditors will look for ways of using the lack of controls to either access sensitive areas or information and the ability of the systems to continue to function during adverse conditions.

Change Management Process

The change management process of an organization can affect the operations of the customer systems dramatically. For example, if a proper change management process does not exist, developers may make changes to production systems without proper testing, thus allowing untested code to make changes to production data.

As part of the SAS-70, the auditors will examine the following:

- The development methodology and the procedures for moving a system from development through testing and into production
- The testing environment (specifically if it is different than the production environment)
- How new developments are documented and whether this documentation carries on through to production
- The approval process for all changes

The scope of the change management process section is rather broad. The auditors will be looking for a documented development methodology and process.

Policy and Procedure

Policies and procedures are examined for two reasons—first, to see that they do in fact exist, and second, they are compared with the actual process to determine if they are actually followed. The auditors will look for documented policies and procedures in the following areas:

- Physical and logical access controls
- Hiring practices

- Change management
- Disaster recovery and continuity planning
- Problem reporting and incident management

Note how the areas where policies are examined mimic the areas where actual processes are examined.

Continuity Planning and Disaster Recovery

There are two parts to the continuity planning section of the audit: the plans for a disaster and the backups necessary to prevent the loss of information. The auditor will look to see how the organization will maintain operations for itself and its customers should a serious event occur. This means that the organization needs to have good plans as well as good backups.

The following items will be examined for disaster recovery:

- The formal disaster recovery plan
- Timelines for recovery matched against various types of disasters
- The availability of redundant facilities and systems
- The testing of the plan

The following items will be examined with regard to backups:

- The frequency of backups
- The information that is backed up
- The storage of the media
- The security around the media
- Media retention periods
- The segregation of the media of different clients

Problem Reporting and Management Process

Problem reporting does not mean responding only to security incidents. It means any type of problem be it security, system, or software. The way that the organization deals with the problems and learns from them is key. In this vein, the auditors will look at the following:

- How problems are tracked
- The information recorded about problems
- The process for approving the resolution of the problem before closing out the report

It should be noted that this process is closely linked with the change management process.

Event Monitoring

Another way to characterize this category is the protection of the system audit trails. The auditors will be looking for the organization's ability to determine what happened. In this vein, they will examine the following:

- What is logged on routers, firewalls, and systems
- Whether the audit logs are ever reviewed and if so, how
- Whether the logs can be tampered with and if so, will the tampering go unnoticed
- Who examines the logs
- How long the logs are kept

The audit trails and logs from systems are maintained so that the organization can review what has happened. If the logs are never reviewed, serious events may go unnoticed for significant periods of time. Likewise, if the people whose actions are being logged are the reviewers of the information, they will have the opportunity to potentially change a log to hide their actions.

SECURITY'S RESPONSE TO THE AUDIT

Several times in this appendix we have mentioned that security may be asked to write a response to an audit report. Let's talk about how that response should be written. We should also be clear that some of the findings in an audit report will be things that security will agree with while other findings may be things that security will disagree with.

If the item is something that security agrees with, then the finding itself is not in dispute. Perhaps it is an area of risk that security has identified but has been unable to manage appropriately due to budget considerations (there are a number of other reasons as well). In this case, security should note that it agrees with the finding and define a specific task or set of tasks that may be accomplished to manage the risk. If resources are needed to accomplish this, they should be clearly spelled out as well as any time frames that are reasonable to meet. This type of response can than translate into projects for the security department and begin to fill the following year's budget requests. It should be noted that some items may be important enough that they must be accomplished immediately. Any such issue must be brought to the attention of management as quickly as possible.

Items that security disagrees with the auditors about must be dealt with carefully. The response needs to be written so that the organization's management understands the issue and why security does not agree with the finding. At the same time, security must word the response in such a way that it does not appear that the security department is protecting itself from criticism. Security must clearly explain the issue and identify other controls that help to manage the risk. It may also be necessary to show how a large added cost to comply will not significantly reduce the risk to the organization or that the added cost is not justified by the risk.

No matter what type of response is called for from security, it is an opportunity for security to show how it can help manage the risk to the organization.

CHECKLIST: KEY POINTS IN HANDLING AUDITS

The following is a checklist of key steps in handling audits:

- ☐ Look at auditors as part of the risk management team of the organization.
- ☐ Help the auditor gather information.
- ☐ Do not expect to see the audit report.
- ☐ If asked for a response, provide it promptly.
- ☐ Work with internal audit to identify key risks for the organization.
- ☐ If an external audit is expected, talk with system administrators to learn how they are implementing security policies and procedures.
- ☐ Conduct a mock audit before a real one to identify potential findings.
- ☐ When writing a response, identify projects that can manage risk identified in the audit findings.
- ☐ If you disagree with a finding, make sure to clearly state your objections and your measurement of the risk.

APPENDIX B

Outsourcing Security

The outsourcing of security has become a lively topic recently. Many new security firms exist that sell some type of service. The outsourcing of security by an organization may be a cost-effective way to fulfill the responsibilities of the security department or it may actually increase the overall security risk to the organization.

As with any type of outsourcing, it is important for the organization to carefully define what type of services are desired and how they can best be accomplished. An outsourcing arrangement can only be successful if the company doing the outsourcing understands *exactly* what their security issues and risks are. Outsourcing can't be successfully done with the expectation that all the company has to do is sign a PO. Outsourcing certainly has the potential to help an organization manage its security risk and this appendix will discuss the issues surrounding outsourcing security services.

SERVICES TO OUTSOURCE

Not every type of security service is appropriate to outsource for every organization. The reason that an organization chooses to outsource some services (see "Reasons for Outsourcing," later in this appendix) will affect the types of services that may be outsourced for that organization. Before we consider the reasons to outsource, let's talk about the various services that may be candidates for outsourcing.

Figure B-1 shows a representation of different types of security services and how they are provided. Please note that this characterization of security has almost nothing to do with how the services manage risk but instead how the service is provided to the organization.

TIP It is important to recognize that the delivery of the service is important. Different organizations like to receive services differently. For example, some organizations might prefer to have employees actually attend security awareness training while other organizations might prefer some type of computer-based training. This preference will influence the type of delivery the organization will opt for and thus the security department needs to understand the organization's preference.

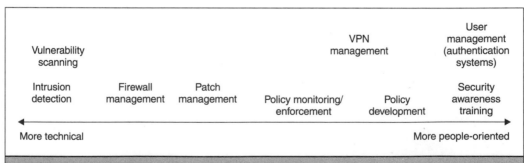

Figure B-1. Technical vs. people services: how the security service is provided to the organization

"Technical" Security Services

We will define "technical" security services as those that can be provided in a mostly automated, analytical manner. In other words, these are services that can be automated to a large extent. No service can be provided without any human intervention but technical security services tend not to require much in the way of interaction with the organization's employees.

Some examples of very technical security services include

- Monitoring intrusion detection systems and alerting on certain types of events
- Periodically scanning systems for vulnerabilities and reporting the results
- Managing firewalls by monitoring the firewall logs and making changes to rule sets in response to a request from the organization
- Managing incident response
- Performing forensics

If you examine these examples closely, you can see that the service provider will have to interact with the organization's security or IT departments, but the vast majority of the organization's employees will have no interaction with the service provider. Therefore, the ability of the provider to properly interact with employees is not necessary (obviously, the service provider must work with the security or IT department in an appropriate manner). The focus is on the service provider's ability to perform the technical function.

"People" Security Services

"People" security services are those services that require a large amount of interaction between the organization's employees and the service provider. The ability of the service provider to properly handle employees by showing proper respect and by being sensitive to the needs of the employees may be the most important part of the service provider's job.

Some services such as security awareness training and the management of user authentication systems will require daily interaction between the service provider and the employees of the organization. If either type of service is to be successful, the employees must feel that they are listened to and understood. If this is not the case, a significant number of complaints will find their way to the ears of management.

Other services, such as policy development will require the service provider to have a good working relationship with some employees. In the case of policy development, the success of the policy may rely on the fact that employees are consulted and made to feel like they contributed to the project.

CHOOSING WHAT TO OUTSOURCE

The first question to ask when looking to outsource security services is: "Why do I want to outsource my security?" Keep in mind that there are many security service providers and you will be able to find a vendor to provide just about every type of security service that you might need up to and including outsourcing the entire security department.

In the end, any decision to outsource security services should match the risk management goals of the organization. In other words, the use of a security services vendor should help the organization manage its information security risk.

Reasons for Outsourcing

When it comes right down to it, there is really only one reason for outsourcing security and that is better risk management. That being said, if we break down this reason, we can see that there are three primary factors: reduced costs, better expertise, or some requirement for a third-party examination.

Costs

The reduction in cost is an easy reason to understand. An organization feels that they can reduce expenses by outsourcing and yet still provide the same security services. Thus information security risk is managed and the costs to the organization are reduced.

Keep in mind that organizations should compare like service levels to compare costs (see Figure B-2). If the organization was paying $1,000 per month for a part-time intrusion detection analyst, it would not appear cost-effective to outsource the management of the intrusion detection for $2,000 per month. However, the vendor is providing 24/7 coverage and a 15-minute guaranteed response to any serious event. In order for the organization to provide the same coverage it would require significantly more than the $1,000 per month that it is currently paying.

Before the costs can truly be compared, the organization must define the level of service that it requires and compare what it would cost to provide that service internally with what a vendor would charge to provide the service. When you define what is

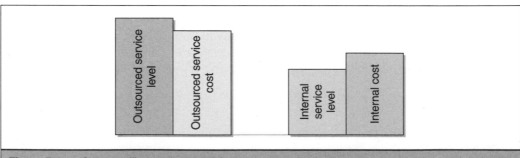

Figure B-2.   Compare like service levels for proper cost comparison

required, try to define the service needed in a realistic manner. If your organization has no means to respond to a security alert in the middle of the night, does it really pay to find a vendor who can provide 24/7 coverage? Or does this mean that you will need the vendor to provide not only the alert but the response during the night as well?

Expertise

The second reason that an organization may choose to outsource security services is lack of expertise within the organization. This is not to say that the internal staff is incapable of performing the task, but that the organization may see the time and resources necessary to perform the task more efficiently spent elsewhere.

In this case, the organization is looking for a vendor who can provide the expertise necessary much faster than the organization could build it organically. This situation may also occur with regard to a specific product (as opposed to a specific type of expertise). Of course, the vendor will have to provide the service at a reasonable cost to the organization for this to be worthwhile. Assuming that the costs are not out of line, the organization sees the vendor as an expert in providing the particular service.

Third-Party Examination

Many organizations are faced with customers or regulators who require some form of third-party examination to verify that security is being performed properly. This requirement may come from insurance providers, customers (who wish to make sure that the organization is safeguarding their information or systems), or regulators on the part of the general public.

In any case, the organization requires some form of third-party validation or examination to prove that they are handling security properly. The security services provider can be the third party that provides this validation. The organization may provide reports generated by the vendor to clients or auditors to show the level of security of the organization.

Costs Involved in Outsourcing

Since it is hard to get something for nothing, we must talk about the costs involved in outsourcing security services. There will be some direct costs to be paid to the vendor. However, there will also be some indirect costs that the organization will have to bear.

Direct Costs

So how much should it cost to outsource security services? It depends on the types of service and the service-level agreements that are provided by the vendor. At the time of this writing, the cost for the management of a single intrusion detection system or firewall is approximately $1,500 per month (this is based on offerings that are available). Please note that this is an estimate. Various vendors charge differently for service. Some will be higher and some will be lower. Look very carefully at the type of service that will be provided.

Prices will also vary depending on how much of the equipment and software is provided by the vendor. If the vendor is providing both the hardware and the software for the managed device, expect to pay significantly more per month to cover the cost of the hardware and software.

Indirect Costs

Any organization that outsources security services will also incur indirect costs associated with the services. By indirect costs, we are talking of costs that are not paid directly to the vendor. These are things that are required in order to have a good relationship with the vendor and to use the services that are provided.

As an example, some vendors may require special communication paths. This may mean that the organization will have to pay for a leased line between the organization's network and the vendor. Some vendors may roll this into their monthly fee but others may not.

There will also be the costs of managing the vendor. It makes no sense for an organization to pay for security services from a vendor and then leave the vendor to its own devices. The type of management that we are speaking of will vary with the type of service that is provided, but let's look at a few examples.

In the case of managed intrusion detection systems, the vendor will provide information back to the organization about the types of events that are being seen. Some will come in the form of a regular report while others will come in the form of emergency notifications. The organization will have to identify specific points of contact to respond to emergencies (for obvious reasons) and the organization will also need to designate someone to receive and review the reports. While this will generally take less time than managing the IDS in the first place, there is still time that needs to be spent (and thus a cost that must be incurred).

If an organization chooses to outsource the development and delivery of security awareness training, someone must manage the project and act as a liaison between the vendor and the employees. When the vendor delivers the training material, someone must review the material and make sure that it is appropriate. During the training, someone must determine if the vendor is providing the training in an appropriate manner.

Clearly, there are indirect costs associated with the outsourcing of security services. When an organization calculates the cost of the services, these costs should be factored into the equation.

Back to Risk Management

In the final analysis, the reasons to outsource any security service need to come back to the management of risk to the organization. If the outsourcing of a particular service does not help in the management of risk, then there is little reason to do it (we will grant that a simple reduction in cost may also be worth doing but this is a decision that the organization must make during budgeting).

The question then is, how does outsourcing help the organization in the management of risk? Outsourcing can help in a number of ways, such as:

- Increasing the level of service and thus reducing potential gaps in coverage
- Increasing the expertise of the operators or analysts
- Increasing the pace of a project by providing additional resources
- Increasing the employees' confidence or knowledge by showing greater knowledge or expertise than is available within the organization
- Decreasing gaps in knowledge of existing security countermeasures by providing an unbiased eye

The organization that is thinking about outsourcing security should carefully examine the risks to the organization and act accordingly. It is also possible that outsourcing security services may increase the risks to the organization in some ways. For example, employees of the vendor may now be able to see sensitive information. The employees of the vendor may not undergo the same background checks as those the organization requires and thus the organization may be open to additional risk of information compromise. All of this must be taken into consideration during the process of outsourcing security services.

 SECURITY ALERT!   The issue of who has access to information is becoming more and more important. Make sure that if you choose to outsource security services that you understand the agreements that your organization may have with customers as they relate to customer information.

CHOOSING A VENDOR

Choosing a vendor to provide security services is primarily a business decision. Certainly, there are service and price issues to evaluate and compare, but in most cases the "other" issues will impact the decision and the working relationship extensively. Let's take a look at the issues involved in choosing a security services vendor. Remember as we go through this that these services may not only be technical services.

Services

The appropriate vendor must provide the services that the organization needs in order to manage its risk appropriately. This may be a combination of technical services such as managed IDS and managed firewalls as well as people services such as security awareness training and policy development.

Vendors who provide a range of services may be more appropriate than single-service vendors simply because your organization may need additional services in the future. Let's take a look at a possible progression. Your organization has determined that an intrusion detection system is needed to help manage the information security risk. It is also determined that outsourcing the system is preferable to hiring the appropriate staff and providing the service internally. In the course of identifying a vendor, it becomes clear that an incident response procedure is needed. The organization decides that it needs assistance in developing this procedure and conducting the appropriate training. The logical choice to provide that service is the managed IDS vendor. Therefore, if the vendor is able to provide this "people" service, the organization can use the same vendor. If not, a new vendor must be identified and contracted.

Another aspect of the services issue is the types of products that are supported by a vendor. If an organization wishes to contract out the service, hardware, and software, it may not matter. On the other hand, if the organization has already purchased the hardware and software, this choice of product will govern the choice of vendor since you will want the vendor to be knowledgeable about that specific product.

TIP When looking at the services that are provided by the vendor, ask the vendor how many clients of your size and complexity they have. You may find that the vendor does not have many clients like you and thus may not completely understand all of the aspects of how your business works.

Price

The cost of the service is an important component of choosing a vendor. In the current market, the prices for outsourced security services range from less than $1,000 per month for each managed firewall to over $5,000 per month for each managed intrusion detection system. The same is true for vendors who provide security expertise to your organization. The costs per day of service can range from $800 to over $3,000.

As you evaluate the cost proposals from vendors make sure that you are comparing like levels of service or like experience levels of consultants. Going with the least expensive service does not always mean that you are getting what you need to help you manage the risk to your organization.

Other Issues

While the services that are offered and the price that each vendor will charge are important components of any decision to outsource security services, there are other issues that should be examined. Services may look good on the surface and in the vendor's promotional materials but how do the services really work? Does the vendor have sufficient internal controls and backup systems to sustain the service in the event of a problem? Does the vendor's location suit your needs? If the vendor is offering several services, is there internal coordination that will enable the services to be offered in a more efficient manner?

Vendor Internal Issues

Your security vendor is helping you to manage the risk to your organization. In providing these services, the vendor should not create additional areas of concern. For example, your organization has installed firewalls in a fail-over configuration so as to eliminate a single point of failure. You have contracted with a managed security services company to manage and monitor the firewalls so that you can identify any issues quickly. Since you have given total control of the firewalls to the vendor, the vendor should have sufficient backup and recovery procedures in place so as to not have single points of failure in its network as this would preclude your being able to manage your own firewalls. At the same time, the staff that the vendor uses to manage the firewalls should not be making unauthorized changes to rule sets that may allow an intruder into your network.

Any security services vendor should be willing to define its internal procedures and show you its recovery plan in the event of a problem.

Location

The location of the vendor may be more important in some cases than in others. In the case of a managed services vendor, location may not matter. It is unlikely that the managed services provider will need to visit your site once the equipment is installed.

On the other hand, if the vendor is providing consultants or security experts to your site, the location of the vendor may be very important. If the vendor is local, it will be much easier for the vendor to provide fast incident response, for example. It will also be less expensive for the vendor to provide on-site services as the travel costs will be lower.

One other item that is often forgotten when dealing with vendors who provide staff on site is the ability to schedule the staff. If the vendor is local, it tends to be much easier to schedule time, especially in small blocks (such as for meetings) than if the vendor is remote. Once travel plans are made, it is often difficult for the vendor to change them.

Coordination

Coordination is something that is hard to measure but it is very important if the vendor is providing different types of services to your organization. What we mean by coordination is the ability of the vendor to share knowledge about your organization with the various consultants or services that are provided. Let's take a look at an example. Your organization is contracting with a vendor for three services: vulnerability scanning, intrusion detection system management, and on-site technical security assistance. If these three services are performed according to contract and without coordination, you may get three sets of reports and results. They may meet all of your requirements.

However, if the vendor is coordinating his services to you, you may see additional benefits. The results of the vulnerability scanning are provided to the managed IDS service. This enables the managed IDS to be more efficient in reporting serious attacks as the staff there now knows where the vulnerabilities truly lie. The results of the vulnerability scans are also provided to the on-site team so that they know where to concentrate their efforts to improve the technical security of the organization.

This is only a small example of how coordination can work. Vendors that do this well can provide great benefits to your organization. Vendors who do not do this well can still provide value but it is value that would grow if the information were used better.

WORKING WITH THE VENDOR

Choosing the vendor is only a small part of using outsourced security services to manage your organization's risk. Once the vendor is chosen, your organization must work with the vendor to get the most out of the services that are being paid for.

Day-to-Day Interaction

As was mentioned previously, when security services are outsourced, your organization should expect to see some of the work related to that service offloaded to the vendor. However, there is some work that must be performed by the staff of the organization.

It is easy to have regular interaction with the vendor when the vendor is sending consultants to your site. The consultants are there so you talk with them and have lunch with them and generally work together to solve whatever problem is the issue. When the consultants are not there, you still have a name (or names) and a face to remember and call as you need to. The consultant is likely to call periodically to check information or to schedule time on site.

It is harder to have these interactions with managed services vendors. Often, you will not know which people at the vendor are providing your service. There is no one name or face to call or to have lunch with. The vendor takes on the image of a group or large company. About the only interaction you may have is when the vendor delivers a report or when you call for a change to a firewall rule. However, it is almost more important to have regular interactions with your managed services vendors. The more information you can give to them about your networks and systems, the better the service the vendor will be able to provide.

Take, for example, a managed IDS vendor. The vendor will be delivering reports to you and may periodically call about a serious event that requires your attention. If this is the only interaction you have with the vendor, you will eventually see the number of false alerts growing. The reason is that the vendor is working with the information you have provided to them. If you never update the information, you cannot expect the service to improve. On the other hand, if you notify the vendor whenever you change a system or network, you will see the vendor being able to sort out more of the false alerts and thus provide better service overall.

Setting Expectations

As you begin to work with a vendor you should make sure that your expectations are made clear. There is nothing wrong with restating your expectations with regard to deliverables, scheduling, interaction, and so on once the contracts are signed. What you may find is that some of your expectations were not set down in the contract or that the vendor does not work the way you thought they did.

Missed expectations are one of the most frequent reasons for the failure of any relationship. If both parties clearly state their expectations at the beginning, there is little room for assumptions to cause problems later.

TIP   It is best to get the final agreement of expectations in writing at the beginning of the relationship.

At the same time that you set out your expectations for the vendor, make sure to listen for the vendor's expectations from you. The vendor will expect that you are working together to manage risk. He will not expect an adversarial relationship with any of the organization's staff. If you are unwilling to comply with the vendor's expectations as far as information and communication are concerned, do not expect the vendor to be able to meet your expectations.

Managing Risk

In the end, the vendor of outsourced security services and the contracting organization are forming a partnership to manage the information security risk to the organization. Both parties need to understand what this means and how the risk will be monitored and measured.

Discuss with the vendor the key issues that need attention. Find out from the vendor how it views risk and measures it with its clients. At the same time, make it clear that it is your risk that must be managed, not the vendor's.

CHECKLIST: KEY POINTS IN OUTSOURCING

The following is a checklist of key steps in outsourcing security:

- ☐ Identify the "technical" security services that you may wish to outsource.
- ☐ Identify the "people" security services that you may wish to outsource.
- ☐ Identify the primary reason for outsourcing security services. Make sure that this meets your risk management approach.
- ☐ Based on the primary reason, identify the services that you should outsource.
- ☐ Identify the costs associated with outsourcing security services and budget appropriately.
- ☐ Identify vendors who provide the services you need.
- ☐ Evaluate the costs of the services, keeping in mind that costs will vary based on the type of service.
- ☐ Evaluate the vendor's "other issues" and determine if the vendor can help you to manage your risk.
- ☐ Set proper expectations once the vendor is selected.
- ☐ Interact on a regular basis with the vendor.
- ☐ Identify ways in which the vendor assists you in managing your risk.

APPENDIX C

Managing New Security Projects

The steps of developing and deploying new security projects are much the same as with new business projects (see Chapter 6) with one difference: the security department is the one running the project. This means that instead of satisfying business needs first while managing risk, the security projects must manage the risk to the organization while not causing problems for the business systems.

For the purposes of this discussion, we will assume that the security department follows the same development methodology as the rest of the organization. That means that the same steps (requirements, design, development, test, pilot, full production) apply. Since we have already gone into great detail on each of these steps, we will discuss the primary differences for the security department when developing a security system.

 SECURITY ALERT!   The security department should absolutely follow the same methodology as the rest of the organization. This is not only good system development but it also serves to help the security department avoid problems when implementing these new systems.

DEFINING REQUIREMENTS

As with any system, a security system needs to meet general security requirements. However, since the security department is developing a system, care must be taken to meet other requirements including those for performance, manageability, and integration. In short, all of the business issues and business requirements that are normally developed by the business unit must now be developed by the security department.

In the following sections, we will cover the major requirements that the security department should not forget when developing a new system. Unfortunately, it is very common for the security department to get tied up in their own systems without spending time working on how their systems will affect the rest of the organization.

Security Requirements

Let's start with the basics. The same security requirements that must be imposed upon business systems should also be imposed upon security systems. This means that the security systems must identify sensitive information that will be included in the system. Appropriate confidentiality and integrity mechanisms must be put in place to assure that the risk of disclosure and unauthorized modification are properly managed.

Likewise, requirements for availability must take into account the effect of the security system on other business systems. It is very likely that a new security system will be used directly by some other business systems in the organization. Therefore, if the security system has an outage, it may affect how the business of the organization is conducted. Keep in mind that if the security system affects the availability of business systems, the organization may choose to forego that additional security.

The accountability requirements of a new security system are perhaps the most important. The reason for this is that security systems may allow the capture of sensitive information or access to privileged operations. In either case it is extremely important that the system be able to properly identify and authenticate the individual.

The same is true of the audit requirements of the security system. Since the security department is often the group within the organization that monitors audit records, audit records that pertain to individuals within the security department must be protected from modification by the same individuals.

TIP Talk to some of the business units and system administrators to find out how a proposed security system may impact business systems.

Fail-over Requirements

Normally, fail-over requirements would be part of the availability requirements of a system. Due to the criticality of many security systems, we thought making special mention of fail-over requirements would be appropriate. Often the security department will deploy a system (internally developed or purchased) that incorporates some requirements for high availability. Unfortunately, the way the system is designed does not necessarily allow its functions to be highly available.

To explain our point further, let's take a look at an example. The security department deploys a system for single sign-on authentication (see Figure C-1). As part of the design the security department notes that this is a key part of the overall security system for the organization and therefore requires a system to run on a high-availability platform. As the system is deployed, every server in the organization comes to rely upon the single sign-on system for the authentication of users. Therefore, not only the computer on which the single sign-on system runs is important, but the communications between the single sign-on computer and the various servers is also important. If the security department fails to note that communications are also extremely important in this example, the ability of users to access various servers throughout the organization may be compromised anytime there is a communication problem.

Performance Requirements

There are two major requirements regarding the performance of the security system. First, the security system must perform the task for which it is built in a timely manner. This means that the system must be sized appropriately. For example, if we look back at Figure C-1, the single sign-on server must be sized to handle the expected number of users and servers. If the system is not sized properly there will be an impact on the users of every other server in the organization.

The second requirement for performance is to consider how a security system may impact the performance of other business systems. There are a number of security systems that require the placement of agent software on business servers. The purpose of the software may be to monitor policy, examine audit files, or even identify potential intrusions. Any such software will by necessity use some CPU time on the server. How much time is used and therefore how much impact on the performance of the server the new security software will have are important considerations. This is not to say that such software should never be loaded on business servers, but the security department

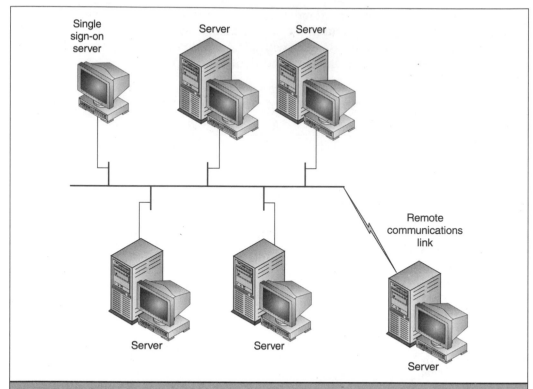

Figure C-1. Availability for a security system may also require the availability of communications.

must take into account the current performance of the business server as well as the impact the security software will have on performance. It may also be possible that the impact of the security software can be modified based upon procedural requirements.

As an example, consider the use of software (such as Tripwire) that checks for modifications to important files. For this example, let us assume that the software uses cryptographic checksums to detect a modification. This means that periodically these checksums must be computed and compared to existing checksums. This process is mathematically intense and thus may impact the performance of the server anytime that the checksums are computed. In order to lessen the impact of competing checksums, the procedural requirement is to run the checksums against the entire system (the most computationally intensive) only when the server is least active.

Manageability Requirements

Any new system must be manageable and security systems are no exception. Most security departments have a limited staff. Therefore, the new system must either be manageable by the existing staff or additional resources must be made available. It is very likely that no new staff members will be available to manage the new system. It is also possible that parts of the new system may need to be managed by system administration departments. Therefore, the coordination between the system administration and the security administration of the system must be identified as part of the manageability requirements.

Another twist on the manageability of the system is that there may be requirements not only for *how* the system is to be managed but *when* the system is to be managed. For example, the security department wishes to deploy a new intrusion detection system. The requirements for the system state that the network will be monitored for intrusions by a security staff member. This requirement means that at least one member of the security staff must be trained on this intrusion detection system. If we also assume that a staff member is to respond to any alerts on a 24-hour basis, we may now have added a whole new dimension to the security department.

Integration Requirements

When a security system is deployed, the requirements should specify how this new system would be integrated into the organization. Integration of some systems will be relatively simple. For example, the intrusion detection system mentioned in the previous section may only require a connection to a network in order to function. The necessity for this connection should be specified in the system requirements.

Other security systems (such as the single sign-on system shown in Figure C-1) may have much more stringent integration requirements. In this case, the details of how the security system will work with other business systems must be clearly worked out with the owners of those business systems prior to any design work. The responsibility for this coordination lies with the security department.

 SECURITY ALERT!   Do not assume that the business unit will understand the impact of a new security system. The security department needs to be proactive and seek out the business units to determine the issues.

WRITING THE RFP

Once the requirements have been developed, research will begin for the proper vendor and the proper product. This is not to say that security projects are never developed internally (we will discuss internal development later). However, given the size and workload of most security departments, it is unlikely that internal development will be the most efficient way to deploy a new project.

Therefore, it is extremely likely that the security department will write a request for proposals (RFP). The RFP should be written with an understanding not only of the organization's requirements but also with knowledge of available products. This does not mean that the RFP should be written for a particular product, but it makes no sense to request capabilities that no vendor can meet.

RFP Requirements

The requirements defined in the requirements definition phase of the project should be written into the RFP. If possible, divide the requirements into categories. A good set of categories might be:

- Functional security requirements
- Fail-over requirements
- Performance requirements
- Integration requirements

Requirements that are absolute (meaning that they must be met in order for the vendor to be considered) should be identified. There may be some requirements that are somewhat flexible. For example, an RFP for a single sign-on system may list as a requirement the ability to handle 100 logins per second. However, this may in fact be a goal rather than a hard requirement and thus something lower than 100 logins per second may be acceptable if a product can fulfill the majority of the other requirements.

The RFP should tell the vendors to explain how their system can meet all of the requirements. Do not ask the vendors only if their systems meet the requirements but specifically ask them to specify computer or network speeds if these will affect the performance of the system.

RFP Conditions of Acceptance

The RFP should explain to the vendors what the conditions for acceptance of their proposal would be. Depending upon the type of project, the RFP may specify that the vendor should provide evaluation copies of the product and support a pilot program before the product will be completely accepted. By specifying these terms upfront, the vendor will be made aware of non-technical issues that may affect the bid price.

Most organizations require various other conditions to be met by a vendor. Make sure that any RFP that is given to vendors contains all these conditions. It is usually a good idea to have the RFP reviewed by the organization's general counsel or procurement departments.

EVALUATING RESPONSES

Assuming that the RFP is well put together, at some point vendors will provide proposals in response to it. It then becomes the job of the security department to evaluate the responses. The responses will have technical portions and non-technical portions. All parts of the response must be evaluated.

Technical Responses

It would seem that evaluating the technical response to an RFP is rather straightforward. Unfortunately, there will usually be some requirements that are not completely met in each response. The question then becomes which response is the most appropriate for the organization.

Figure C-2 shows a flow chart of an evaluation process. Notice that the technical response is only part of the evaluation process. The absolute requirements are identified and each response is examined to see if these are met. If so, the proposal is evaluated against the "flexible" requirements to see which proposal meets these requirements the best. This evaluation assumes that some of the flexible requirements will not be fully met by any one product.

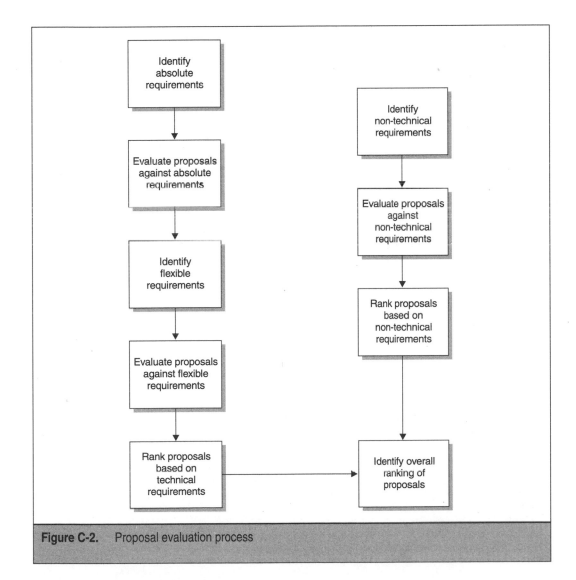

Figure C-2.   Proposal evaluation process

Once the evaluation is complete, the proposals should be ranked from the best proposal (meaning the one that met the most requirements) to the worst (the one that met the fewest requirements).

Non-technical Responses

From a strict engineering viewpoint, it is unfortunate that the non-technical requirements are as important (and sometimes more important) than the technical requirements. Be that as it may, the non-technical aspects of each proposal must also be evaluated against the requirements.

The non-technical aspects will include the price of the product, the cost of ongoing support, and the willingness of the vendor to support the testing and pilot portions of the project. Also, do not forget to evaluate the ability of the vendor to remain in business and support the product over the long term. As with the technical evaluation, the proposals are ranked based on the vendor's ability to meet the requirements. Keep in mind that there have been plenty of small vendors with awesome products that don't live to see their second or third birthdays. A major consideration when dealing with small vendors is how likely they are to be in business down the road.

Tradeoffs

Now comes the fun part. It is highly unlikely (unless the project is very small and simple) that any one vendor will meet all the requirements (both technical and non-technical) to the satisfaction of the organization. Therefore, the security department, in cooperation with procurement and the general counsel, will need to make trade-offs to determine which vendor will best meet the needs of the organization. In many cases this may require technical requirements to be trade-offs with non-technical requirements. For example, one vendor may provide a product that meets the majority of the technical requirements. However, further investigation indicates that this vendor is not financially well off and therefore may not be able to meet the long-term support requirements of the project. In this case, the trade-off will be between the technical sophistication of the product and its long-term viability.

It should be noted that some non-technical issues might be solvable through the use of legal or contractual agreements. In the example above, it may be acceptable to include in the contract with the vendor a clause that places the source code for the product in escrow so that if the vendor fails, the organization can gain access to the source code and thus continue to use and support the product.

CHOOSING THE VENDOR

Once the proposals have been evaluated, the vendor of choice should be notified that they have won the contract. At this point, the actual legal and contractual negotiations begin. It is possible that the selected vendor may not be willing to agree to all the contractual requirements of the organization. If this occurs, it may be necessary to identify an alternative choice.

The chosen product should then be tested (if it has not been already as part of the evaluation process) to make sure that it actually meets the requirements as stated in the proposal. If the product does not meet the requirements it may be necessary to choose another vendor.

At some point in the project the product may be deployed in a pilot phase. As part of the pilot phase, performance, integration, and usability will be tested in a live environment so that flaws in the product will become evident. If these flaws cannot be corrected, it may be necessary to identify another vendor.

DEVELOPING NEW SECURITY PROJECTS INTERNALLY

In some cases, developing a security product in-house is a more cost-effective choice than purchasing a product from a vendor. Often these situations will arise when there is a very specific need for security in a system designed and built solely for the organization. When the situation occurs, the security department should follow the same development methodology used to develop other in-house systems.

The primary difference between this type of development and normal business systems development is that the security department is now the primary requirements driver. The security department thus must take a center role rather than a supporting role in the project.

INTEGRATING THE PRODUCTS WITH THE ORGANIZATION

The new security project is moving along. A vendor and product have been chosen, testing is complete, and an assistant is ready to move into full production. One issue that is often overlooked by security departments is the integration of the product into the organization. There are two types of integration that must be managed for the project to complete successfully: technology integration and procedural integration.

Technology Integration

With technology integration the technical aspects of the new project will successfully work with existing systems in the organization. There are many different types of technical integration that range from ensuring that the products run on the platforms required to ensuring that the network architecture of the organization allows a new security project to function. The following two examples will illustrate these points.

The security department wishes to deploy a single sign-on system. The product that is chosen requires agent software to be loaded on each server. During the requirements phase of the project, the server operating systems were identified as Solaris 2.6 and 2.7,

Windows NT 4.0 and 2000, and AIX 4.3. The chosen vendor produces a product that runs on all five of the required operating systems. However, during testing it was determined that the configurations of Solaris that are used in the organization cause the product to fail. During the testing process, the problem is identified and a configuration change is determined to allow the new system to work properly.

As a second example, consider the following situation. The security department wishes to deploy a network intrusion detection system around the organization's Internet connection. A vendor that meets all of the stated requirements was found and the product was tested. During deployment it was found that the network administration group was using switches rather than hubs around the firewall, thus preventing the network intrusion detection system from functioning correctly. The security department was faced with the choice of using a network tap or trying to force the network administration group to use hubs instead of switches. Further testing showed that the network taps would perform satisfactorily and thus taps were procured and deployed.

In both of these examples, the issues of technology integration with the existing environment became key to the success of the projects.

Procedural Integration

New security systems may require new procedures or changes to existing procedures. Since procedures govern the way users and administrators perform their jobs, it is very important to make sure that the new system integrates procedurally into the organization.

If we consider the previous example of the single sign-on system, there are two procedural integration issues that must be dealt with. The first is rather obvious: the administration of users on servers will change because of the single sign-on system. This means that the procedures for adding and removing users from the systems must be modified to reflect the new system.

The second procedural change may not be quite as obvious. As mentioned in the example, the configuration of the Solaris systems has been modified to allow the single sign-on system to work properly. This means that the Solaris system configuration procedure must be modified to reflect this change. Failure to modify the configuration procedure will mean that every new Solaris server that needs to work with the single sign-on system will not work properly as first configured.

Procedural integration may take many forms depending upon the type of security system that is deployed. Some security systems may only require new procedures for the security department. Others may require changes to existing administration end-user procedures. If the procedural changes are forgotten, is likely that the new project will not be successful.

SECURITY PRODUCT INTEGRATION

One last issue should be discussed before we conclude the discussion of new security products. The issue is the integration of a new security system into the existing security department. Often new security systems are put into place with the promise of greater automation and the need for fewer highly skilled security staff. In order to fulfill this promise, new systems must somehow work together. The most common way for security systems to work together is by integrating their information so that the security state of the organization can be reflected in a single report. Unfortunately, this promise of security information integration has been left unfulfilled by most vendors.

If the security department is unlikely to find the necessary integration directly from vendors, it may be up to the department itself to coordinate and integrate information from various products. In its simplest form, this integration may mean placing security events into one database. More complex integration may be needed to allow the correlation of security events from various products and systems.

However the security department chooses to integrate new products into its operations, time spent on long-term plans for such integration will be well spent.

CHECKLIST: KEY POINTS IN DEPLOYING NEW SECURITY TECHNOLOGY

The following is a checklist of key steps in deploying new security technology:

- [ ] Identify the organization's development methodology and determine how the security department will meet all of the methodology's requirements.
- [ ] Identify the project manager for the new project.
- [ ] Develop the system security requirements.
- [ ] Develop the system fail-over and availability requirements.
- [ ] Develop the system performance requirements.
- [ ] Develop the system manageability requirements.
- [ ] Develop the system integration requirements.
- [ ] If the product is to be purchased, write the RFP.
- [ ] Have the RFP reviewed by legal and procurement.
- [ ] Evaluate the technical responses and rank them.
- [ ] Evaluate the non-technical responses and rank them.
- [ ] Conduct trade offs and create a final ranking of responses.
- [ ] Begin contract negotiations with the chosen vendor.
- [ ] Develop an integration test and pilot program for the new system into the organization's IT environment.
- [ ] Identify procedures and policies that need to be updated because of the new system.
- [ ] Develop an integration plan for the new system into the security department's operations.

Index

References to figures and illustrations are in italics.

❖ A

INTERNATIONAL CONTACT INFORMATION

AUSTRALIA
McGraw-Hill Book Company Australia Pty. Ltd.
TEL +61-2-9417-9899
FAX +61-2-9417-5687
http://www.mcgraw-hill.com.au
books-it_sydney@mcgraw-hill.com

CANADA
McGraw-Hill Ryerson Ltd.
TEL +905-430-5000
FAX +905-430-5020
http://www.mcgrawhill.ca

GREECE, MIDDLE EAST,
NORTHERN AFRICA
McGraw-Hill Hellas
TEL +30-1-656-0990-3-4
FAX +30-1-654-5525

MEXICO (Also serving Latin America)
McGraw-Hill Interamericana Editores S.A. de C.V.
TEL +525-117-1583
FAX +525-117-1589
http://www.mcgraw-hill.com.mx
fernando_castellanos@mcgraw-hill.com

SINGAPORE (Serving Asia)
McGraw-Hill Book Company
TEL +65-863-1580
FAX +65-862-3354
http://www.mcgraw-hill.com.sg
mghasia@mcgraw-hill.com

SOUTH AFRICA
McGraw-Hill South Africa
TEL +27-11-622-7512
FAX +27-11-622-9045
robyn_swanepoel@mcgraw-hill.com

UNITED KINGDOM & EUROPE
(Excluding Southern Europe)
McGraw-Hill Education Europe
TEL +44-1-628-502500
FAX +44-1-628-770224
http://www.mcgraw-hill.co.uk
computing_neurope@mcgraw-hill.com

ALL OTHER INQUIRIES Contact:
Osborne/McGraw-Hill
TEL +1-510-549-6600
FAX +1-510-883-7600
http://www.osborne.com
omg_international@mcgraw-hill.com